HOW TO LOSE A BATTLE

FOOLISH PLANS AND GREAT MILITARY BLUNDERS

Edited by

BILL FAWCETT

HARPER

NEW YORK • LONDON • TORONTO • SYDNEY

HARPER

HarperCollins books may be purchased for educational, business, or sales promotional use. For information please write: Special Markets Department, HarperCollins Publishers, 10 East 53rd Street, New York, NY 10022.

FIRST EDITION

Designed by Joy O'Meara

Library of Congress Cataloging-in-Publication Data

How to lose a battle: foolish plans and great military blunders/edited by Bill Fawcett.—1st ed.
p. cm.
ISBN-10: 0-06-076024-9
ISBN-13: 978-0-06-076024-3

1. Battles. 2. Military art and science—History. 3. Military history—Case studies. 4. Errors. 5. Operational art (Military Science)—Case studies. I. Fawcett, Bill.

U27.H69 2006
355.4'8—dc22

2005054727

10 ❖/RRD 20 19 18 17 16 15 14 13 12

ABOUT THE EDITOR

BILL FAWCETT is the editor of *Hunters & Shooters* and *The Teams,* two oral histories of the SEALs in Vietnam. He has written or collaborated on several science fiction and mystery novels, including the authorized Mycroft Holmes mysteries and the Madame Vernet Investigates series. As an anthologist, Fawcett has put together more than fifty fiction and nonfiction anthologies and collections ranging in subject from UFOs and U.S. Special Forces to cats and space combat. He also designs both computer and board games. Fawcett's most recently published works are *It Seemed Like a Good Idea* and *You Did What?*, humorous looks at the why and who of history's greatest mistakes.

Dedicated to the men and women who served under the commanders described herein. They are a constant reminder that, when everything is considered, it is the courage, professionalism, and determination of the soldier that wins the wars.

CONTENTS

HOW TO LOSE A BATTLE

THE BATTLE OF ARBELA

Near the Village of Gaugamela in Persia, 331 BC

BILL FAWCETT

In the fourth century BC there was only one real world power, Persia. That empire had already conquered all of the Greek cities along the eastern shore of the Aegean. When Athens dared to involve itself in the revolt of one of these formerly Greek cities, the Persian emperors felt they had no option but to conquer all of Greece. Twice they tried, and, to the amazement of even the Greek city-states, failed. Eventually the many fractious cities were united under the military control of Philip of Macedon. His son, Alexander, saw it as his divine duty to protect all of Greece. The conquest of the Persian Empire by Alexander the Great was an astounding feat, and there is no question of the brilliance of his generalship or the organizational brilliance of Alexander's father, Philip. His supply system alone was centuries ahead of anyone else's. Reinforcements of Macedonian troops arrived even as he prepared to cross into India. The conquest is even more amazing when you compare the relative populations and wealth of all Greece and Macedon to that of the Persian Empire ruled by Darius III: there were at least ten times as many subjects in Persia as Alexander controlled. Worse yet, Greece was poor, while Persia had a rich and thriving economy. With so little work at home, many Greeks found it necessary to hire themselves as mercenaries, often to Darius.

In modern terms, Alexander's invasion of the Persian Empire would be the equivalent of Canada invading the United States, but only being able to move troops over the bridges near Detroit. So how did Alexander win and Darius lose? The Macedonian king had three advantages that made all the difference. First, he inherited a truly first-class and innovative military machine from another military and political genius, his father, Philip. The next advantage was the men he led. Man for man, Alexander's Greek mounted and infantry forces were both better armed, better trained, and often better supplied than any force they met. The phalanxes, massive formations often sixteen men deep, were armed with the sarissa, a metal-tipped spear eighteen feet long. This far outreached any weapon they faced, even the twelve-foot spears of the Greek mercenaries. The man-for-man superiority of the Greek infantry was recognized by Darius and his predecessors, who made phalanxes of Greek mercenaries a key element in all of the armies they formed. Interestingly, and to Alexander's disadvantage, Darius III had been able to hire several thousand Greeks to fight for him at Issus only a year earlier. Still Alexander's Greek soldiers were superior in training, weapons, and attitude. The final advantage Alexander had was himself. He was not only a brilliant tactician and strategist, but also charismatic and courageous.

Darius III was fighting to retain his throne, and after losing to Alexander the year before at Issus, the Persian emperor needed to prove himself capable of defending his empire. Darius III was by no means either inexperienced or stupid. In fact, he managed to choose the ground for this pivotal battle and had several days to prepare it. His army was at least three times the size of Alexander's, and had exotic weapons, such as elephants and scythe-bladed chariots, which the invading Macedonian army did not. In the decisive arm, cavalry, Darius had nearly five times the number of horsemen Alexander led. Many of Darius's horsemen were also much more heavily armored, covered head to toe in scale mail, and were armed with lances. So the battle was fought at the place Darius III chose, the field he had leveled for his chariots, near his capital, and he made the first moves, so, in theory, he had the initiative. Darius did almost everything needed to ensure a victory, but all of this could not overcome what turned out to be a fatal flaw, one which lost him both this battle and his empire.

Once they were close to where Darius's army waited near the town of Arbela, the Macedonians moved cautiously to within a few miles of the Persian army, which stood ready to meet them. They arrived just as the sun was setting. Rather than rush into battle, they camped and rested. Every Greek knew they were greatly outnumbered and far from home. If defeated, their nearest safe haven lay over a thousand miles away. This could have caused morale to collapse, but combined with their faith in their commander, the situation instead engendered great resolve among Alexander's men. In contrast, Darius III had gathered forces from all parts of the empire, including Indian cavalry and slingers from the mountains of what is today Afghanistan. They did not all speak the same language, and most had never even seen Darius III. The first manifestation of Darius's great flaw revealed itself as the Greek army approached.

Darius was sitting in camp less than seven miles from Alexander's army with an army that was relatively rested and ready for battle, and even though his opponent's men were exhausted from several days of hard marching, he did nothing. Rather than move to attack the camp, Darius allowed the Greek army three full days to recover from what had been a difficult march. You could rationalize that the Persian emperor felt that the advantage of fighting on a large, smooth battlefield he had prepared outweighed the tactic of hitting his enemy when they were vulnerable. Whatever the reason, by not even sending a part of his army to harass the Greeks, Darius gave up the strategic initiative. In effect he committed his much larger army to waiting for the Greeks to come to them.

Finally, on the third day after arriving, the Greeks formed up and marched onto a set of hills that afforded almost every man a good look at the massive number of soldiers arrayed against them. After studying the Persian army before him, Alexander made the risky decision to withdraw into his camp once more. This might have compromised the vital morale of the men, who were now aware of how badly they were outnumbered. The decision appears to have been the right one, however, for there is no record of the Greeks losing any of their confidence. Perhaps this is in part because the Persians had the much smaller army of Alexander in plain sight and yet simply allowed it to march away. The Persians also returned to their camp, having stood ready for a fourth long day awaiting Alexander's attack.

Still, the night before the battle had to be a difficult one for every Greek in Alexander's army, as well as for the commander himself. One of the classic methods for a smaller force to defeat a much larger one is to attack at night. The confusion and guaranteed lack of control could enable an inferior force to disrupt and scatter their opponents. It was said that this was suggested by Parmenion, Alexander's trusted second in command. But confidently the Macedonian king simply stated that he would not "steal" an empire through such a victory. Pickets were ordered out and the Greek army was able to get another night's rest. Alexander himself remained awake until he had formulated a plan, and then was said to have slept soundly, having to be awakened long after sunrise by his generals.

The Persian emperor was also aware of the possibility of a night attack. His reaction was to order his entire army to stand to arms all night. This loss of nerve meant that by the time the battle started, men and horses had already been awake and in their armor almost twenty-four hours. Compare this to driving all night and then competing as the center in an NFL football game. Before the first arrow flew at Arbela, the Persian side was already tired. Not only had Darius failed to harass the Greek army when it was exhausted from marching, but now his fear of a night attack had reversed the situation, with well-rested Greeks now facing physically depleted Persians.

Darius, his army still at arms from the night before, seems to have waited unmoving as the Greek army formed up and marched onto his chosen battlefield. He had selected and carefully prepared the area so it was smooth and contained no hidden hazards for his chariots, elephants, or cavalry. His army, if tired from standing at arms all day, was in place. The Persian emperor had a massive superiority in the numbers, if not the quality, of his army. At this point, nearly everything seemed to have gone Darius's way. But this appearance was most certainly deceiving.

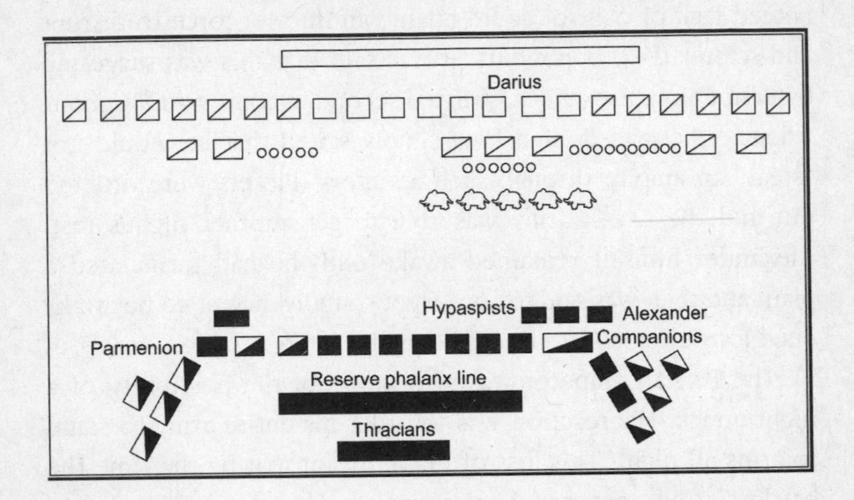

Alexander marched his army out in an "oblique order"—that is, with one side farther forward than the other. The left side of his line was "refused," or held back, and was also much shorter than the Persian right (each side being described as if you were looking forward from the center of that side). So Alexander's left side would be to Darius's right flank, or side. Darius did not order his longer and larger right to attack and envelop the shorter Greek left. Instead, he waited. Alexander then continued to extend his line even wider (facing the right side of Darius's army), and even angled his advance so that he threatened to shift the entire battle off the battlefield Darius III had sacrificed so much to fight upon.

The Persian army was too large and difficult to command to shift as easily in reaction. To prevent the movement of the Greeks, Darius chose to thin the forces in the center to extend his line and send them to reinforce his extending right, rather than move his entire army. Finally Darius acted, probably to stop the shift by Alexander's army. The Persian emperor ordered much of the cavalry on his left wing to attack and halt Alexander's sidestepping movement. In reaction to this new Persian attack, Minedas, commander of the Greek left, counterattacked at the head of a much smaller force of horsemen. These riders suddenly halted well short of the attacking Persians and seemed to then turn and run.

Trained cavalry can maintain its formation at almost any pace so long as the riders make an effort to stay together. But if you are pursuing a fleeing enemy, each rider urges his mount to its greatest speed and the formation is lost. This seems to have happened when the formed Persian units broke ranks to pursue the "fleeing" Greek horsemen. Then, as planned, Minedas's Greek horsemen rode back, moving through corridors left by a large force of infantry that had moved forward unseen behind his cavalry. These phalanxes then closed ranks. The unformed and thus even more than normally vulnerable Persian cavalry slammed into an unexpected wall of spears. Bravely, the Persian horsemen threw themselves at the phalanxes again and again. This Alexandrian infantry was only four to six ranks deep, far less deep than the traditional sixteen-man-deep formation, so it must have appeared tantalizingly vulnerable. More Persian units followed, both cavalry and infantry, hoping to break through the thin Greek line. But the Greeks under Parmenion held, just barely. Minedas's horsemen reformed and attacked to protect the flanks of their infantry, and most movement stopped. The Greeks' left flank held and the reinforced right flank of Darius's army was soon completely committed.

In reaction to seeing his right tied up and making little progress, Darius released his chariots and elephants. The faster chariots moved quickly across the smoothed battlefield, the scythes on their wheels flashing in the morning sunlight. Chariots were already falling from favor because the horses pulling them were so vulnerable; so it proved in this case, as Macedonian javelins brought down the horses of almost every chariot before they could reach the phalanxes. Then the elephants arrived, but, forewarned, the Greeks were prepared and opened paths the frightened elephants could pass through. Agonized by javelins and arrows, the elephants ran right through and past Alexander's entire army, doing little harm.

Darius then ordered a general advance, supporting the melee on his right. Soon, Parmenion on the Greek left was involved with the Persian right, once again fighting the much larger force to a standstill. When the Macedonian right had advanced, it left a gap where it had joined with their center. Seeing this gap, a large unit of Indian horse charged through. But even these horsemen were just as quickly engaged and defeated by Greek phalanxes that had been stationed in reserve behind the army and stopped. Later another Persian cavalry unit managed to fight its way around one flank, and they made for the camp where Darius's family, who had always traveled with and been well treated by Alexander since their capture the year before at Issus, were held. Those riders were repulsed by light infantry left behind at the camp, and also had no effect on the battle.

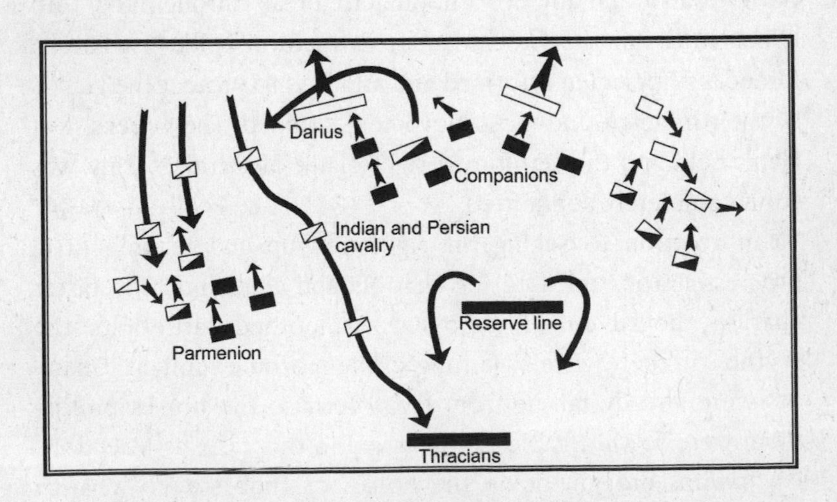

At this point, both flanks of Alexander's army were under immense pressure. Badly outnumbered, both wings fought to hold their own and no longer advanced. Hard pressed by what seemed an endless supply of Persians, the Greeks and Macedonians were tiring, and there were no reserves to take their places. The strategy Darius used, that of overwhelming the flanks of a smaller army, is sound and has many times been successful. It almost was this time. But in his efforts to collapse either flank of the Macedonian army, Darius had continually sent units away from the center, where he stood, to reinforce both attacks. At this point, understanding his opponent, Alexander led his last uncommitted phalanxes and the best of his cavalry, including his bodyguards, the elite Companions, into an all-out attack against the center of the Persian line.

Formed into a giant wedge comprised of both cavalry and infantry, with Alexander and his Companions at the point, they smashed into the still large mass of Persian infantry in the center and began to cut their way through to where Darius himself sat enthroned. The Companions arced around, angling to penetrate to where the Persian emperor and his generals stood. As the Macedonian phalanxes accompanying the Companions pushed back less-well-armored and outclassed Persian foot soldiers, there was a good chance that Darius would be caught between the Companions and the Greek foot. His own elite infantry, three thousand Royal Guards, or Immortals, formed up, braced for the impact of the Companions, and were swept aside after just a few minutes of hard fighting. As he had a year before when hard pressed, Darius III, emperor of the largest empire in the world, turned tail and fled. The battle was hardly decided, much less lost, but seeing himself at risk, Darius ran with the Greek horsemen close behind. Alexander broke off his pursuit of Darius to save Parmenion and his left flank from being overwhelmed. At every point, the thinner Greek line was hard pressed to hold on. But when word spread through the ranks of the Persians that Darius had deserted, the army units began to withdraw or simply disintegrate. Amazingly, Darius continued to run, even though he was soon able to gather around him almost thirty thousand infantry who had yet to fight. That thirty thousand was almost as many infantry as Alexander had started with. So, with the loss of his nerve, Darius III also lost his empire. Darius continued to run, and his remaining army soon melted away. Several weeks later his own generals killed him.

Why did Darius III lose? The battle was fought where he wanted, how he wanted (at least at first), and he had massive superiority in numbers. But Alexander based his plan on one fact: when they had battled the year before at Issus, the conflict had been decided when Darius III fled the field. Simply put, it appears the Persian emperor was unable to face personal danger. Darius III lost two battles and the largest empire in the world because he was a coward.

EXODUS

The Exodus as a Military Mistake

Biblical Egypt

BRIAN THOMSEN

Normally, a military contingent dispatched to return runaway slaves might be considered an overwhelming force, and in the pre-Spartacus days of the Book of Exodus, the idea of the Israelite slaves fighting back was about as remote as the chance that the pharaoh's funeral would be a quiet and humble affair.

But the pharaoh's forces failed against Moses and his supreme commander.

According to the good book (via King James):

> *15 And the LORD said unto Moses, Wherefore criest thou unto me? speak unto the children of Israel, that they go forward:*
>
> *16 But lift thou up thy rod, and stretch out thine hand over the sea, and divide it: and the children of Israel shall go on dry ground through the midst of the sea.*
>
> *17 And I, behold, I will harden the hearts of the Egyptians, and they shall follow them: and I will get me honour upon Pharaoh, and upon all his host, upon his chariots, and upon his horsemen.*

18 And the Egyptians shall know that I am the LORD, when I have gotten me honour upon Pharaoh, upon his chariots, and upon his horsemen.

19 And the angel of God, which went before the camp of Israel, removed and went behind them; and the pillar of the cloud went from before their face, and stood behind them:

20 And it came between the camp of the Egyptians and the camp of Israel; and it was a cloud and darkness to them, but it gave light by night to these: so that the one came not near the other all the night.

21 And Moses stretched out his hand over the sea; and the LORD caused the sea to go back by a strong east wind all that night, and made the sea dry land, and the waters were divided.

22 And the children of Israel went into the midst of the sea upon the dry ground: and the waters were a wall unto them on their right hand, and on their left.

23 And the Egyptians pursued, and went in after them to the midst of the sea, even all Pharaoh's horses, his chariots, and his horsemen.

24 And it came to pass, that in the morning watch the LORD looked unto the host of the Egyptians through the pillar of fire and of the cloud, and troubled the host of the Egyptians,

25 And took off their chariot wheels, that they drave them heavily: so that the Egyptians said, Let us flee from the face of Israel; for the LORD fighteth for them against the Egyptians.

26 And the LORD said unto Moses, Stretch out thine hand over the sea, that the waters may come again upon the Egyptians, upon their chariots, and upon their horsemen.

27 And Moses stretched forth his hand over the sea, and the sea returned to his strength when the morning appeared; and the Egyptians fled against it; and the LORD overthrew the Egyptians in the midst of the sea.

28 And the waters returned, and covered the chariots, and the horsemen, and all the host of Pharaoh that came into the sea after them; there remained not so much as one of them.

Whether one is willing to accept the quite literal deus ex machina intervention on behalf of the fleeing Israelites or discount it altogether, it is nonetheless fair to point out several examples of gross incompetence on the part of the pharaoh's forces that doomed their recovery mission from the very beginning.

To begin with, the pharaoh assumed that his slave nation would realize life and survival outside of his domain would be even tougher than their slavery existence. This was both naïve and very wrong. The Israelites had been welcomed into Egypt as a free people fleeing a famine. Later, they had been enslaved to prevent them from someday dominating the country. But there were simply far too many Israelites to keep enslaved by just the supervisors. So when, led by Moses, they up and left (possibly assisted by a series of natural disasters, like maybe ten plagues), that is what happened.

If even the most conservative estimates are correct, the number of Israelites involved in the Exodus was large enough that a simple changing of minds would not have been possible in an immediate enough time. There were too many to persuade. By the time the pharaoh realized the Chosen People were well on their way, an off-site retrieval strategy became necessary, rather than a simple act of herding them back within the city, as one would errant goats and sheep.

The cavalry and chariot force should have been adequate for this task.

Moving out in pursuit they would also be fine . . . obviously overtaking the escaping Israelites in a fraction of the time the mass of fleeing former slaves could cover ground, since they would have been forced to travel at the rate of their slowest member.

The problem and fatal flaw in the plan was the delay in pursuit, which not only allowed the Israelites to put enough distance between themselves and their pursuers, but also allowed them the chance to arrive at a different terrain. The delay may have resulted from hesitation, or the time it took to mobilize the army, or the confusion caused by the plagues, or even the loss of so many Jewish scribes and assistants. But it occurred.

The biblical authors claim they made it to the Red Sea, which the Lord parted for them.

Biblical scholars argue that it was really the Reed Sea, or perhaps the Bitter Lakes. In either case, the problem is the same—marshy terrain.

On one hand, you have the slaves traveling on foot, with the occasional minor beast of burden bearing their meager possessions.

On the other hand, you have the pursuers: armored charioteers mastering strong steeds with maximum agility.

Sure, they can make up for lost time and perhaps show off their great agility by herding the wayward slaves back from whence they came . . . until they reach "the sea," which is a problem—a problem that soon becomes insurmountable. The chariots, with their own weight and the weight of their armor-laden drivers over wheels designed for speed on sand or stone, sank into the soft ground. The chariot-mounted units, the most elite of all Egyptian forces, soon slowed to a standstill, or, perhaps more accurately, to a "sinkstill." Following the Israelites, they would have bogged down in the marsh and mud, tripping their steeds, halting their pursuit, and thwarting their mission.

The delay of the pursuit allowed the change of terrain, a military mistake of biblical proportion. The Israelites escaped from the finest military unit of their day and marched on into the desert, saved by swamp and by a mistake in timing and organization—a case where there may have been divine intervention, but earthly incompetence was miracle enough.

THE BATTLE OF CANNAE

Italy, 216 BC

BILL FAWCETT

It takes a lot to be the poster battle in all of ancient history, not only for losing big-time, but for being the prime example for two thousand years of a total and complete disaster. The Punic War Battle of Cannae between the armies of Rome and Carthage, without dispute, holds this dubious distinction. The slaughter of Rome's largest and best-equipped army to date was the result of several factors—including some good old-fashioned bullheaded ignorance by the Roman commander—all of which conspired to make this encounter one of the great stupidity-based defeats in history. Even measured against the Roman military disasters of Carrhae and Teutoburg Wald, the Battle of Cannae was not only the most bungled, but also brought Rome closer to destruction than any other loss in that empire's history.

By the time of the battle in 216 BC, Hannibal had already crossed the Alps, gained allies among the Gauls, and devastated one entire Roman army at Trebia, in 218 BC. (Remember, BC years count down so 218 BC is two years before 216 BC. In that period, dating was more local, and most dates were recorded as something like "the fourth year of the Reign of Pyrrhus." The AD/BC system was imposed on all dates only in recent history, in order to give historians a common dating baseline.)

As the Carthaginian commander arrived in what we now call northern Italy, he was able to add thousands of local warriors to the Spanish and Numidian troops that survived the march from Spain and across the Alps. The area had been conquered only recently by Rome and was still restive under their rule. Hannibal next defeated a large Roman army at Trebia, where he used tactics similar to those he had used at Cannae two years later, so no Roman commander should have been surprised to see them again. Hannibal then went on to threaten many of Rome's allied cities in the vain hope they would join his side. The Carthaginian then returned north to camp in the Gallic territories just south of the Alps. Unable to defeat the Romans, Hannibal still needed to remain a threat so Rome could not raise armies to attack Carthage or Spain. So he and his army waited. Two years later, Hannibal's welcome in the friendly Gallic states had worn thin, primarily due to the effects of feeding an army of almost forty thousand men. Food shortages, inflation, and the occasional pillaging by his soldiers had taken their toll. Because of rising pressure from Gauls where he was camped in the lands of leaders, the Carthaginian had to start moving his army as soon as possible. This meant they began to threaten Rome and her allies earlier in the spring than normal. But in the two years that had passed, Rome had doubled the size of their army, so they too were anxious for a battle, where the consuls were sure they would defeat Hannibal. All of Rome was eager for a battle, and also, it was shown, very overconfident.

To understand why Rome lost at Cannae, you have to understand the nature of the Roman army in the third century BC. The flexible, responsive Roman legion known as unquestionably the best army in the world for four hundred years was still more than a century away. The army of Rome at this time was comprised of levies of citizens, and, since each person had to supply his own equipment, only the richest could afford to become cavalry. This resulted in mounted units that were small and not highly disciplined. It's always hard to tell the rich and important to shape up and obey orders. Hannibal's cavalry, in contrast, was one of his strongest arms, employing highly skilled and experienced African and Spanish horsemen.

The short sword and pila (throwing spears) had by this time replaced the pike as the main Roman infantry weapon. Some of the triari, the back line formed by the most experienced troops, however, still occasionally carried a long spear. More important, the smaller, flexible formations were still evolving, and the leadership skills to command such movements simply hadn't been developed yet. Before Cannae and Trebia, Roman armies had usually won by simply overwhelming their opponents. This led to the overconfidence and a feeling that the one-sided loss at Trebia had been a fluke. Yet two years earlier at Trebia, Rome had also lost most of her experienced soldiers and commanders. The new army was larger, well equipped, and confident, but inexperienced at nearly every level. The Roman army of 216 B.C. was merely a hammer, not yet a sword.

The leadership of their army showed the Greek roots of Rome. When threatened or at war, the Greek city-states had for centuries appointed a dictator. They gave this man total power for the crisis, including command of the army and control of the government. But too often these dictators liked the power the crisis gave them, and often declared the situation, and their near-absolute control of the city, to be ongoing for years. While the office was supposed to be held only for a limited time, normally a year, there was the slight problem of who told the man who controlled the army, the navy, the economy, and bureaucrats it was time to give up all that power. Many didn't, even in that bastion of democracy, Athens. As a result of this problem, a system evolved in Rome where each year the Senate elected two men, not one, called consuls, who split the control of the army. When operating separately, each controlled the legions that were with them. When together, they were equals, alternating command daily. Sometimes this obviously awkward system of command rotation would work. But when it didn't, as at Cannae, it set the stage for disaster.

The two consuls commanding the Roman army at Cannae were L. Aemilius Paullus and C. Terentius Varro. Aemilius Paullus was an experienced soldier. Varro was a politician eager for the military glory that would further his status in the Senate. Varro had no military experience on any level. Still, the men got along, and for some time Aemilius was able to moderate Varro's lust for glory. Aemilius was unwilling to face Hannibal's army on a flat battlefield, which favored Carthage's more numerous and experienced cavalry, so the experienced soldier resisted the urge to fight Hannibal when that leader's smaller army offered the Romans battle several times.

Between them, the consuls commanded over fifty thousand Romans, versus Hannibal's forty thousand, half of whom were undependable Gauls and other locals enlisted mostly at the promise of loot. For weeks, the two armies waited within a few miles of each other, the Romans on the hills and the Carthaginians on the level river plain below them. Aemilius's continued refusal to be drawn into battle on the field of Hannibal's choice irked Varro. Since the loss at Trebia, the Roman army had been under the command of Fabius the Delayer. The rebuilt Roman legions were felt to have been, man for man, inferior to Hannibal's army. Because of this, Fabius had spent the last two years shadowing the Carthaginians without directly engaging them. A large part of the Senate never liked this strategy, including Senator Varro, and he chafed at Aemilius continuing to avoid battle even though Rome clearly had the larger army.

Interestingly, though his army was famous for them, records show that no elephants remained with Hannibal's army by this time, and so no elephants took part in the Battle of Cannae. Not that they were needed.

After spending Aemilius's day as commander on nearby heights where they were safe from the far-superior Carthaginian cavalry, it was Varro's turn in control. He decided to force the other consul to fight. Varro led the entire Roman army down onto the plains adjacent to the Aufidus (now called the Ofanto) River. Night fell and the Romans camped on the plain. The next day it was Aemilius's turn to command, and, with his entire army already deployed near the river, it was impossible to withdraw. Varro had forced the battle, and it would be fought in terrain that favored Hannibal and his cavalry.

To maximize the impact of their superior numbers, the Romans formed into a massive column, deeper than it was wide, and prepared to smash through the center of the Carthaginian army. If the Carthaginians had tried to face this in the traditional manner of placing their best units in the center as well, the strategy just might have worked. But Hannibal used his numerous Numidian light cavalry, allies from Africa, to screen the fact that he had reorganized his formation. The change should not have been a surprise to the Romans, as he had used a similar formation to defeat them at Trebia two years earlier, but no one seems to have considered that he might do it again. The Carthaginian placed his best armored and trained troops, mostly raised in what is today Spain, on both flanks. On the far ends of his line, opposite the weaker Roman horsemen, were Hannibal's cavalry, who were better trained, more heavily armored, and much greater in number than the patrician Roman horsemen. This left the numerous but least well trained and armed Gauls facing the Roman column. Once Hannibal had completed organizing his army, and without the Romans having time to react to how his forces were now placed, the Carthaginian pulled his light troops back into reserve and the Gauls rushed forward. And the battle began.

The Roman light infantry, the velites, also fell back, and the superior Roman infantry smashed into the Gauls at the center of Hannibal's line. The Romans' plan to make their column deeper, in order to give it even greater impact and put more pressure to the front, left the flanks open. Aemilius and Varro's plan was to smash right through the Carthaginian center, then turn both ways to surround both flanks.

The flanks of the Roman army, now moving forward in its long column, were to be protected by their cavalry. No one expected the Roman cavalry to defeat the Africans' horsemen, only to hold long enough to break through the center. Instead, the Roman horsemen collapsed almost instantly and fled from battle toward their camp in the hills, most not even stopping there. The light Numidian horsemen kept after the Roman horsemen. The Carthaginian armored Spanish and Celtic horsemen, after a short pursuit, turned back toward the infantry battle.

Long swords swung against the large Roman shields and armor to little effect. Meanwhile, the more tightly packed legionnaires' short swords thrust out from behind the wall of Roman shields to slaughter the lightly armored Gallic infantry in front of their massive column. The Roman legions pushed forward in their thick mass, constantly pressing back the Gauls. The Roman infantry was now separated from their fleeing cavalry, and soon also their light infantry, which had also been driven away by the Carthaginian horsemen. The determined Roman infantry ignored these setbacks and drove forward. The Gauls continued to fall back grudgingly, and their formation began to bend. After some time, the inevitable result of the uneven duel was that the Gauls were being forced back. The Roman infantry kept slowly advancing over the bodies of the dead or dying Gauls.

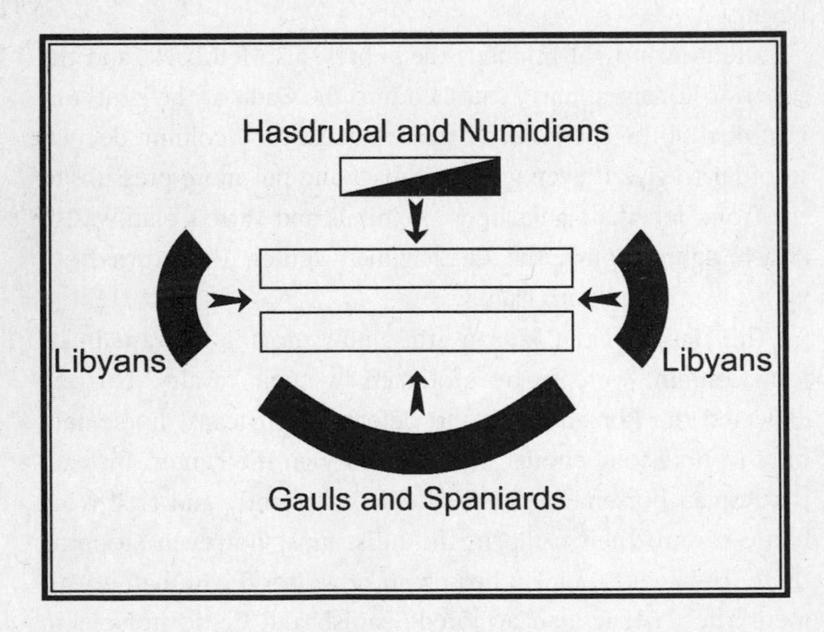

It was only at this point that Hannibal finally set his best infantry into motion. They were not used to reinforce the collapsing center of the Carthaginian line, which by now had bent back and was near breaking, but rather against the sides of the ponderous Roman column. The Roman advance stopped as men turned to deal with the new threat on both flanks. Suddenly, the Romans found themselves surrounded on three sides, but with such a deep and wide formation most of the men were too far behind their comrades to fight. Their thick, deep column meant that less than ten percent of them, those on the outside, could actually fight.

The inexperienced Roman soldiers and officers were unable to change formations in the middle of the battle, and so they pushed harder. The apparent hope was to smash out the Gauls before the two flank attacks could have any effect. It was the worst decision they could have made, because continuing to push forward doomed the army.

Hannibal, having personally held back from the fighting, saw the Romans continue forward, and sent his light infantry around behind the tightly packed Roman formation. Fortunately for Hannibal, the heavy horsemen also returned at this point and attacked the rear of the Roman column. The triari, the back line of the Roman army, was forced to turn about and face the cavalry. This stopped the forward movement of the entire army. The Roman army was surrounded, most of its men packed into the center and unable to fight, its superior numbers wasted and everyone trapped. What followed was a slaughter. Of the more than fifty thousand men who marched down from the hills under Varro, less than ten thousand, perhaps as few as three thousand, survived.

So how did the Romans lose this battle? It started with a system that allowed Varro, a politician with no military experience and a personal agenda, to command Rome's only major field army. In addition, they fought the battle on terrain that definitely worked in Hannibal's favor, allowing his cavalry to be used to its full advantage. *Plus*, they chose arguably the worst possible formation to make use of their better infantry and greater numbers. There were no tactics, much less any finesse, to the Roman movements once the battle started. They simply formed up in what resembled a giant phalanx and pushed forward, allowing a smaller army to completely surround them.

Rome survived, which must have amazed Hannibal, and Varro actually showed great courage and presence over the next few days while rallying the remnants of his army. Then, in 204 BC, Scipio Africanus and yet another Roman army defeated the last of those veteran African and Spanish soldiers who had enveloped the Romans at Cannae in a battle near Carthage itself. The city and empire of Carthage surrendered and the second Punic War ended.

There is no question that Hannibal was a genius, perhaps one of the greatest commanders in history. But at Cannae he had a lot of help. There was the split in command that made no military sense, and this put in control an inexperienced commander who used unimaginative tactics. Then Varro's movement into the valley ensured that they fought on the opponent's battlefield and terrain of choice. Any one of these command errors could cause the loss of a battle. Finally, neither Varro nor any of the Roman commanders seems to have reacted in any way to the Carthaginian change in formation or flank attacks. Together these mistakes created what may well have been the most one-sided military defeat in all history.

THE BATTLE OF CARRHAE

Parthia, 53 BC

BILL FAWCETT

There is little to question about the motives that drove Marcus Crassus to one of the worst defeats in Roman history. He was one of the Triumvirate, three equal leaders who ruled Rome jointly. The other two members were Gaius Julius Caesar and Gnaeus Pompeius (Pompey), already known because of his many military victories as Magnus the Great. Crassus was the richest man in Rome, which was the wealthiest city in the world. But more than wealth, Romans valued power and prestige. Neither the Senate nor his fellow triumvirs wanted a war with Parthia, located mostly in present-day Turkey. There was a neutrality treaty between the countries, and Parthia had grown to as large an area as the semifeudal nobility could govern and was no real threat to Rome itself. But Crassus, even after leading the legions that defeated the slave rebellion of Spartacus, detested being in the shadow of both Caesar and Pompey. So he gathered a large army and set off to conquer Parthia.

The army Crassus formed looked, on paper, to be able to overwhelm Parthia. Marcus Crassus had seven legions (perhaps twenty thousand of the best infantry in the world), a thousand Gallic, and three thousand Asian light horsemen armed primarily with spears. Before leaving, he was joined by an additional six thousand lightly armored horsemen under the Roman ally Artabazus, the king of Armenia. This force was twice as large as the total of all Parthian forces. There was one major difference. Whereas the Roman force was primarily an infantry army with light cavalry supporting it, the Parthian armies were all comprised of cataphracts, heavily armored horsemen similar to medieval knights, riding horses also protected by armor (called barding). The bulk of the Parthian army consisted of horse archers. And these horse archers were equipped with a composite bow, one that fired an arrow farther and harder than any other type of bow—hard enough, the Romans found to their great consternation, to penetrate even the armor worn by the legionnaires.

Having decided his defeat of Spartacus made him a military genius on the same level as Caesar and Pompey, Crassus proceeded to ignore the advice of not only his local allies, but even the augeries of the priests, who were an integral part of every Roman army.

Crassus's first bad decision was to pursue an unnecessary war, but his big mistake was how he went about it. Everyone seems to have advised him to take his infantry into Parthia by way of a chain of mountains and hills. This would have put the Parthian cavalry at a disadvantage, as they could neither form up nor charge effectively. But the desire for instant glory seems to have blinded Marcus Crassus to the risks of taking the faster route across the flat river valleys of Mesopotamia. His desire to do so was encouraged by the local leader of a kingdom on the border of Parthia, the chieftain Arimanes. Arimanes "reinforced" the Romans with nearly six thousand of his own horsemen. The local noble also assured Crassus that the Parthian army was already beaten and retreating at the mere rumor that the Roman commander was coming. Unknown to Crassus, Arimanes was actually allied to the Parthians and, when push came to shove, neither he nor his horsemen could be found. Crassus's desire to take this desert route was reinforced by the fact that he would be able to add a few thousand more men to his army by picking them up from the border fort garrisons that lay along his chosen route—garrisons put there because the level terrain made it the obvious route for a Parthian cavalry to invade going the other way.

Convinced that he had to move into Parthia quickly or the entire Parthian army would escape, taking with it his bid for military glory, Crassus ordered the Roman army onto the perfect terrain for cavalry—terrain that was also the worst type possible for his infantry to meet a mobile foe on.

As the campaign started, Crassus felt his military genius was being proven again. Making a river crossing into hostile territory has always been hard, but by using the cover of a major thunderstorm, Crassus was able to cross the river that marked the border of Parthia without opposition and occupy the minor city of Teugama. His brilliance proven, to himself at least, Crassus never made another good decision.

In reaction to the Romans' treaty-breaking invasion, the Parthian king, Orodes II, took half his army into Armenia to punish Artabazus for his assistance to the Romans. The other half of the Parthian army remained behind under the command of a noble named Surena, often called just Suren, who was also the head of one of the seven clans that shared power in Parthia. Accompanying Suren's less than three thousand cataphracts were thousands of horse archers. It is likely that Suren was simply planning to slow down the Roman army in order to buy time for Orodes II to drive Armenia from the war and reunite the entire army for a final battle against the Romans.

So the Roman army sat near a river in a desert, and they needed only to follow this same river to eventually reach the two capitals of Parthia. But rather than follow the meandering river and take a few extra weeks to arrive at the capital, Crassus allowed himself to be convinced by Arimanes to take the "faster" route across country. He was told that this would enable him to reach the Parthian capitals before they could be reinforced. Nearly all of Crassus's lieutenants advised against this, but he ordered them to march. At first things went well; the land near the river was lush and green, and the wells frequent. But as they pushed inland, the land turned to empty desert. After convincing Crassus to push into this waste even more quickly, Arimanes took his entire force away, promising to disrupt the "retreating" Parthians—supposedly to delay them so the Romans could have their battle, but more likely just to have a good laugh and collect his rewards.

The Roman commander then received a letter from Artabazus saying he could not send the rest of the army he had promised. Orodes II had invaded Armenia and all of Artabazus's forces were needed to defend his own country. But this did not cause Crassus to hesitate. All he wanted was a fast and glorious victory, so that was all he saw. No argument by his second in command, Cassius, who later made the unkindest cut of Shakespearean fame, could sway the triumvir.

After several more thirsty days the Romans approached the

town of Carrhae. Near it sat the half of the Parthian army that had remained behind and their commander, Suren. Crassus now went from being obstinately in command to indecisive. At first, he ordered a line formed with cavalry at each side, this being the classic Roman attack formation. But as the light Parthian horsemen swept easily around the flanks, he ordered the entire army into a large square. This change may have been necessary, but the square meant that the whole army was now barely able to move.

Suren is said to have prepared his cataphracts for a massive charge. Before it could start, he saw the depth of the Roman line and their numbers, and ordered the heavy horsemen to hold, presenting a constant threat that held the Roman army in its square formation. Instead of charging the square, Suren ordered his horse archers to begin firing into the static Roman force. It was an unpleasant surprise to the Romans that the Parthians' arrows were delivered with enough force that they could penetrate the legionnaires' armor. After an intense barrage, the fire slackened and the Romans took heart, knowing that a horseman could only carry a limited number of arrows. But their joy was short-lived, as Suren brought up camels carrying tens of thousands of additional arrows, and the arrow storm began again, continuing for hours.

When a large Parthian force appeared at the rear of the Roman square, Crassus ordered his son, Publius, to take the Gallic horsemen, his best cavalry, five hundred foot archers, and seven cohorts of infantry to drive off and destroy the smaller Parthian force. This force appeared to be comprised of mostly unarmored horse archers. The Parthian archers fled and Publius followed. When both forces were some distance from the main battle, the Parthians turned and charged into the Romans with what cataphracts accompanied them, while both Roman flanks were suddenly fired upon by the horse archers. The Gauls rode forward to meet the Parthian heavy cavalry, and discovered that their spears could not penetrate the cataphracts' armor. In desperation they began to grab hold of the heavily armored Parthians' lances, if they survived to do it, dragging both Gaul and Parthian to the ground. Missing your dive at the metal-tipped twelve-foot lance often meant being skewered by it, and most of the Gauls eventually were. Soon the Gauls and the light infantry tried another desperate measure to stop the heavily armored horsemen. They dived under the cataphracts' horses to stab the animals where they weren't protected. This was also a near-suicidal attack. As his position worsened, Publius sent his father a desperate request for reinforcements.

Before long, most of the remaining Gauls were on foot, and both flanks of the Roman detachment's battle line were collapsing under the rain of arrows. Publius ordered the entire force to retreat to and form up on a small hill. Facing outward in every direction, they soon thwarted the cataphracts. The trouble was that a thick clump of men capping a single hill created a nearly ideal target for the horse archers. As his men fell around him, it became apparent no help was coming and Crassus's son committed suicide. He chose the traditional manner and ordered his armor bearer to stab him. After Publius died, those who remained surrendered. The survivors numbered less than five hundred out of the force of four thousand that had marched out just a few hours earlier.

While Publius's force was being slaughtered, Crassus was changing formation. With the pressure on the back of the Roman square gone, with all the Parthian cavalry off slaughtering Publius, Crassus ordered a return to an attack formation. When he received the message telling of his son's plight, Crassus ordered the entire army forward. The front of the army was hit by cataphracts and showered in arrows. The attack halted almost as it began.

At this point, the accounts of all of the survivors agree, Crassus simply lost it. He raved madly and generally panicked. While he still commanded an army at least twice as large as the Parthians opposing him, he lost hope. Seeing this, the two highest-ranking surviving commanders, Cassius and Octavius, took control of the army. They ordered a careful retreat to the city of Carrhae a few miles distant. Seeing that the army was retreating, virtually all of the remaining Roman cavalry, mostly locally recruited light horsemen, sped off. They paused just long enough to spread rumors in Carrhae of a total Roman disaster, panicking the city. Since they were engaged in a fighting retreat to Carrhae, the Romans were forced to leave their wounded where they fell. Plutarch states that four thousand wounded men were killed by the Parthians the following dawn. When darkness finally fell, the Romans continued to retreat as the constant rain of arrows slowed.

Even at night, the Roman army was still surrounded and occasionally attacked by the nimble Parthian horsemen, who emerged from the darkness, struck, and retreated before an alert could even sound. In the darkness, a tribune named Varguntiniuis led four cohorts off on his own volition. Separated from the main Roman army, Varguntiniuis and his small force was quickly surrounded and overwhelmed the next dawn. Of the nearly three thousand men in those four cohorts, only twenty survived. The Parthians, impressed by the valor of these last survivors, who stood prepared to fight to the end, allowed those few remaining to live and go free.

Crassus's army continued its retreat through the night and finally reached Carrhae with over thirty thousand men still in the ranks. The Parthians arrived the next day, but were in no position to assault the city. Crassus was once more in command, but soon learned that there was not enough food in Carrhae to feed his army for more than a few days. The next day he ordered a further retreat. Not having learned his lesson, Crassus trusted yet another local guide who was in the pay of the Parthians. He led the army by the worst and driest route possible. Soon the Romans found themselves trapped by the Parthians against the first real water they had found—a marsh they were unable to cross.

The Parthians agreed to parley and negotiate a peace with Rome. This would likely have resulted in an indemnity and the loss of some territory. But this was not to be. Crassus, still on the edge of panic and his will broken, had to be forced by his troops to even talk with Suren. When one of the Parthians grabbed Crassus's reins, a fight began between the Roman delegates, which were all of the surviving Roman commanders, and Suren's bodyguard. Crassus was killed, and those few Romans who survived fled into a nearby marsh. The Parthian army attacked the leaderless Romans, whose morale broke almost instantly. Twenty thousand died, and the remaining ten thousand were taken prisoner. These last were settled as a group in the distant Parthian province of Sagdia, where archaeologists today still find Roman-style artifacts.

The Roman legion, when properly employed, was able to defeat almost any enemy. The Romans had not only a tradition, but an expectation of victory. But this attitude, and his personal quest for glory and military fame, led an inexperienced and overconfident Marcus Crassus to place his legions in a position where their strengths of organization and tactics could not make a difference. The result at Carrhae was that the vaunted legionnaire became simply another target unable to bring the enemy to grip. Then again, Crassus assured this defeat with blatant and continual failures of command, reconnaissance, and intelligence. He could not even surrender well enough to end the slaughter.

You have to wonder at the ego that could disable and then lead to destruction of the world's best fighting machine. Marcus Crassus created and then lost a war that he did not have to fight. He chose to fight this war on terrain that gave the enemy every advantage. The Roman triumvir seems to have gathered no intelligence about the enemy and their tactics, or the terrain his army would cross. Perhaps most foolishly, a commander who had just one battle's worth of experience chose to constantly ignore the advice of more experienced officers and trust instead the wrong local advisor every time, all because they told him what he wanted to hear. Over forty thousand legionnaires died or were sold into slavery in Crassus's vain quest to equal in glory two of the most brilliant military minds of all times, Caesar and Pompey. He managed instead to establish his own place in history as one of the worst commanders ever.

Marcus Crassus did leave a very large estate.

TEUTOBURG FOREST

Germany, AD 7

BILL FAWCETT

Contrary to what most grade school textbooks say, Rome actually did expand into Germania, today's Germany, almost to the Elbe River, under the reign of the emperor Augustus. The expansion did not last very long, however, and, unlike most Roman expansions, this one was not cemented by any major military victories. In fact, the opposite was true. Unlike anywhere else the Roman empire occupied, Germania did not adopt Roman culture or become a part of the widespread Roman economic structure. There are always many reasons for such a political and social failure. A clash of cultures or lack of mutual understanding is often the cause when two peoples fail to reconcile. The Roman failure to hold Germania was basically about the economy, and, even more, it can be explained by one Roman commander being consistently and arrogantly dense.

The economic part of the picture was that the Roman empire needed to make a profit on its wars. The professional and long-term-service Roman army was expensive to maintain and recruit. Unlike the earlier Roman legions at Cannae and Carrhae, the army under Augustus had changed from one of citizen levies and volunteers to a full-time and truly professional force, where being in the legion was a twenty- or twenty-five-year commitment. Rather than weeks of training, it took many months to train and indoctrinate a Roman legionnaire of the first century. Men were paid for their service based upon their rank and given a substantial retirement bonus, often in the form of land in some frontier area. With a professional army and large bureaucracy, there were a lot of expenses, and the only way to get the money was either taxes or loot.

For the means of transport and communications available at this time, the Roman Empire under Caesar Augustus was too big. It would take a messenger as long as two months to travel the length of it by horseback and ship, and a legion needed twice as long to cross the empire under the best conditions. This meant the governors had a lot of discretion and no real check on the decisions they made in the emperor's name. It also meant that if something went wrong, they were on their own for several weeks.

Just maintaining the status quo was expensive. So for a war to have any appeal, there had to be the potential of sufficient booty, or expansion into fertile lands where settlers could be sent, then taxed, so the effort more than paid for itself. This requirement, more than anything else, is why the expansion of the Roman empire slowed. In the east, as you read about in Carrhae, the Parthian empire was too much trouble to beat and hold. (Their capitals were actually captured by a later emperor, but even then they were merely pillaged and abandoned.) To the south were the empty wastes of the Sahara Desert. To the west, the Atlantic Ocean and the unknown. Only to the north could there be a chance of more expansion. But there was a problem, as the lands of the Germanic tribes beyond the Rhine were simply not worth invading. The tribes were poor compared to those that Augustus's father, Julius Caesar, had conquered in Gaul. Nor were the German lands very fertile or attractive to settlers. Even so, the sheer force of Roman culture and the strength of its earlier victories allowed Augustus to claim the lands with the grudging acceptance of the German tribes, and even to appoint a governor over them, Publius Quinctilius Varus. So for a short time, in name and form, Germania was a Roman province.

Garrisons were mostly comprised of Frank or German auxiliaries located in small strongholds all over the new province of Germania. Three full legions were assigned to Varus. Those were stationed in the south of Germania, near the borders of the established Roman provinces. So the bulk of the new province of Germania was lightly occupied, but Rome still expected it to show a profit. Another incentive for taxes was that Augustan governors were not paid, but instead were allowed to keep a part of the taxes they collected. So Varus decided to institute taxes on all the tribes, a new and unpleasant concept for most of the warriors affected. While the entire occupation of Germania was accomplished on the strength of the Roman reputation and not conquest, Varus began treating the province as if it had been conquered and subdued. Varus had earlier been the governor of a thoroughly subdued African province and had no trouble with it, so he was merely treating the Germans in the same manner he had others under his command. He began ordering chieftains about and meddling in tribal affairs, acting just like any normal Roman governor. In short, Varus acted like a conqueror, which had been true in Africa, but the German tribes had never been conquered. This was, to put it mildly, the first of many mistakes.

Perhaps the most Romanized, and also one of the most southern, German tribes was the Cherusci under the leadership of Arminius, who spent much of his youth as a hostage in Rome, and then as an officer in the Roman auxiliaries. This meant that he was well trained by Rome itself in how to conduct a battle. Arminius soon showed that he had learned well the military lessons Varus disregarded or failed to remember. Arminius and many other local leaders regularly met and dined with Varus, attesting their perpetual loyalty to him and the empire. Varus took this to heart. After all, he represented Rome, whose legions were without question the most effective fighting force in their world.

Varus was confident of his military situation because he had three top legions under his command, the XVII, XVIII, and XIX (17th, 18th, and 19th). So when word came of some local uprisings in the farthest parts of his province, Varus brought all three legions together and marched north. This was the normal Roman procedure in reaction to any form of rebellion, to use overwhelming force and make an example of the rebels. In this way, Rome was able to dominate 20 million highly varied people from Britain to Egypt with an army of less than 220,000 legionnaires and about that many more auxiliaries.

Confident that at first he would be moving through the "friendly" territory of his loyal ally and frequent dinner companion Arminius, Varus was little concerned by the fact that his column was badly organized and cluttered with noncombatants. Accompanying every officer were one or even a dozen servants. Women followed, some "wives" and others there for professional purposes. Droves of merchants and their servants joined the column in order to be ready to buy the spoils and slaves at the best prices. Thus, with three legions, three squadrons of cavalry, and six additional cohorts (about twenty thousand men), Varus marched off in a long, strung-out column that contained more civilians than soldiers.

Now, the roads in Germania were primarily trails, and most of Germania was heavily forested. This made it very difficult to throw out units to the sides of the march column. Those not on the trails simply could not keep up, and often encountered ravines or rivers that forced them back into the main body. So scouting was limited to seeing what was on the path ahead.

Marching on a trail only a few meters wide also meant that if you paused, pressure from those who followed forced you to keep moving. Within a few days, the mixture of unruly civilians and narrow trails further broke down the march discipline of the column. The Roman legions, combat units of cohorts and centuries were split into small groups intermingled with women and merchants, all moving in a jumble along the forest trails. Marching at its head, Varus was aware of the disorganized situation of his legions, but was confident that he would have the time to rectify the confusion when they got closer to the rebels. The Roman governor soon felt even more secure knowing that Arminius had somehow managed to muster his tribe in record time (the German chief had actually started mustering his warriors even before the legions were gathered). Arminius had then led his several thousand German warriors off for the announced purpose of harassing the rebels and clearing Varus's route. This already bad tactical situation was further complicated by a steady rain, with occasional thunderstorms.

This rain is important in understanding the fate of Varus's legions. Already the Roman governor had made the classic mistakes of accepting the intelligence reports of a potential enemy as accurate, and of putting his legions into a marching order in terrain where their single greatest strength, the ability to fight in a tight formation, was nullified. The unrelenting rain made the legionnaires, whose advantages as a formed unit were already nullified, less effective individually as well. The rain drenched the leather straps that held the Romans' armor, causing it to stretch, and to shift when hit or while marching. The constant rainfall soaked in and made leather- or cloth-covered wooden shields heavier and harder to hold high. Finally, the rain made the Romans' only distance weapon, a wood-and-metal javelin called the pilus, slippery and harder to throw. On top of all this was the sheer exhaustion that comes from marching in wet clothes over bad trails while getting wetter and more chilled with every step.

Only a few rainy days into the march, and deep into the territory of the Cherusci, the column was suddenly attacked by the thousands of warriors that Arminius had gathered earlier. Varus now knew the folly of trusting his dinner companion, but it was too late. Spread out and forming up only with difficulty, the legionnaires drove off this attack by their "allies," but only after taking significant losses. Many of the civilians were killed or ran into the forest, where they were quickly either slain or enslaved. Every soldier in the column now knew that the entire force was strung out in hostile territory. The entire army retreated to a wood-covered hill, where they burned most of their wagons to prevent them from slowing the pace. The legions also destroyed anything else of value that they or the merchants carried to keep it from becoming spoils for the Germans. The legionnaires also reduced what each man carried with him to nothing but weapons and a few days' food. The next day, the march renewed. Left behind were the wounded and those many civilians who feared to continue marching. Lightly guarded and with the forest only a few meters away, the fortified camp on the hill was impossible to defend. It fell within days and everyone left behind was slaughtered.

The three legions had been stung, but they were still essentially intact as a fighting force and continued the march. They were hoping to reach a friendly city or suitably open country. In open country they knew they could defeat anyone. But the Germans knew this as well and avoided all of the large clearings. Ahead of them, the Romans knew there were small cities and open spaces. So the march continued onward through the rain, the unarmored and faster-moving German warriors attacking first one section of the column, then another. Pausing only to drive off each marauding group of German warriors, the legions continued to make slow progress past the dripping trees. With no wagons or men to spare, the wounded had to be left behind and were lucky if they died quickly.

A Roman historian, one Cassius Dio, tells the story of the march. He recorded that Varus finally did reach open country, but there were no settlements or strong defensive positions. With limited food, there was no choice but to continue marching. Upon setting out from the open terrain, the legions again plunged into the trails that wound through the Teutoburg Forest, where they suffered their heaviest losses. The superior tactics and training of the legionnaires were useless, "for since the Romans had to form their lines in a narrow space, in order that the cavalry and infantry together might run down the enemy, they collided frequently with one another and with the trees." There was simply no place to deploy and no way to create the solid shield-to-shield formation against which so many opponents had been ground down and defeated. The Germans, used to fighting as individuals, were familiar with this type of constant hit-and-run skirmishing.

By the end of the third day after the attacks had begun, it was apparent the legions were falling apart. In an almost unheard-of breach of discipline, one cavalry commander, a Numonius Vaala, abandoned the infantry and tried to make it back to the Rhine with his unit alone. They never had a chance. The mounted squadron died to a man. Still, the column, now depleted by serious losses, continued to slog ahead, and what remained of the legions fought on. Once the running battle had started, a call had gone out from Arminius for warriors from every German tribe to join in. There was loot to be had and revenge to be garnered. In small groups and large, they attacked the struggling Romans almost constantly. There was little coordination between the German units, but none was needed. The march slowed to a crawl, yet there was no choice but to struggle on, hoping to reach a defensible settlement or city.

It rained even harder on the fourth day, and the wind increased to a fierce gale. Finally, the column began to disintegrate. As officers died and centurions lost control, men deserted or surrendered. Yet others fought on, exhausted, with sodden equipment and little hope. They were overwhelmed, as more and more Germans were arriving every day. By the fifth day, all that remained were fugitives. A small number of legionnaires reached the fortress of Aliso, which held out against a determined German attack, and thus they survived. Everyone else in the three legions was killed or enslaved. Varus committed suicide, as did most of his officers.

It was recorded that when Augustus was told he had just lost three full legions, about a tenth of his entire army, he exclaimed, "Quinctilius Varus, give me back my legions." For the next five hundred years, no legion ever was raised under the numbers XVII, XVIII, or XIX.

The Roman army returned to Germania a few years later under better commanders, and from AD 10 to 12, punished the German tribes and drove them away from the new Roman border of the Rhine River. But after the loss of three legions in the Teutoburg Wald, it was considered too costly for them to stay and reclaim Germania as a Roman province.

It is harder to find what Varus did right than to list all he did wrong. Almost every mistake he made can be attributed to overconfidence. But we can try to list his errors. The list reads like a catalog of all the "must do" things you need for losing a battle: He had insufficient intelligence regarding the enemy, and even less on his "friends." There was a lack of planning for the march, and disregard for flank scouts and units protecting the column from attack on the sides. Much of the early problems were caused by allowing the unusually large civilian components to separate his combat units, making them less effective and often outnumbered locally. But perhaps most important, this defeat was once again caused by making the legions fight in terrain that nullified every advantage the legionnaire had from his armor, thrusting sword, and greater training.

THE HORNS OF HATTIN

Holy Land, AD 1186

BILL FAWCETT

Okay, here is a hard question. You are Guy of Lusignan, recently elected king of Outremer, the Christian kingdom of the Holy Land. The Islamic forces facing you have found a brilliant leader in Saladin and an army has been gathered under his command. You know that your forces are outnumbered by the enemy by a factor of five to one, and it is even worse if you just look at the most important combat arm of your age, cavalry. You are also aware that several of your leaders have been marked for death by the enemy king. Located between you and the enemy army is a waterless desert, and your cities are all protected by some of the greatest fortresses ever built. This means that in a castle or walled city, even a few hundred men could withstand an attack by thousands of the enemy. This had been proven many times by AD 1186. So what do you do? Stay in the fortresses or march out to meet Saladin's army in the open?

There seems to be an obvious answer, but it was apparently

not as obvious to the king of Outremer. Guy was new to the throne, and his kingship had been contested by many of the very nobles who now made up his army. He may have correctly assumed that in his age of chivalry, where personal courage was valued over all else, any sign of hesitation could be interpreted as cowardice. Even the accusation would cost him his kingship—and his life. The leaders of the factions that controlled Outremer were typical nobles for their day: brave, often devout, and not capable of finesse. So, instead of sitting safely behind the walls of the many castles and cities the Christians controlled, King Guy decided to advance against Saladin.

Now, Saladin had as his army about twenty thousand armored or partially armored cavalry and a smaller number of horse archers. There was very little Islamic infantry beyond supporting elements, who provided food and fodder, brought up supplies, and guarded the camp. Guy controlled a much smaller force of horsemen, perhaps as few as a thousand and certainly less than fifteen hundred, but he had with them twenty thousand foot soldiers who had been assembled by stripping the garrisons of every castle and city in Outremer. The Christian cavalry were outnumbered thirteen to one. Such odds sound long, but they were no worse than other Christian kings, such as Richard the Lionheart, had later won battles with. Most of the Outremer horsemen were knights and men-at-arms in armor, while most of Saladin's were unarmored horse archers. This army was also the largest the Christian kingdom had seen in almost 50 years, and so everyone in command of the Christian army was full of confidence. So on July 2, 1186, the entire Christian army marched out, leaving behind cities and castles occupied by so few men they would be unable to defend themselves.

Between the two armies was a stretch of desert containing

few wells. Regardless, it seems that Guy was expecting a quick victory and made little provision to carry water with his army. In theory, the troops were marching through territory Guy had once commanded, so the thirty-mile trek must not have seemed that dangerous. The Outremers were so confident as to actually carry with them their most revered relic, the "True Cross," which had been found by the mother of Constantine. The target of this march was Tiberius, a small city that Saladin had recently captured and was camped near.

Within a day, it was clear things were not going well. Constant attacks by small bands of Saladin's heavy horsemen had slowed the movement of the Outremer infantry. By the end of that first day the men and horses were exhausted, and the wells they had planned to reach were still miles away. It was decided by the leaders of the fighting orders and nobles to make a dry camp.

The march continued the next day, with the Islamic horsemen still harassing the army, but doing little real damage to the Outremer force. The knights' armor and the padded coats of the infantry protected them from most of the arrows fired by the horse archers. Islamic chroniclers tell of Christian infantry soldiers as having so many arrows sticking into them that, while they remained unharmed, they looked like porcupines. Still, the constant threat from the unarmored horse archers meant that everyone in the Christian army had to stay in their armor in the hot sun, and that took its toll in thirst and exhaustion. What little water the men carried for themselves was quickly consumed.

By the end of the second day, the army was just a few miles short of a lake and near two hills called the Horns of Hattin. These hundred-foot-high prominences provided a strong defensive position. One was known to have had a well near its summit. Unfortunately, only after they began to make camp on that hill was the well found to have been blocked. By this point, the knight's horses had been weakened by dehydration, and many of the infantry were beginning to collapse. Most of the twenty-two thousand soldiers camped on the hills were so thirsty that they had trouble sleeping, and a general sense of defeat was said to have pervaded the infantry. It didn't take a tactical genius for every common soldier to realize something was very wrong. By the time the unexpectedly dry camp was established, Saladin's army had completely surrounded the two hills, keeping them under constant arrow fire. There would be no water and no real rest.

As the light of dawn appeared, one of the nobles, Balian of Ibelin, could stand no more. He led his vassals and mounted sergeants into a headlong charge down the hill. The attack slashed through the entire Islamic army, which closed again behind it. When Balian turned to go back, he found his few dozen horsemen faced by hundreds of Islamic cavalry. He wisely turned and fled. A short time later, Reynard of Sidon, unaware of Balian's escape, led his own mounted men in a similar suicidal charge. He was also able to fight his way through Saladin's less heavily armored horsemen and flee. It is an irony that those two men, who had sought a noble death, were among the few survivors.

Without orders, the surviving infantry formed up and moved en masse toward the lake that sat within plain sight of the hill. Without the protection of their own heavy horse, and in no real formation, this mob of Christian infantry was torn apart and slaughtered by Saladin's armored cavalry. This left perhaps a thousand fully armored knights on the waterless hill surrounded by thousands of hostile horsemen and archers.

The armored Islamic heavy horsemen charged up the hill from all sides. The sun beat down and dust rose, but thirsty and exhausted as they were, the Christian knights held on and drove them back. Saladin sent them back up time after time. Each attack killed more of the defenders, until by that afternoon only a few hundred knights remained. They gathered for a last stand around Guy's tent and their relic of the True Cross. When the Moslem knights made their final attack, they found that most of the remaining Christians were too weak to fight or had collapsed from thirst and exhaustion. Those who remained alive or could be revived when given water were taken prisoner. The exception to this was a few of those knights who were notorious for attacking and pillaging helpless Islamic pilgrims: they were executed on the spot by Saladin.

With their garrisons lost at the Horns of Hattin, the cities and castles of Outremer fell quickly. There were more Crusades and even many Christian victories, but the control of the Holy Land, and Constantine's mother's True Cross, were both lost at Hattin.

It is easy to see what Guy of Outremer, being big on courage and short on wisdom, did wrong. In a common theme for defeat, he fought the battle when and where the opposition desired and in terrain that favored the Moslem horse over the Christian infantry. Guy even failed to effectively scout the route of his march to determine which wells were viable. Certainly, the blocked well on the Horns of Hattin should not have been a surprise. Guy lost control of his infantry and failed to prevent their suicidal movement toward water. But mostly he could have won by staying behind the walls of his fortresses. To retain his crown and lands, Guy of Outremer simply should not have gotten out of bed at all, or at least never have left his castles.

THE BATTLE OF AGINCOURT

Just About the Perfect Disaster

France, 1415

BILL FAWCETT

It would be much easier to list what, if anything, the French king John did right in combating the invasion of Henry V of England than to list what he did wrong. Ever since a Norman noble holding major lands and titles in France conquered Britain in 1066, the English kings had lands and claims in France. The 1415 invasion of France that ended in the Battle at Agincourt was inspired by another similar expedition across France seventy years earlier by the Black Prince. This time Henry V decided to try to enforce his claim of sovereignty over much of what is today modern-day France. To do so Henry V landed with thirty thousand men at the mouth of the Seine River and quickly placed the rich and strategic city of Harfleur under siege. In response to this challenge to one of his major ports, King John and Charles d'Albret, the constable of France, reacted with an impressive lethargy. Finally, after some weeks, they began to call up all of the chivalry of France, bidding everyone to join them in Paris.

While the French army assembled, the siege of Harfleur wound to its inevitable end with the capture of the city, though not before disease had struck the English camp and Henry's army was reduced to less than twenty thousand effectives. Of those who were left, some remained behind as a garrison in Harfleur, while others returned to England. This left Henry V with an estimated seventeen thousand soldiers of all types. Except for knights and nobles, it is hard to accurately determine the size of a fifthteenth-century army. There were no pay lists, or any pay at all for that matter, as most men fought for the right to loot and pillage.

Knowing that John was gathering a much larger army to meet him, King Henry, in what appears today to be a bit of ultimate chutzpah, decided to lead his army in a great raid across western France to Calais. This move exposed his army to being trapped or destroyed far from any bases or friendly cities, but somehow must have made sense to the feudal mind. This march was to follow a route similar to that of the Black Prince's army seventy years earlier; that choice may be a hint as to why Henry V took such a chance. It may have been inspired by a desire to share in the fame and success the Black Prince gained from his sweeping raid, which ended in another one-sided English victory at Crecy.

As a result, a few weeks after taking Harfleur, Henry and his men marched south. They quickly discovered that all of the closer bridges across the Somme were heavily guarded, which meant it would take too long to fight across them. But they had to cross the river to reach Calais. For the next few weeks, the entire army marched east along the Somme, looking for a crossing point. Each day's march brought them closer to Paris, where John had finally assembled an army of sixty thousand knights and retainers. This did not include the six thousand Parisian militia crossbowmen who had volunteered to go and were disdainfully sent away. The crossbowmen were dismissed as "shopkeepers," who were of low social status, and told that they would be useless in combat. Of course, by the time this massive army had been assembled, the English had spent nineteen days pillaging their way across the center of France while looking for an undefended ford or bridge across the Somme. But finally and belatedly, the assembled might of France moved toward the English.

Now, Henry V was having his own problems. There just wasn't enough food to feed his army, and there were few targets left worth looting on the north side of the Somme. Worse yet, the patriotic spirit of French nationalism remained strong among the French, and this inspired the peasants to attack Henry's foraging parties, which slowed their gathering food. The situation was made even worse when many of the lesser French castles bravely chose to resist even his large army. Losses from exhaustion and even starvation began to take their toll. Men also deserted, and less than fifteen thousand still remained under the British banner. Much less confident than when he started his great raid, the English king maintained his march southeast along the Somme until the two armies literally blundered into each other near the small city of Agincourt.

Amazingly, it appears that neither side bothered to set scouts or have outer flank guards. The French benefited from this oversight the most. A stag ran into one of the leading elements of Henry's army. The hunting cries and horns that were subsequently blown by the excited British chivalry warned the French that the English were nearby. No one told the English that the French were close, so the French had the vital element of surprise. Unfortunately, the constable of France did nothing for the rest of the day and the advantage was lost.

Finally the British became aware that the French army was nearby, and had in fact blocked their line of march. When the size of the French force became apparent, Henry V realized that there was a good chance the sheer bulk of the opposing army would crush his smaller, exhausted force. He sent word to King John that he was willing to give up all his loot and make peace in any but the most humbling terms. Confident of his superior army, d'Albret refused to allow his sovereign to consider the offer. The constable of France had worked hard assembling the greatest army his nation had seen since the days of Caesar, and he was going to have his battle. And, to the regret of all of France, the next day he did.

The clouds from the rain the night before cleared early, and it was a sunny day as Marshal d'Albret sent his first division straight at the position Henry V's tired and hungry army had hurriedly prepared. There seems to have been no scouting, no flank movements, no taking any advantage of having a relatively rested army four times the size of the one he was facing, no nothing. He was going straight in to smash them without further ado, or apparently any additional thought. The French did take one step to show they had learned something from Crecy: since the horses seven decades earlier were less well armored than the men they carried, it was arrows wounding the horses that knocked most of the French knights from the saddle; to avoid this now, most of the French attacked on foot, leaving their horses tethered far from the battle. That done, no other planning or preparation seems to have been made. D'Albret simply sat within a few miles of the British. Having already sacrificed the element of surprise the day before, he did not even bother to send forward his several thousand crossbowmen to soften up the English for his dismounted knights.

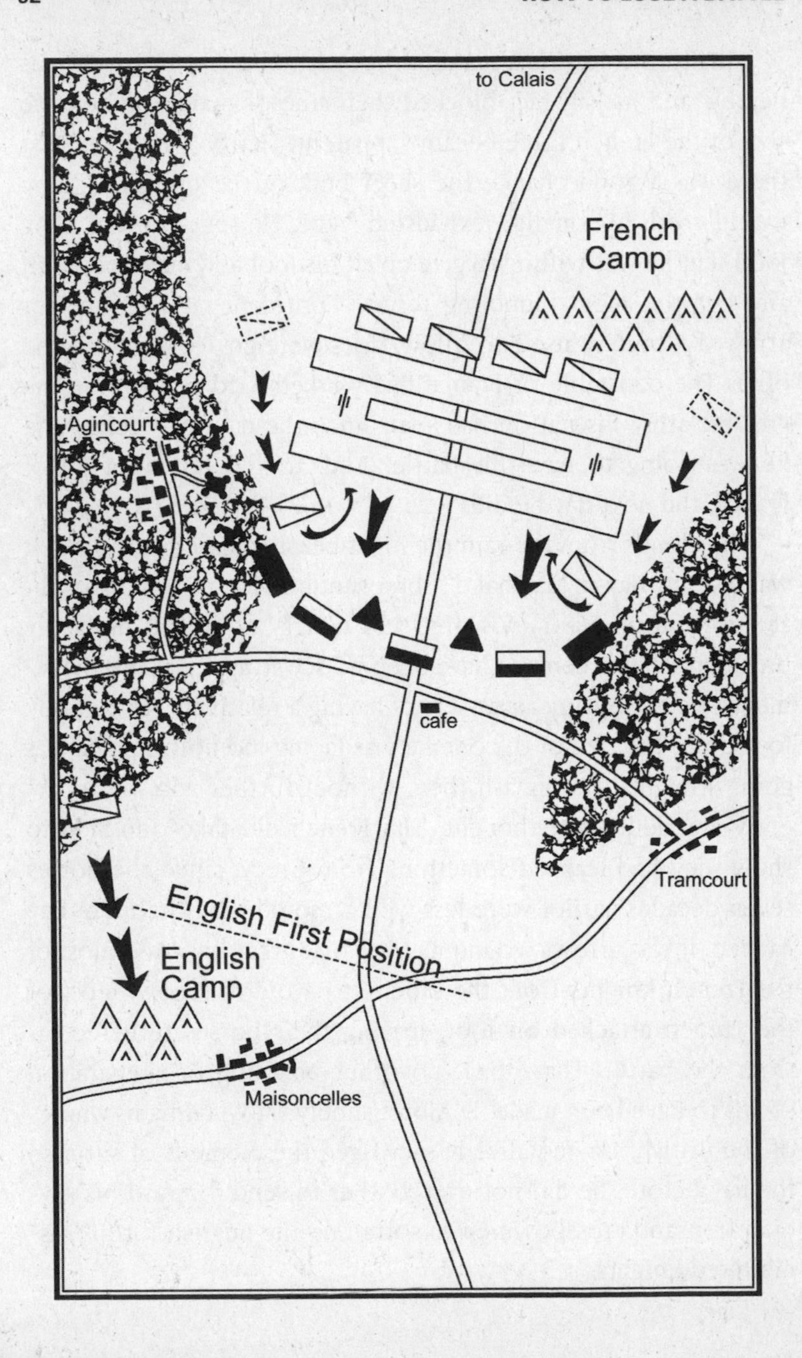
to Calais
French
Camp
Agincourt
cafe
Tramcourt
English First Position
English
Camp
Maisoncelles

Henry, whose grandstanding was the reason his army seemed about to be wiped out, made better decisions, and the French constable paid for every one of his mistakes. By securing both flanks on a forest and the river, Henry managed to allow only a narrow front into which the French could attack. This situation was made even worse when the constable made no effort to move any of his mounted forces around the sides or to the rear of the English, even after seeing the narrow battlefield, dismounting them instead. D'Albret remained confident that the armored chivalry of France would easily march right up (running any distance wasn't a good idea in a full suit of armor) and overwhelm the British. Henry also sent a few hundred archers, all he could spare, into the forest, positioned to fire into the flank of any attack. Constable D'Albret does not seem to have bothered to even send scouts into those same woods. Only a few dozen knights were all that would have been needed to clear the forest, but at no point were any sent. As a result, every French attack was subjected to demoralizing flanking fire during its entire approach to the English position.

Of course, the more than ten thousand French archers could have fired back at the forest or the English position, but since none of the titled knights would allow men of such lower classes to precede them (and likely win the battle without them), it was decided to place the archers behind each division, effectively masking their fire and rendering them useless.

So, having missed every chance to use his advantages, the constable of France then lined his three battles up one behind the other and sent them straight in against the prepared British position. This meant only a small part of the French army could engage the English at one time, essentially negating the French advantage of being a much larger army.

The first division of the French army moved forward toward

the English. To say that they charged would be inappropriate. Heavily armored men-at-arms and knights on foot can't run. The weight of their armor, shields, and weapons slowed them to, at best, a fast walk. Their movement toward the British was slowed even further by the rain the night before; the ground over which they attacked was quickly churned into a mass of slippery mud. This slower pace meant that there was more time for the English longbowmen to wreak their slaughter. The air was soon filled with the hum of arrows. At first, the arrows fell at a steep angle as the archers fired at their maximum range. But the French were packed so tightly that many of those found victims. When the remaining soldiers got closer, the flights of arrows could be aimed at individuals, and these struck with such force that they easily penetrated the chain mail and hardened leather of the French men-at-arms. Arrows continued sleeting in from the archers in the woods to the side, meaning there was simply no shelter from the deadly shafts. Men fell by the thousands, making it even harder to advance over their bodies. Few of the French knights or men-at-arms actually reached the British lines. Those who did found that it was protected by lines of sharp stakes. Before the second French division could arrive, the French in the first division could take no more and had begun to withdraw. The unarmored and lightly armored English then left the protection of the stakes and charged after the retreating French, easily overtaking and killing the heavily burdened and often exhausted men who remained. The second and then the third French division continued to frontally attack the English, until it became apparent that there was no chance of recovering the battle. As it became obvious that the attack had failed, most of those who remained back fled to the safety of the walls of Paris.

Tens of thousands of Frenchmen died. A few hundred Englishmen were lost. The French king John was captured and spent the next five years in the Tower of London. The treaty he signed to finally be set free ceded much of northern France. The expense of ransoming their king and all of the captured nobles depressed the French economy for a decade. Henry certainly had made a strategic error that put his army where the Battle of Agincourt was fought, but his tactics, combined with d'Albret's hesitance and incompetence, worked together to make the English king look good.

So what did King John and Charles d'Albret, constable of France, do wrong? It might be easier to list what he did right. Okay, he was brave and courageous once the battle started. The French army took much too long to assemble, effectively ceding the vital port of Harfleur by default. The constable refused to even consider what was effectively a surrender by Henry V. Both forces lacked even rudimentary scouts or intelligence on the enemy or their movement; in fact, there seems to have been little effort to even determine where the enemy was by either side. The French failed to attack on the first day when they could have surprised, and smashed in open order, the vanguard of the English army. The French allowed the British to determine the battlefield and fight from a prepared position. The British were starving and there was no need to accept the battle on any terms other than those that favored the French. But the French accepted the battle and then fought it in such a way as to lose the advantage they had in numbers. Then, the constable made no use of the one arm he feared most in the enemy, his own archers. Remember, he refused to allow six thousand Parisian crossbowmen to join the army, but still had another ten thousand crossbowmen there. Most never fired a single bolt. The French totally failed to clear or even scout the flanks along the line they knew they were going to attack on, and paid dearly for not doing so. Finally, the French constable did not take the wet ground or weight of armor into account when he dismounted most of his armored men-at-arms and knights.

To give Henry V such an infamously lopsided victory as the Battle of Agincourt, Charles d'Albret had to make about every mistake an army commander could . . . and he did.

THE BATTLE OF TRENTON

The Hangover Heard Round the World

Trenton, New Jersey, 1776

BILL FAWCETT

This is a small battle, and really there is only one—well, maybe two—real mistakes an otherwise competent and professional officer made. So why is it here? It's here because those mistakes made as much or more difference in history than most of the battles in this book.

By the winter of 1776, the rebel cause in the American colonies was not doing well. Things had gone from bad to worse. Since August the rebel army had lost battles at Fort Lee, Fort Washington, White Plains, Kip's Bay, and Long Island. On top of this, it had been driven out of most of New York, and the Continental Congress had been forced to flee Philadelphia. In today's terms the entire Revolution was in danger of being marginalized, with the rebels controlling only a few thinly populated areas and popular support waning. To make matters worse, the enlistments for half of the men in the one real remaining army in the field were due to end on New Year's Day. General George Washington had to act and act quickly, or the war would be over and he, along with all of those who today in the United States are called the founding fathers, would be landless and would become hunted fugitives.

Numbers were a problem as well. Washington had barely over two thousand men in his camp at Valley Forge to face the twenty thousand British soldiers in New Jersey and New York. Combining every other Revolutionary garrison spread along the Delaware, there were still less than seven thousand Continental soldiers facing three times their number in New Jersey alone, with more British troops occupying New York behind them. Worse yet, many of these Continentals were militia, and most were far less well trained for a stand-up battle than the British units they faced. Most of the British, and their paid mercenary troops, the Hessians, felt with some cause that the war was over. Even most of those living in the colonies were fairly sure all that remained for the spring was for the British to smash a few pockets of die-hard rebels. This sentiment was spreading even among those sympathetic to the rebel cause.

The winter of 1775–1776 was one of the worst in centuries. In fact, the Northern Hemisphere was in the middle of what is referred to today as the Little Ice Age. Growing seasons had been unusually short in both North America and Europe, with rivers that normally don't even see ice on them freezing over. The men in Washington's poorly financed army suffered from the savage cold; some had worn out their shoes and really did have to march with rag-covered feet to this battle. (After the battle they had Hessian boots to select from, as well as many other needed supplies.) Now, northern European armies rarely fought in winter. Napoleon would teach them differently, but that is twenty years in the future. Between the harshness of the weather and the tradition of not fighting in the winter, no one on the British side had any reason to expect any action by Washington's outnumbered and ill-equipped troops.

With his army falling apart, his cause faltering, and morale low, Washington had to act. His one advantage was that he knew the British were aware of his situation and would discount what remained of his army. So he planned a surprise attack on the day he felt the Hessians would be least alert, Christmas Day. A holiday attack was hardly a novel tactic, though it continues to work, even as recently as the Arab-Israeli Yom Kippur War.

In Trenton, Washington's target, were camped three regiments (nearly twenty thousand men), all Hessian mercenaries. The British used these Hanoverian soldiers as shock troops, and they were feared for their fierce bayonet charges and strict discipline. The Hessians mostly spoke German, not English, which made them ideal occupation troops, since they were unlikely to sympathize with the rebels, as they could barely communicate with them. The Hessians also tended to act as if they were in a European-style war and not a revolt. This meant they confiscated what they needed and treated every colonist as an enemy. So among all the British troops, excepting maybe Tarleton's Legion, the Hessians were by far the most hated. This was also the closest enemy position, and Washington decided that their winter quarters in Trenton was the ideal target. If they won it would end his five-battle losing streak in spectacular fashion.

Gathering every combatant he could, Washington ordered a crossing of the Delaware on Christmas Eve night. Immediately things began to go wrong. The Delaware was a mass of large ice floes, and this slowed the efforts of the Marbleheaders, fishermen from Marblehead, Massachusetts, to bring the army across in the small boats. If you look closely at that famous picture of Washington standing as he is carried across the Delaware, you can see that most of the men in the boat are using their oars to push the ice away, not to row. This and problems getting the artillery over the Delaware meant that rather than an attack in the late hours of the night, the army would arrive at Trenton after sunrise. Any pickets would see them at a distance, so it was likely surprise would be lost. If what remained of the Continental Army found itself in a stand-up battle with the Hessians, they would likely lose. They would also have nowhere to retreat, with their backs against a river. Still, understanding there was no alternative, Washington ordered his army on. Fighting no battle would have been just as disastrous to the rebel cause as losing one.

Meanwhile, in the Hessian camp it was party time. They were comfortably settled into the houses of Trenton, and expected to be paid a bonus and sent home by the next summer. Their opponents were starving and freezing and badly outnumbered. So it was time to break out the schnapps. Playing cards, drinking, and doing those things soldiers far from home do to party, the entire Hessian force went at it. The officers were just as overconfident as the men. No sensible army would move away from their warm camp in such weather. If they did, they could not cross the ice-filled Delaware River. This war was over and it was time to celebrate the holiday and a job well done.

As the Hessians partied, several things went wrong on the colonial side. There was a second Hessian regiment camped in a town near Trenton; this is called being in a mutually supporting position. If the battle lasted more than a few hours, this second Hessian regiment would likely arrive and Washington's army would be suddenly, badly outnumbered. A second military force of another two thousand colonials had been ordered to cross the Delaware and attack this regiment, but they were unable to get past the ice floes and never got across the river. Then a Tory farmer saw the rebels advancing that night and sent a warning note to Colonel Rall, commanding the Hessians. It went unread because of the officer's interest in a card game and possibly an already advanced state of inebriation.

As the Continentals approached the town, they should have been discovered in plenty of time for the Hessians to form up and make a battle of it. But they weren't. Everyone had drunk heavily the night before, and many of the pickets were never placed. Worse yet, when a Lieutenant Weiderholt raised the alarm and his nineteen-man picket did fire on the advancing rebels, no one else was awake or sober enough to notice. Brushing aside those few pickets, it was just after dawn when Washington's forces attacked Trenton from both sides. Strangely, the sounds of volleying muskets and even cannon failed to awaken Colonel Rall. The Hessian resistance was at first disorganized and fragmented. Groups of Hessians attempted to rally at several points, but were either overwhelmed by numbers or broken up by the skilled use of cannons. Half the town was soon taken, and many of the Hessian soldiers scattered or were captured half dressed and confused. Still confident, and likely less than fully awake, the officer was slow to react and then dressed carefully. By the time he appeared and took command of his grenadier regiment, the rebel troops were preparing to assault a barricade that was reinforced with two cannon near his quarters. The mercenaries were in no better shape than their commander. The Hessians fired early and high. Not a single man on the Continental side fell. With a yell the colonials charged, stopping to fire their muskets as they ran. The barricade was taken, and with it the last cannon still in Hessian hands. Rall led a counterattack, but Washington himself led a new force in that drove off Rall and retained the captured cannon.

Even with most of their regiment captured or hiding, the Hessians were tough, professional soldiers. Unwilling to concede the battle, Rall ordered his band to play, and this helped him to rally men from all the units. But with most of the town occupied, the rebel soldiers could take cover and shoot from the houses on every side of the Hessian units trying to form in the streets. Most of the German officers were killed, and no counterattack could get started. Even after all this, the Hessians continued to fight. Rall ordered what was left of the rallied men into an open field nearby, where the Continentals could not use the buildings as cover. Calling together all of his surviving troops, Rall found he had about seven hundred men ready to fight. Even with two-thirds of the regiment lost, the mercenaries fought on. But Rall now had a problem. The colonials had cannons, and he had lost his. What remained of the regiment in the open field would be cut to pieces by those cannon and be unable to respond. So he ordered an attack back into the town. The attack was shot to pieces and dozens more Hessians fell. One regiment failed to get the order and remained in the open. This gave those who survived the ill-advised attack back into Trenton no place to retreat to. Rall himself was wounded and died just after the remnants of his command, soon surrounded by Continentals and faced with a battery of cannon, surrendered.

Had Rall paid any heed to the farmer's warning, even just ensuring his pickets were in place and alert, it is likely that Washington would have been driven off or defeated and the American Revolution ended by the failure.

So the Revolution of 1776 was saved by three mistakes we see on so many of these lists:

overconfidence;

failure to view intelligence; and

lapse of discipline and basic security procedures.

THE BATTLE OF BALLYNAMUCK

Not Exactly 1066

Ireland, 1798

BILL FAWCETT

There was just one time since William the Bastard changed his moniker to William the Conqueror that someone actually landed an army on the British Isles. It was in Ireland, and the invasion was more a farce on the level of Peter Sellers's *The Mouse That Roared* than any real threat to the British occupation of Ireland. So, here we have an invasion that began with a fury, but ended with a whimper.

The year 1798 was a time of great strain between France and England. The revolution controlled France and threatened all monarchies, while Britain led the way in opposing it. Ireland, occupied and oppressed for hundreds of years, continued to resent English domination and discrimination. Rebels from Ireland saw in France both a kindred spirit and an ally who could provide the muscle needed to finally drive the hated English off their island. Many Irish rebels had fled to France, including Wolfe Tone, the effective leader of the resistance, and were actively encouraging the Directory (the transitional governing authority during the ongoing revolution) with promises, which proved to be true, of Irishmen flocking to join any effort to throw the British out. The idea of taking the war to their enemy, the Crown, had strong appeal, and a Britain deeply involved against the Irish would have few resources to spend on continuing its war against the emerging Republic in France.

The first mistake made was the choice of who would lead the expedition to invade Ireland and support the Irish insurgents. The choice was General Jean Joseph Amable Humbert. While he had followed orders well and fought with courage, General Humbert was not used to independent command. If the other choice had been sent, history would likely be very different now, but that less-than-qualified French general was encouraged to lead a venture even farther away from Paris, the conquest of Egypt. Had Napoleon Bonaparte, not Amable Humbert, led the French armies into Ireland, who knows what might have resulted. But the polite, careful Humbert was chosen to lead one force, and the more proven General Jean Hardy the larger one.

The plan was simple: the two armies were to be transported by the French navy to Donegal, a hotbed of anti-British action. There, a total of somewhat under five thousand soldiers would use thousands of additional muskets to arm those Irishmen expected to flock to Wolfe Tone under his green flag with a harp and "Ireland Forever" on it. Perhaps the only thing they did judge correctly was the enthusiasm of the Irish. From the beginning, everything else went wrong.

Like too many plans, this one did not take into account changes that might be needed as a result of the unexpected. Considering the English weather, there should have been some thought as to what to do if poor wind or other obstacles prevented one of the forces from joining immediately. The prevailing winds are westerly, but westerly winds prevent ships from leaving French harbors. But there wasn't any plan for this, and when steady, contrary winds trapped Hardy's larger force with Wolfe Tone in their French harbor, Humbert was basically on his own.

Humbert, without knowing that Hardy and the larger force would not appear, chose to land at Killala rather than Donegal, where the rebels were expecting him. So Humbert and his thousand soldiers landed, politely notifying the local vicar and others. He then waited several days for news of Hardy. It didn't matter that he was in the wrong place, because there was no one to join up with. Those rebels who had been organizing in Donegal were left waiting.

Now, when invading a hostile shore where you are likely to be outnumbered by the defenders, it is important to take the initiative. Amable Humbert paraded around Killala for several days, during which approximately a thousand Irishmen joined his army. He was taking a few days to train these recruits, when word arrived that he was on his own. At this point, the combined Irish-French force began a leisurely march toward Castlebar, the seat of County Mayo.

By this time, General Cornwallis, who commanded all of Ireland from Dublin, had learned of the French landing. Yes, the same Cornwallis who led the failed British army that had tried to occupy the Southern states in the American Revolution two decades earlier. Cornwallis dispatched what seemed to be a large enough force consisting of almost four thousand regulars taken from a number of garrisons. There is a problem with garrison duty—being garrisoned becomes as monotonous as your average nine-to-five day job. It is usually safe and secure, and as a result it dulls the troops and affects morale. This is reflected by the fact that, while outnumbered by more than two to one, Humbert and the Irish volunteers managed to rout the British in a short battle just outside Castlebar. The British broke almost immediately, and the battle was soon known all over the world as the Castlebar Races, referring to the speed with which the British units ran in disorder to Athlone, leaving behind their baggage and nine guns and covering the sixty-three miles in less than a day. That's an amazing rate for anyone to travel on foot, most having to run all night to get there in so short a time.

No longer waiting for support from the two other planned expeditions and making no effort to communicate or coordinate with them, Humbert had every reason to fall back and wait. The troops under Hardy alone would quadruple the number of regulars in his force. The Irish were moving toward Killala from all directions, ready to join his army. The ships that had dropped his force off had promised to return with more regulars. And, finally, Amable Humbert knew there were almost fifty thousand British soldiers occupying Ireland.

After enough hesitation to give Cornwallis time to reorganize his forces to meet the threat, General Humbert, with a whole eight hundred soldiers and perhaps fifteen hundred Irishmen, marched on Dublin and the largest concentration of British troops without stopping to train or recruit more men. Cornwallis had no problem knowing where Humbert was, as the village garrisons in towns he passed near sent a constant stream of reports on his progress. By the time the French and their Irish volunteers had reached the town of Ballynamuck, almost forty thousand British troops were closing in from all sides. Humbert ordered his forces to attack when outnumbered twenty to one. After several minutes of the French making more a gesture than an attack and the Irish taking severe casualties, the French general surrendered.

Humbert and his French soldiers were treated well, the general being entertained in high style for some weeks before returning to France. His men were also soon paroled back to France, carried by Royal Navy ships. As for the Irish, Humbert had to know what awaited them if he attacked. They were slaughtered to the man by dragoons before the day of the battle was over.

By the time Hardy and Tone arrived, the Irish had lost heart. The two never landed, with Tone suffering the indignity of being captured at sea and hanged by the British as well. A third small raid came to nothing, and so ended the last invasion of British soil.

One has to wonder just what General Amable Humbert intended. He cannot be blamed for the failed plan; he was only one of several commanders. But he can be blamed for indecisiveness followed by a suicidal (for the Irish at least) lack of sense as he moved toward a far superior army's strength. There is the definite possibility that even he would not have been able to explain his intentions. His actions were neither those needed to foster a major rebellion, nor militarily sound once he left Castlebar. The final result was that the Irish rebels were thoroughly suppressed.

An inflexible plan, where even a likely complication of bad weather was not accounted for, coupled with indecisive leadership, which evolved into impulsive leadership, led to an action that lost focus on its original objective (to foment the Irish rebellion), resulting in the expedition blindly moving toward an unachievable objective—a mission destined for failure.

BAD LUCK OF BILLY BAINBRIDGE

Tripoli, 1803

BRIAN THOMSEN

The so-called Barbary pirates patrolled the seas around Tunis, Tripoli, Algiers, and Morocco from the Middle Ages to the early part of the nineteenth century. (Their name derived from the Berber people of North Africa.) Primarily sea raiders, initially they made a nice living plundering merchant ships for fun and profit, but during the era of colonial expansion and conflicting European empire, they opened up a profitable sideline privateering for various powers, setting targets for political reasons as well as commercial gain, while negotiating treaties with all sides of the western conflicts, extracting duties and tribute in exchange for not privateering various interests.

When the United States was slow to deliver the tribute due to the changeover from the Adams to the Jefferson administration, Tripoli's pasha all but declared war.

Captain William Bainbridge was anchored in Algiers Harbor with the tribute in hand, having just completed the forty-day crossing from Philadelphia, when he was summoned by the dey (sultan or pasha) to his castle. That worthy instructed him that the tribute would have to be delivered to the sultan himself, and that Bainbridge and his crew must convey him and his entourage to the sultan's castle under the Algerian flag, in essence chauffeuring and catering the excursion, or have his ship destroyed and his crew and himself sold into slavery.

Bainbridge's ship, the *George Washington*, was a twenty-four-gun vessel and more than a match for the dey's forces. Unfortunately, Bainbridge had docked her directly in front of the guns of the castle, which were ready to fire even as the meeting was taking place.

With no chance to reposition his ship or even alter the placement of his crew, Bainbridge had no choice but to accept the mission and incur the embarrassment as his ship's colors were temporarily replaced by the Algerian flag. According to Max Boot's *Savage Wars of Peace*, not only was he compelled to take the tribute (close to $800,000 in coin and jewelry) and the dey's ambassador to the sultan in Constantinople, "but also the ambassador's suite of 100 black slaves and 60 harem women and a veritable menagerie consisting of twenty lions, three tigers, five antelopes, two ostriches, and twenty parrots." His only revenge was the bedeviling of the unwelcome contingent with frequent and sudden shifts in tack along the way, disrupting the Muslims' prayer rituals, as they continually had to reposition themselves to face Mecca during their devotions.

The new president, Thomas Jefferson, was incensed by such indignities to the representatives of his newfound nation, but was unable to interest Congress in a declaration of war, thus hampering the resources available to him to deal with the situation.

By September 1801, the situation had gotten much worse.

Not only were the sultan's forces demanding higher levels of tribute, they were also conspicuously not honoring their parts in any bargains, and, as a result, the piracy continued, necessitating more intervention and stabilization by the novice American naval forces. Soon supplies and crew enlistments began running short, which resulted in a four-ship force being cut in half, with the *Essex* and the *Philadelphia* left behind to continue a basically ineffective blockade at Tripoli.

The following year, though falling short of declaring war, Congress authorized the president to secure by any means necessary the protection of American shipping abroad. As a result, six more ships were dispatched to the Mediterranean, under the command of a political appointee, Richard Valentine Morris, who decided to bring along his family, thus signaling to the world interests that actual "fighting" might not be high on the agenda, no matter what armament the boats possessed. He took the better part of a year to actually make it to Tripoli.

Morris met with the sultan to negotiate and balked at the terms, thus offending the warlord, whose expectation was that he would be receiving new tribute at once, as well as the guarantee of annual payments down the road. Morris then turned around and headed back to America, nonplussed by the whole affair.

Thus after two years of undeclared war between Tripoli and the novice United States Navy, the new appointee did little to enhance the safety of her ships or even the respectability of the newly formed republic role as a world power. Worse yet, before a new commander could arrive on the scene, Bad Luck Billy Bainbridge once again reared his unfortunate head.

Bainbridge was now commanding the *Philadelphia* as part of a blockade that had been ordered by Washington to put pressure on

Tripoli and discourage piracy against U.S. ships in the Mediterranean, when, on October 31, 1803, he spotted a sail to the east and set off in pursuit.

In no time at all, these eager pirate hunters ran aground on the Kailiusa Reef off the harbor of Tripoli.

Bainbridge ordered the jettisoning of anything that might reduce their load, allowing them to ride higher in the water and perhaps disengage from the grounding that held them immobile.

First the water, then the stores, then the cannons, and then the mast itself, but nothing lifted them free as Barbary pirate agents of the pasha closed in.

Realizing that capture was inevitable, Bainbridge had holes drilled in the hull to assure that his ship would never be sailed again, and then surrendered to the pirates at hand.

Bainbridge and his men would spend the next twenty months in captivity in Tripoli, but none of the tortures they faced was as great as seeing their stores and weapons salvaged by the pirates. Not to mention that the pirates were able to repair the boat, which was freed from the reef with the rising tide of a storm that had come in.

The U.S. Navy now had one of its own ships to contend with in its war against the pirates.

So what went wrong?

Well, if Bainbridge was representative of the caliber of naval commanders dispatched to Tripoli, one need look no further.

And there seemed to be a misconception all along the way that the United States was dealing and negotiating with honorable men.

They weren't.

They were dealing with pirates.

At Algiers, Bainbridge should have been more careful in placing the ship and in keeping his men ready at arms, so that when the "pissing contest" began the United States of America would be able to put their best face forward and show a pattern of strength instead of one of weakness. Instead, they again and again returned, never seeming willing to fight, and allowed themselves to be taken advantage of.

At Tripoli, Bainbridge should have quite literally watched where he was going.

Did the pirates intentionally run him aground?

Probably.

And the feeble attempt at rendering the ship useless to the enemy was as bad as if they had done nothing, when a well-placed fire would have taken care of the ship and the ammunition at hand as well, depriving the Barbary raiders of their booty.

Though a new peace was struck, and the United States did indeed have several valorous victories in the campaign (though probably not enough to have merited its inclusion in the "Marines' Hymn" with the line "to the shores of Tripoli"), the Barbary pirates incident was a lackluster venture for the fledgling U.S. Navy, and about as effective as the tour of duty performed by Bad Luck Billy Bainbridge.

AUSTERLITZ

They Fell for It?

Austria, 1805

BILL FAWCETT

One of the reasons Napoleon won the Battle of Austerlitz was that he outthought and his marshals simply out*fought* the enemy. But the main reason for his victory was that two other emperors and their generals "fell for it," big-time. There is a military maxim that no battle plan survives contact with the enemy, but, in the case of the Battle of Austerlitz, this one did.

In 1805, Austria, hurting from earlier defeats by Napoleon Buonaparte, decided once more to challenge the newly proclaimed French emperor. The English and Russians joined with Austria in declaring war. A yet-to-be-chastised Prussia was also hovering menacingly close to joining this alliance against France at the first sign of weakness. This coalition to defeat Napoleon was known as the Third Coalition, and represented the premier and monetary power, Britain, allied with the two largest land armies of Europe, those of Austria and Russia. Once more, the French were surrounded and outnumbered by their enemies.

Napoleon was the leading figure of his day, dominating everything that happened in Europe and greatly affecting the newly formed United States as well. (The War of 1812 was primarily a result or extension of the Napoleonic Wars.) The man was undoubtedly brilliant and a great general. He also evolved into a competent ruler. But the confidence and egotism that made Napoleon a great general eventually led to his downfall. A useful insight into Napoleon's personal vanity was that, up until being made emperor, his name had been spelled "Buonaparte," and at about this time he dropped the "u" to make his family name sound less provincial.

The Grand Army had been stationed on the coast of France facing England, but when word came of the Austrian preparations, Napoleon ordered it to march east. A few weeks later, Nelson's naval victory at Trafalgar ensured that only the British navy controlled the English Channel, and so England would never again be threatened with invasion by the Corsican emperor. By then, the Grand Army was already several hundred miles away. Even with the newly trained and named Grand Army marching toward Austria, the situation was hardly in France's favor. A substantial Austrian army under General Mack sat threatening France and protecting their border at the city of Ulm. A larger Austrian army was being concentrated a few days' march behind Mack, and yet another powerful Austrian force was marching north from Italy. Two Russian armies were also on their way to reinforce Austria, and, while still technically neutral, the Prussians were quietly mobilizing their entire army.

The French were outnumbered, had lost control of the seas, and were threatened with invasion from Austria. So, of course, Napoleon attacked. In the first few weeks, the Grand Army maneuvered at speeds not seen since the days of the Roman legions, completely surrounding Mack and over thirty thousand of Austria's best soldiers in Ulm. Only a few units were able to break out before the old Austrian general, whose error had been to do nothing, was forced to surrender. Taking Ulm without any real battle, this was an impressive victory for Napoleon, but another almost 200,000 Austrian and Russian soldiers were still on the march. Afraid of being outmaneuvered again, the Austrians continually fell back before the French advance. One of the Russian armies was still weeks away, but their main army and many other Austrian units managed to concentrate at the same time as Napoleon captured the Austrian capital of Vienna at the start of November. This combined allied force was commanded jointly by both the czar of Russia and Francis I of Austria.

Napoleon, the newest emperor in Europe, marched to face this combined army before it could be further reinforced. When the three emperors finally met in battle, their armies faced each other across a small stream known as the Goldbach, a few days' march from what would be the bloody battlefield of Wagram in 1809. (At Wagram, only the courage of Napoleon's men and generals saved a divided Grand Army from destruction. Thanks to the blunders and predictability of his opponents in this 1805 battle, things were far less desperate for the French.)

The combined Austrian and Russian army had almost ninety thousand soldiers in it. Facing them were only fifty-three thousand men under Napoleon; there were another twenty thousand Frenchmen marching hard, but the allied commanders disregarded them and felt sure they had an overwhelming superiority. That was their first mistake. The traditional European army marched at a very sedate pace, designed more to keep the unit intact and battle-ready at all times. Massive supply trains further slowed any movement, so that the Austrian armies moved slowly when viewed in comparison to the French, who marched everywhere at a grueling pace and often lived on only what they could forage (read find and steal). The Russians, though, made the Austrians look fast, moving at a nearly glacial pace. But both the czar and Francis I and their generals at Austerlitz acted as if the French moved no more quickly than they could.

Napoleon had scouted this very battlefield only weeks before. He had found it to be ideal for his purpose, which was to hoodwink the allies into doing what he wanted and then to take advantage of their mistake. To one side were swamps, effectively impassible to any formed unit. On the other side of the battlefield was equally difficult hilly terrain. This meant there was a limited front, which took one advantage away from the allies. Their much larger allied army was not able to use their numbers to flank the French. Dominating this battlefield was the Pratzen Heights. This steep hill with a large, flat summit faced the French right and center. Traditional military thought, even today, equates being on higher ground with being in a superior position. This did not worry the French emperor. Napoleon was always a believer in "his star," and he felt confident that if he could just bring an enemy to battle, he would prevail even if he conceded the Heights from the start. Doing so was, in fact, a vital part of his battle plan. So the French formed up on the ground below the Pratzen Heights, with their army in the rolling fields along the Goldbach. Napoleon was ready to fight the battle he wanted, and, confident in their superior numbers, the Austrians and Russians were eager to give it to him.

There was another factor that drove Napoleon to feel it was a necessity to force a battle there and then. While he had virtually no further reinforcements coming, there were two more entire armies, whose combined strength were almost as great as the larger force he was facing, marching to join up with the two emperors. In fact, Kutusov, the Russian military commander, strongly argued that they should wait for these additional men, but most of the other generals and both emperors felt that they had the numbers and a position that assured them victory. Knowing this, they were also easily led to believe that the French morale had failed. Morale in the Grand Army, miles from any base and doomed if defeated, was a major concern for its commander and yet another reason Napoleon felt he had to fight as soon as possible. He actually faked an attempt to withdraw his army the day before the battle, and this further raised the allies' expectations. Certainly the French soldiers knew they had to win or they would find themselves hunted fugitives hundreds of miles from safety, but the faith of the men in their emperor was still strong.

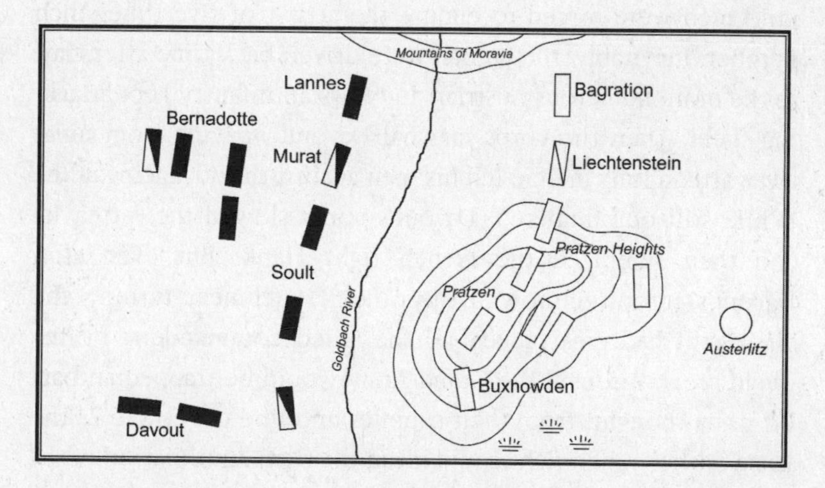

When the battle began, the French left flank was commanded by Marshals Lannes and Murat, who were among Napoleon's best generals. It had in front of it a wide, flat plain. Across this open field were the forces commanded by two of the best Russian commanders, the princes Bagration and Liechtenstein. These four skilled commanders had with them most of the cavalry from both armies. Evenly matched, both sides showed courage and determination as they fought over what would later be called the Cavalry Plain of Austerlitz. A mini-battle in itself, the advantage changed back and forth without a decision until Bagration received the order to retreat and act as rear guard for the rest of the two nations' army. Even then, this capable Russian prince was able to break and maintain his army intact as a rear guard as most of the rest of the allied soldiers turned into fugitives.

For much of the Battle of Austerlitz, Napoleon sat with the reserves and Soult's corps in the center of the French position and did little. It was on the French right flank that the battle could have been lost, though not won. Here, at first, ten thousand men were forced to endure the attack of five times their number. Inevitably, the French were driven back time after time as the more numerous Austrian and Russian infantry kept attacking them. Then the corps marshal Davout, arriving from miles away after a long march, led his men against the advancing allies. While still outnumbered, Davout's corps slowed the retreat of and then stabilized the French right flank. But even after Davout's troops reinforced the other Frenchmen, turning this flank still had great appeal to the allied commanders. If they could break through, the Grand Army would be trapped and cut off, they thought, from their supplies and line of retreat. A collapse of the French right could mean the total annihilation of the Grand Army. This was, as Napoleon had planned, an irresistible temptation. Indeed, if Davout failed to hold, there was a good chance that the Grand Army would have been shattered.

The allied center and part of the allied left flank had been located at the start of the battle on the Pratzen Heights. As the battle to break through the French right flank developed, it constantly must have appeared to those commanding the combined army that just one more push by fresh troops would smash through the Frenchmen there and bring the allies victory. The general on that flank (the allied left), Buxhowden, could taste triumph with each new push. But somehow every attack fell just short of success. Eventually, every man and gun he commanded was committed, with each new effort driving the French back just a bit more. He asked for, and got, a constant stream of reinforcements from the only uncommitted units in the allied army, those occupying the center of the army on the Pratzen Heights. As Napoleon and the French reserves under Marshal Soult, another experienced corps commander, sat watching, the Austrian and Russian regiments and battalions from the allied center streamed down off the top of the Pratzen Heights to attack Davout. As thousands of allies marched down to attack the French right flank, Napoleon and a large part of his army waited, watching and hoping that Davout would hold.

Finally, it reached a point where it was apparent to Napoleon that almost every regiment and battalion the Russians and Austrians had on the Pratzen Heights at the start of the battle had been sent marching down the hill toward Marshal Davout and his brave men. The allies had taken the bait: by sending everyone off to make just one more attack against the French right flank, they had left a big hole right in the center of their army. They did not realize this because they felt falsely secure on the Heights. Soon their army was really split into two parts held together by only a thin line of soldiers. Bonaparte unleashed his own center against the few units still holding the allied army's center on the Pratzen Heights. The attack was made with Soult's entire corps, which was still fresh and rested, and even elements of the Imperial Guard. Drums rapped and bugles screamed commands as Soult and the entire French reserve marched forward. They brushed aside those few units still posted on the forward slopes of the Pratzen Heights, and were astonished to find that when they reached the top it was empty. There was no longer a center to the allied army. Instead, both halves of the allied force found that there were not only Frenchmen in front of them, but on their side and even behind them. The Russian Guard made a desperate counterattack to try to retake the Pratzen Heights, and failed. Napoleon now firmly controlled the middle of the allied position. The way was open for Soult's entire corps to march off the Heights and attack Buxhowden's mass of Russians and Austrians, who were jammed against Davout's corps from the side and rear. Davout then ordered his own battalions to stop their slow retreat and charge as well. With a swamp on one side and fresh French battalions attacking on the other three, over half the combined Austrian and Russian army collapsed into a mob interested only in escape. Some tried to cross the frozen lakes that dotted the swamp, often falling through the thin November ice. More surrendered or were ridden down. The battle was over and Napoleon Bonaparte had won his most impressive victory. This was made possible by the decisions and overconfidence of the general and two emperors he faced.

From the beginning, Napoleon had manipulated the commanders of the larger Russian-Austrian army. By offering them the superior position of the Pratzen Heights, he got them to fight the battle where he chose, and, most important, attack how he wanted. The two emperors, Kutusov, Buxhowden, and all the allies attacked exactly where Napoleon wanted, against his right flank. But their massive attack was to no avail due to Davout's steadfast defense. The allies continually reinforcing their flanking attack with troops from their center opened the way for what today is often considered Napoleon Bonaparte's greatest victory. All because it was, from the beginning, a carefully planned trap . . . and they fell for it.

THE BATTLE OF SAN JACINTO

The Mexican Province of Texas, 1836

BILL FAWCETT

In 1835 Santa Anna, one of the generals who had led the Mexican people in throwing out the Spanish, was elected president and almost immediately abolished the constitution, making himself a dictator. Like their neighbors to the north, many Mexicans felt strongly about their freedom and constitution. Within a year, the dictator Santa Anna Perez de Lebron reacted to the first resistance to his rule and his having abolished the constitution by leading an army into the formerly prosperous province of Zacatecas. It was an army that burnt, pillaged, and raped its way across the land until the province was both devastated and virtually unpopulated. Santa Anna then made sure that his statement "If you execute your enemies, it saves you the trouble of having to forgive them" was known to every person in Mexico. It was a stern warning, but also showed his total disregard for the "rights of man" and other freedoms lost when he abolished the constitution.

Now, if there was one part of all Mexico that was still willing to revolt against Santa Anna, it was Texas. It was far from the centers of the dictator's power, and two-thirds of the thirty thousand citizens living in what was then the Mexican province of Texas were immigrants from the United States. The remainder were either established Mexican families with an independent spirit or men who had fled there when Santa Anna took over. The abolition of the constitution angered most Mexicans, and the "Texicans" more than most. Many of the men and officers who fought against Santa Anna, from the Alamo to San Jacinto, were of Mexican descent, and many risked lands that had been in their families for generations. By 1836, things had come to a head and a revolt started in Texas, with a few hundred ill-organized men easily driving out the local garrisons. So far this was all being done in the name of the abolished constitution. But revolution was revolution, and, having led a successful one against the French that freed all Mexico only a few years before, Santa Anna knew he could not allow another revolt to start, even in the distant and relatively poor province of Texas.

The population of Texas was only a tiny fraction of Mexico's; the Mexican army itself was nearly as large as the entire population of the distant province. Santa Anna had beaten the French army and suppressed much larger revolutions, so it took him several mistakes in Texas to lose both the battle and a war. That he lost at all is more surprising, since Santa Anna was leading battle-tested veterans against men who had no more than a few months at best to train together, and were much more independent-minded and difficult to lead than good soldiers should be. So how did, as Texans so proudly point out, Texas win its independence rather than end up the wasteland that Zacatecas had become?

Santa Anna had been called the Napoleon of Mexico, and he quickly took the name to heart. He was confident, or, as we shall see, *overconfident*, in the face of any "rabble" in thinly populated Texas. Still, he decided to bring against Texas an army of six thousand of his best troops, most having taken part in devastating Zacatecas the year before. Public statements assured everyone in Mexico City that Texas would meet the same fate as Zacatecas, and that every former citizen from the United States would be killed or driven out of that province permanently. Like Napoleon, Santa Anna felt maneuver was a most important part of warfare. So he carefully directed each march and the routes of every column in his army. Unlike Napoleon, the Mexican dictator took little interest in supplying his army. Determined to put down the revolt before any effective opposition could organize, the dictator ordered his army to move north with forced marches. It being winter, the journey soon took its toll, and more resembled the retreat from Moscow than the start of a new campaign. By the time the army neared the Rio Grande, only about four thousand effectives remained. Two thousand men had fallen from exhaustion, had gotten sick, or had simply deserted during the hard march from the capital to the Rio Grande. These remaining troops were reinforced to slightly more than the six-thousand-man army Santa Anna had started with by adding to them the survivors of the Texas garrisons. This meant that there was one Mexican soldier for every five men, women, and children in all of Texas. No one, not even those who wanted it to, such as the president of the United States, expected the Texican revolution to succeed.

The first opposition came on February 23 at the abandoned mission near San Antonio de Bexar, known as the Alamo. As with Zacatecas, Santa Anna quickly made it known that he would take no prisoners. The defenders fought with desperate courage, but by March 6 were unable to hold the large length of walls and were eventually overwhelmed. Those who did survive the assault may have been executed; evidence is mixed. But the final result was that no defender survived.

A few weeks later a mixed force of cavalry and horse artillery caught the largest single force of rebels under Colonel Fannin near Goliad. Trapped in the open, the Texans formed a defense position and drove off the first attacks by the horsemen. Then the horse artillery unlimbered and began punishing them with shot and grapeshot, packets of hundreds of musket balls fired from the cannon like a giant shotgun. Seeing his position was indefensible, Fannin negotiated a surrender. His men would lay down their arms in exchange for being able to return to their homes and the promise to never take up arms against Santa Anna again. These terms being accepted, the Texans surrendered. At this point, Santa Anna ordered that they all be executed. The officers who accepted the surrender protested and were sent away. On March 27, the Napoleon of Mexico forced the prisoners onto an open area and had his men open fire: 342 died, but 28 escaped to spread the tale.

Having destroyed both the only fortress occupied by the Texans and their largest single force, Santa Anna seems to have decided that the revolt was over. Sam Houston was desperately trying to organize what remained of the resistance, but this force of less than a thousand men (at its peak) was being constantly forced north away from the centers of population and their families. So Santa Anna split his force into a number of "flying columns," which mostly meant they were just small enough to march fairly quickly and live off the land. These columns began to recreate in Texas the atrocities of Zacatecas. You could follow their movement by the smoke from the homes and towns they burnt.

Leading the largest column, about a thousand soldiers, Santa Anna pursued and eventually drove the rebel government completely out of Texas (onto a ship). He continued moving in the general direction of Sam Houston, more concerned with driving the former U.S. citizens out of Texas and burning every building he found than fighting a battle against an already defeated foe.

This overconfidence, and the general exhaustion from a long march and months of campaigning, led to a relaxation of procedures that the *real* Napoleon would have never tolerated. Pickets and scouts were used only occasionally, and orders were often sent by unescorted couriers.

Sam Houston's scouts captured a courier riding to the dictator's camp. The message told him two things. One was that the column Santa Anna led was much closer than he had thought, less than a day's march away. The second was that in less than a week the Mexican column was to be strongly reinforced. With his own men more than restive, and some ready to mutiny due to inaction, Houston knew that it was finally time to act. He had already stopped running and was marching closer to Santa Anna. Seeing that the weeks of retreating were over, the Texican army's spirits rose as they marched to meet the men who were burning their homes and towns. When they realized that the battle was imminent, they cheered.

Unknown to Houston, the Mexican reinforcements had arrived earlier than expected. Sam Houston had at most eight hundred men ready to fight, and the additional arrivals meant that Santa Anna had under his command over fifteen hundred experienced soldiers, including mounted lancers and several guns. This gave Santa Anna, already convinced he was merely completing a mop-up following his victories at the Alamo and Goliad, a false sense of confidence. His army was nearly twice as large as Houston's and in a good defensible position. His men were professionals, and he had heard of the dissention Houston's constant orders to retreat had engendered. The Texans would never dare to attack, and all he had to do was wait until desertions, already a Texican problem, and frustration eliminated the opposition for him. Even though he knew the Texans were close, the dictator's confidence was such that he ordered his army to stand down for the afternoon, relaxing in camp rather than preparing for battle. He joined his officers sipping champagne under the shade of a large tree in the center of the camp and soon everyone but a few guards were enjoying their siesta.

When Houston formed his army for the attack, it numbered 793 men. All were ready for a long-awaited fight, but few had ever really been in a battle. The potential for disaster was great, but the chance to defeat and capture Santa Anna was too great an opportunity to pass up. This was probably Houston's last and only chance for victory. The Texan commander understood that if he held his men from battle much longer they would certainly mutiny or simply desert. So the decision to attack was made, and soon the double line of Texans waited behind a ridge that hid them from the Mexican army's camp. Upon Houston's signal, they moved silently forward.

As the men moved toward the Mexican camp, everyone expected to be spotted and hoped they could gain the relative advantage of the top of the ridge before having to face the Mexican regulars. Amazingly, they approached the ridgeline and nothing happened. No one, especially Sam Houston, could believe their luck. When they finally came into sight of the camp, it was a bare two hundred yards away, and still no alarm was being given. Finally, as the entire double line of Texans came into sight, a few cannonballs were fired at their approaching line, sailing safely overhead but alerting the Mexican soldiers that something was happening. A few musket shots rang out from the camp and drums rolled as men struggled to wake up and form into units.

At this point, a small party of men that Houston had sent to check ahead joined the battle and yelled out that the Texans' only line of retreat, Vince's Bridge, was down. Every Texan now knew it was most certainly victory or death, in a most literal sense. Santa Anna never took prisoners, and there was no way to escape. Just as this cry went up, the army being a mere eighty yards from the edge of the confusion-filled Mexican camp, Colonel Sidney Sherman bellowed, "Remember the Alamo and Goliad." It was both a warning and a rallying cry. "Remember the Alamo" was repeated and he then roared it out in Spanish as the advancing Texans opened fire from only a few yards from where Santa Anna's officers were struggling to bring order to a now-panicky army. The galling fire (most of the Texans were frontiersmen, so many shots hit home) broke the morale of the disorganized men. Resistance stopped except in isolated pockets, and most of the Mexican soldiers ran or tried to surrender. These were the same soldiers who had pillaged and raped their way across Texas for the previous three months, and the units that had taken the Alamo, leaving no one alive. Few surrenders were accepted and panic took over, Santa Anna's officers and men fleeing for their lives.

The battle took less than twenty minutes. The revenge went on for over an hour as Texans pursued and killed the remnants of the column. Riflemen fired into milling mobs and their small cavalry unit was everywhere, slashing the routing soldiers and ensuring no one was able to reform and offer any resistance. It was not until some hours later that Sam Houston was once more in control of his army and some prisoners were taken. But he was worried. While they had broken the column, this was less than a quarter of Santa Anna's total army, and the dictator had escaped. Thanks to Santa Anna's overconfidence, Houston had a victory, but the war was far from won.

The next day, among a few straggling prisoners brought in to join those already under guard, was a dusty, dirty man with a torn shirt that, if anyone had bothered to look closely, was of far higher quality than those of the common soldiers. It was not until his own men began saluting and muttering his name that the Texans realized this prisoner was indeed Santa Anna Perez de Lebron himself. The stained and filthy shirt was, it was later realized, actually held together with diamond studs. Quickly brought before Sam Houston, who was suffering from an ankle shattered in the initial attack, the dictator began negotiating for his life and freedom. Many of the Texans, still desiring revenge for the Alamo and Goliad, wanted to hang Santa Anna right there. But Houston held him prisoner until a month later, when a treaty was signed and Texas became a nation. The deal was that Santa Anna could go free if he let go of Texas. He agreed and returned to Mexico City. After that no one called him the Napoleon of Mexico anymore.

Texas was a thinly inhabited frontier and the Mexican army was nearly as large as the population of the former province. The year before, a much more populous province had been easily turned into a wasteland. Furthermore, Santa Anna was leading battle-tested veterans against men who had no more than a few months, at best, to train and work together. So how did Texas win its independence rather than end up the wasteland the other rebellious province had become? There is one simple reason for this nation-forming defeat: Santa Anna's overconfidence led to a dispersion of forces, and an overly harsh response that rallied opposition. His real failures were to not maintain local security around his camp or even bother to locate the enemy. It all came down to misplaced confidence and a gross underestimation of the Texicans.

THE CHARGE OF THE LIGHT BRIGADE

Balaclava, Crimea, October 25, 1854

BILL FAWCETT

You can't have a book about bad military decisions without including the Charge of the Light Brigade at the Battle of Balaclava. Rarely is there the opportunity to discuss such a complete fiasco. As has been shown so often in this book, the failures of a single person in a key position can lead to disastrous defeat. In this case, the British army was blessed with not one but four different individuals who managed between them to destroy in minutes what was arguably the best cavalry regiment in the world.

The Crimean War started because the Ottoman Empire was weak and Russia, after centuries of warfare with this southern neighbor, saw the opportunity not only for revenge but also a chance to gain a port with direct access to the Mediterranean Sea. This had a lot of appeal, as every other European port Russia controlled was frozen closed a large part of the year, or blocked by the Turks. But the merchants of Europe most certainly did not want what promised to be stiff new competition from Russian merchants suddenly loosed in what had been their captive markets. So when Russia declared war on the Ottoman Empire, both France and Britain were quick to join the fray on the Ottoman Empire's side. Fairly quickly, the three allies took the initiative and invaded the Crimean Peninsula, which was Russian territory and extended into the Black Sea. This meant that their troop and supply ships could sail—well, actually mostly steam by this time—directly from England or France, then past Istanbul through the Bosporus Straights to the battle front. The Crimea was also a very tempting target, as it contained the Russian czar's only real southern port, Sevastopol.

The British army of 1854 was a flawed tool, and its obvious failures on all levels during the Crimean War led to massive and much-needed reforms. But that was after the war. At this point, little had been changed since Napoleon had been defeated forty years earlier. A major problem was that the supply system was fragmented and disorganized. This meant badly needed winter coats sat in the harbor while soldiers froze to death in the lines before Sevastopol. The tactics used were those of Wellington at Waterloo and simply did not take into account the much greater firepower of both the infantry and artillery. There were, effectively, no real medical services. Worse yet, as we will see, the British army of 1854 remained an old boys' club in the truest sense. It was controlled by the Horse Guards in the same manner they had commanded two hundred years earlier, and the membership in this old boys' club was still limited to the aristocracy.

"Old" was also the operative word in the case of the British army's Crimean commander, Lord Raglan. He had lost an army at Waterloo four decades earlier and appears to have long lost his taste for conflict at any level. So here is the first of our four,

FitzRoy James Henry Somerset, Baron Raglan. An indecisive man with little charisma and showing signs of his age, Raglan was appointed because he was next in line for a command and no one objected. Sometimes, not even skilled subordinates could make up for such a commander. Unfortunately, it is now apparent that Lord Raglan did not have any of those either, at least not commanding his cavalry.

For weeks after the landing, due primarily to the tenacity of the common soldiers, the Russians were pushed back. Near the town of Balaclava, the czar's forces counterattacked. On the first day, they were pushed back in disorder. This created the exact situation cavalry excels at: pursuing and destroying a defeated foe. But that did not happen—which leads us to the second of our merry gang of four, George Charles Bingham, the Third Earl of Lucan. He commanded all of the British cavalry in the Crimea, including the Light Brigade, and his favorite, the Heavy Brigade. Now there hadn't been a real war since Napoleon was defeated, and Lucan was the absolute model of a peacetime commander. He had little knowledge of strategy and was unconcerned with actually waging war. Lord Lucan saw his forces, particularly his Heavy Brigade, almost as a personal collection. He was said to spend as much as eleven thousand pounds sterling per year keeping the brigade's appearance sharp and accoutrements new. That would mean at least half a million U.S. dollars a year. More was spent on dress per trooper than most of the men in the regiment were actually paid.

So on the first day, with Russian infantry retreating in a mob and their Cossack cavalry and guns caught in the chaotic mix, it was the ideal opportunity to bag an entire Russian army. The Heavy Brigade sat perfectly formed, supported by the Light Brigade nearby, with both awaiting the order to attack a near-defenseless enemy. And they sat and sat, and the order never came. The Russian army was able to retreat and reform some miles away, and the British cavalry kept their uniforms clean. A similar incident followed, again to Raglan's frustration, when Lucan held his regiments in check while another opportunity for the cavalry to smash the Russians passed. Seemingly, he just didn't understand, or didn't care, what opportunities were missed so long as his brigades looked good on parade. The entire army soon began referring to him as Lord Look-On.

Now we turn to the Light Brigade, who are beside themselves with frustration and probably taking a good deal of ribbing about their forced inaction. The commander of the Light Brigade happened to be Lord Cardigan, another noble who had little skill or experience at command. He also had no real combat experience, and little desire to understand how a charge against the enemy was different from riding to the fox. And just to make things even more fun for Lord Raglan, Cardigan was Lucan's brother-in-law, and Cardigan and Lucan cordially hated and disrespected each other.

Raglan should have done something about the two cavalry brigadiers' animosity, or at least sent one home. Instead, he let things fester in the hopes that they would get better. They didn't. So Raglan did his best to keep the two men apart, a neat trick since Lucan was Cardigan's direct superior.

On October 25, the Heavy Brigade had actually managed to engage in a few successful actions—nothing that really risked the polish on their helmets, but enough to have them lord it over the men and officers of the Light Brigade, who had seen no action at all. It was typical that the dislike of the commanders blossomed into a rather unhealthy competition between the two brigades. This should have been dealt with immediately, as it eventually proved disastrous, but Raglan instead did nothing.

The Russians were once more on the offensive the next day. There was a series of redoubts, little earth and stone forts, along a line of hills in front of the positions that held the bulk of the British army. Columns of Russian infantry managed to approach these and overwhelmed several. This left the Russians free to pull back to their lines one of the most valued trophies of eighteenth- and nineteenth-century warfare, enemy guns. Capturing guns was very prestigious, and losing them a great loss of face. So when Lord Raglan, high on a hill and able to see all this happen, realized the czar was about to receive the gift of a battery of his artillery, he ordered the Light Brigade to recapture them. It should have been fairly easy for the well-mounted unit to drive off the Russians and bring back the lost artillery pieces as the infantry dragged them away. Or it would have been, except for the actions of our fourth man and the vagueness of the order he was given to deliver:

> *Lord Raglan wishes the Cavalry to advance rapidly to the front—follow the enemy and try to prevent the enemy carrying away the guns. Troops Horse artillery may accompany. French cavalry is on your left. Immediate.*

This was an order that made sense if you were on the top of a hill and could see everything or knew what was intended. But the messenger chosen to deliver this message to Cardigan was Captain Lewis Edward Nolan. He was serving as an aide-de-camp and delivering messages because he was considered one of the best horsemen in Britain. He was also an egotist of the first measure, who believed that cavalry, well led by someone like . . . well, himself could accomplish almost any battlefield feat. And Nolan held his beliefs with the fervent strength of a true zealot.

He felt that cavalry could break any square, charge any infantry formation, and overrun any artillery placed against it. The captain wrote all this into a book on this entitled *Cavalry: Its History and Tactics.* Those who were coming to understand and realize that firepower had just about brought an end to an era of stirrup-to-stirrup charges and slashing through enemy infantry with saber and lance publicly disdained the book and the author. But such disputes simply made the man defend his faith in cavalry that much more adamantly.

Nolan also held little respect, with good reason, for either Lucan or Cardigan. A fanatic believer in the mounted trooper as the decisive arm, he had watched as time after time the two bumbling and battling brigadiers missed opportunity after opportunity to prove his points and cover his revered cavalry in glory. Now, it appeared, had come his chance to rectify all this. He raced down to the Light Brigade with the fateful promise that he would lead the charge himself.

When Captain Nolan arrived, Brigadier Cardigan sat with the 607 men and officers of the Light Brigade already arrayed to attack. Ready behind him was the Heavy Brigade in reserve. Its commander, Lord Lucan himself, sat in a valley that ran from the Russian lines to where he waited. Hills on both sides obstructed his vision, although Lucan would have heard the firing and cannon to his right. In a great rush, Nolan rode up to Lord Lucan, whom he knew had failed to follow orders to attack at least twice before. The brigadier rightfully asked what guns he should attack. He could not from the valley floor see the guns being taken away, and the inclusion of the horse artillery in the order implies that infantry was the target, or part of it.

Now, Nolan could have been seeing the opportunity to prove his theories on the continued battlefield superiority of cavalry. Or he might simply have been so frustrated with Lucan, Cardigan, and the farce they had made to date of his favored arm that he could not stand it any longer. He died a few minutes later, so his motives are lost. But what he did was to completely change the nature of the orders he carried.

"There, my lord, is your enemy," Nolan answered, gesturing at a battery of twelve Russian guns at the other end of the valley. What he did not include in his gesture was the actual redoubts and guns Raglan wanted saved, those being much closer and easier to reach.

Since the Russians were advancing, both sides of the valley were filled with the czar's infantry and even some light guns. The distance to these guns Nolan had indicated was close to a mile; an attack on that distant battery was blatantly suicidal. Commanders with sense, or those not chafing from the comments their earlier inaction had caused, might have paused to question such an order. But Lucan did not.

The order went out for the Light Brigade to prepare to charge. Cardigan, unwilling to even talk to Lucan about the order, accepted the order without question. You have to wonder what effect the antipathy between Lucan and Cardigan had on his willingness to follow such an order.

The Russian gunners saw the six hundred horsemen forming into lines and guessed they were the target of the planned attack. They intensified their bombardment, using an improved version of the explosive shells, such as those invented by Henry Shrapnel for Wellington to use in Spain fifty years before. Nolan rode through the formed units, pushing his way to the front, but he never got to lead the charge. A shell burst nearby and a thick piece of metal slammed into his chest. He was dead in moments, his frightened horse bolting to the rear, Nolan's highly trained body maintaining his seat even as he died.

The actual charge has been immortalized by Lord Tennyson in

his epic poem *The Charge of the Light Brigade.* All six hundred men charged for the Russian battery as ordered. Shot and shell poured into the horsemen from every side. A few men actually reached the guns and began to stab at the gunners. A counterattack by Russian horsemen quickly drove them off, and what remained of the Light Brigade was forced to ride back through that same gauntlet. More than Tennyson, the commander of the French cavalry, General Bosquet, probably summed up the entire disaster best: *"C'est magnifique, mais ce n'est pas la guerre."* It is magnificent, but it is not war.

Of the six hundred that charged, only 441 men and 346 horses made it back out of that "valley of death." Cardigan, lightly wounded, was one of them. He lived to have the satisfaction of seeing Lord Lucan receive the blame for the misdirected charge. After all, Nolan was dead and the British public needed someone to blame. Raglan too blamed Lucan, informing him afterward, "You have lost the Light Brigade."

But all four men each conspired to bring about the most notoriously futile and costly cavalry charge in British history. Lord Raglan has to be blamed for indecisive leadership and a failure to control his subordinates, or even his aides. Lord Lucan demonstrated a lack of military skill in his earlier battlefield failures, including failing to obey two different orders to attack. Lord Cardigan, through his own lack of military understanding and antipathy to his commander, blindly followed a mistaken and suicidal order. Captain Nolan, for reasons of his own, changed the order he carried from a reasonable one to "the Charge of the Light Brigade."

ANTIETAM

The Ghost Army That Haunted McClellan

Maryland, 1862

WILLIAM R. FORSTCHEN

Dawn of September 17, 1862, a day that offered the potential of ending the American Civil War.

Across the previous three months, General Robert E. Lee had run riot over the Union's Army of the Potomac and the Army of Virginia, shifting the battle front from the James River before Richmond to the banks of the Potomac in central Maryland.

After brilliant successes in the Seven Days campaign and Second Manassas, he had ventured an invasion into Maryland, and then things had gone awry.

The months of hard campaigning had cost him over forty thousand casualties, many of them his best regimental, brigade, and division commanders. His men were exhausted, and one crucial factor, a shortage of shoes, left most of the army barefoot—not so bad when campaigning on the red clay roads of southern Virginia, but different altogether on the rocky terrain of Maryland and the hard-paved macadamized pikes of that region.

Crossing the Potomac during the first week of September, Lee counted less than forty thousand rifles in his command. Interestingly, the issue of states' rights played against him here. Thousands of men simply fell out of the march when the Potomac was reached. Their reason? They had enlisted to defend Virginia, not invade Maryland, and would sit out the fight until Lee came to his senses and crossed back over the river.

Then came the famous "lost orders." Along the banks of Monocacy Creek, a few miles from Frederick, Maryland, a copy of Lee's marching orders were found by some Indiana troops and quickly passed up to McClellan.

George B. McClellan, the vainglorious Union commander of the Army of the Potomac, was brilliant as an organizer and trainer, but an utter failure on any battlefield. In his hands he held the order of battle for Lee's army, their dispositions and marching plans, revealing that just on the other side of the mountain range before him, the Catoctins and South Mountain, General Lee's thin ranks were spread out along thirty miles of road, while his own tightly ranked army was poised like a spear, ready to slice into the middle and cut Lee's forces in half.

He had, as well, a tremendous numerical advantage, nearly two to one, with better artillery, his troops fairly well rested, and an excellent road to take them into battle.

Of course he blew it, wasting a day more in boasting about impending victory rather than pushing his men forward with a forced march. He delayed another day trying to push aside one thin division that Lee had placed atop the South Mountain range to block ten times their numbers, and then wasted another day slowly bringing his men up toward Antietam Creek.

And yet, on that morning of September 17, 1862, to an unbiased observer judging the potentials simply on numbers, position, and supplies, victory for the Union seemed to be a foregone conclusion.

Counting just infantry, McClellan had a better than two-to-one advantage. With artillery, he had the Union's typical advantage of well-trained gunners and a far greater number of rifled barrels, significant when it came to long-range counter-battery work.

Lee's position, drawn up in an arc before the village of Sharpsburg, was a dangerous one. His only line of retreat was a single ford across the Potomac to his rear.

And yet McClellan went into the battle fearful. His amateur intelligence agents, hired from, of all sources, the Pinkerton Detective Agency, had come in with reports that Lee's army numbered more than 100,000 strong. And he believed it, in spite of the pleadings of his corps and division commanders, who had gained a close-up look at the Confederate lines the evening before and saw that they were thin.

There was a ghost army out there according to George. Most certainly, he saw forty thousand of Lee's men arrayed for battle, but behind them, sixty thousand more phantoms lurked and would counterstrike when the time was right.

McClellan set his headquarters a mile or more back from the front line, atop a good defensive ridge on the far side of Antietam Creek—the perfect position to hold when the phantom army of Lee finally struck back. It was a position that offered only a partial view of the battlefield, while Lee put himself smack in the center, ready to instantly control the field.

On the morning of September 17, George McClellan reluctantly went into the fight, convinced he was facing vastly superior numbers, when every shred of real evidence was to the contrary.

Even with that fear, if he was going to attack, simple military logic dictated that it come as a hammer blow across the entire front, a sharp, sudden unleashing of hell to knock an enemy off balance in the opening move. He did nothing of the sort, and historians now easily define the Battle of Antietam as three distinct and unrelated fights, first on the Union right, then at the center, and finally on the left.

The opening move, into the cornfield and the assault on the west woods, was a botched affair: two Union corps assaulting the open ground in uncoordinated waves, though Joe Hooker's valiant First Corps came close to taking the day. If not for the wounding of "Fighting Joe," the battle might have been decided right there.

Hooker, bleeding from a potentially dangerous wound to his foot, actually went back to McClellan's headquarters and begged him to unleash everything and throw in his reserves. McClellan spoke only of the ghostly troops Lee had hidden away just behind the opposite ridge, and refused to commit.

The fighting in the right sputtered out when there were, frankly, no organized units left to fight for the Union. But the Confederate side was equally shattered, with Lee frantically moving what few men he had into the fight, riding about to rally individual stragglers heading to the rear.

The center fight now opened, completely uncoordinated with the right. This was the infamous Sunken Road, a natural entrenchment created by a farmer's lane, a position that never should have been assaulted. The bloodbath left thousands more dead or wounded on both sides, and yet again, by the time of the last assault, Lee's troops were fought out and broken. All that was needed was one more attack. A Union division commander went back to McClellan, begging him to unleash his reserves, but again, no—Lee would then pounce with tens of thousands. The division commander, furious, begged McClellan to come up to the front and see for himself that Lee was finished. Again McCulellan refused. The division commander rode back to his command, and shortly thereafter died in a vain attempt to push through with the few men left to him.

The folly now unfolded on the left, at the infamous Burnside's Bridge. Burnside, commanding the left, was a general fit for McClellan that day. He was slow, hesitant, and stymied with how to get his men across the river; a disgusted cavalry officer at one point just plunged into the shallow stream to demonstrate that it could be easily forded, but Burnside felt he needed the bridge.

Lee was holding the left with fewer than a thousand men against Burnside's entire corps and the potential reserve of yet another corps behind him, more than twenty thousand men.

The folly is well known: the repeated assaults across the narrow bridge, the final storming of the heights, and then a couple of hours wasted while Burnside's men crossed, dry-footed, then deployed out for the final attack.

Only the timely arrival of fewer than three thousand men, under A. P. Hill, saved Lee, as Burnside advanced to nearly pistol range of Sharpsburg before being repulsed by one-third their numbers.

Over twenty thousand of McClellan's infantry sat out the battle, frustrated observers watching as their comrades were slaughtered, but, in dying, opening a clear path for a solid attack to finish the day and drive what was left of Lee's army into the Potomac.

The bulk of McClellan's rifled guns remained on the far side of Antietam Creek as well, firing at long range, though staff throughout the day begged to move the batteries up close and use them to sweep the field. But no, they were well positioned to turn back the expected counterstrike by Lee and the phantoms haunting George's mind—phantoms that never came.

The day was a tragic waste.

More incredible, however, and rarely spoken of, were the events of September 18, 1862. Come dawn, Lee, his numbers down to less than thirty thousand, defiantly held his ground. He had yet to concede a battlefield, and he would not do so now.

McClellan's corps commanders begged to go in, to finish it off. Two of the army's corps were fresh and had barely seen action. To McClellan, however, Lee's defiance was proof positive that the Confederates outnumbered him. He refused to budge, not even to order skirmishers forward to probe out of fear of provoking his opponent.

The following night, after evacuating the wounded, Lee quit the field. The next day, McClellan cautiously advanced into Sharpsburg. Confederate stragglers and deserters, interrogated by their captors, openly spoke of the disastrous losses inflicted in the battle. Civil War soldiers were notorious for being open-mouthed when taken prisoner; they'd be offered a drink and some hardtack by opponents just like themselves, and would freely gossip.

This intelligence was carried back to George, with pleas to aggressively push forward. Again he refused.

When President Lincoln arrived on the field a couple of weeks later to review what had gone wrong, McClellan was defiant, claiming a great but near run victory over a superior foe. To Lincoln, it was obvious that yet another opportunity had been squandered, and, shortly thereafter, McClellan was relieved of duty. He would become a gadfly of the war effort, pronouncing it a failure, and run as a peace candidate on the Democratic ticket in 1864. Fortunately, his bid for the presidency was as successful as his fight at Antietam.

Historically Antietam is listed as a Union victory. But that's propaganda, actually. Lincoln needed a victory to hang his Emancipation Proclamation on, and thus the encounter at Antietam Creek was "spin-doctored" to fit the bill.

It was, without doubt, one of the great lost opportunities of the war, a true case of seizing defeat from the jaws of victory.

A coordinated assault in the first hour, pinning Lee down on all fronts, would surely have resulted in a collapse of the Confederate position before midday. A commitment of even half of the reserves available would have pinned Lee to the banks of the Potomac and torn him apart before sunset.

The failure, in spite of all evidence given to him that victory was at hand, is attributable only to George B. McClellan and his worst enemy—his own imagination and the phantom army that haunted his nightmares.

CHANCELLORSVILLE

Joe Hooker's Knock on the Head

Virginia, May 1–3, 1863

WILLIAM R. FORSTCHEN

Joe Hooker was called Fighting Joe, but the name was actually the result of a typo in a newspaper. In a report of an earlier action, there was a phrase ending with the word "fighting," and the next line started with the words "Joe Hooker." The comma was left out, a copy editor capitalized the word "Fighting," and the name stuck.

In fact, Hooker did have a good reputation as a fighter, showing brilliance at Antietam and an aggressive spirit.

A long-cherished urban legend maintains that his last name became associated with the world's oldest profession, and stuck because Joe was notorious for having an entourage of "soiled doves" floating about his camp. Sadly (since it is such a great story), it is not true. The word "hooker" was already being used decades before the Civil War. Perhaps the name, however, inspired his notorious immoral behavior off the field, behavior that scandalized Victorian America, but most likely was secretly cheered on by many of his troops, typical soldiers and Americans all.

When he took command of the Army of the Potomac early in 1863, he was handed a demoralized wreck. Burnside had created a disaster at Fredericksburg, and again a month later with the notorious "mud march," a failed attempt at a winter campaign. Typical of poor Burnside and his luck, as his troops broke camp and started to move, the January skies opened with a torrential, freezing four-day downpour. The army stalled in the mud, and hundreds died from exposure and exhaustion.

Hooker ordered his demoralized troops back into winter quarters. He flooded the camps with fresh food, winter clothing, generous furloughs, and light duty. Morale began to climb.

Next, he took a major step toward a more modern concept of war: he kicked out the amateur civilian Pinkerton agents who had handled intelligence for McClellan and created a modern intelligence-gathering network. Trained observers were posted along the front line to count troops on the other side. Charts of order of battle were drawn up. Every deserter and prisoner was systematically talked to in a friendly way and information was cross-checked.

Within a few months, for the first time, the Union Army of the Potomac had an accurate read on Lee's army, his order of battle, his troop strength by regiment, and most important, the information that Lee's forces were so woefully short of supplies that nearly half his forces, under Longstreet, had been pulled back as far as Richmond so they could be fed and the horses pastured.

A manned observation balloon tethered to the ground with a thousand feet of rope was used to great effect monitoring daily movements on the other side and very carefully observing Confederate semaphore stations. In short order, the simple code used by the rebels was broken and daily communications along Lee's front lines were read in Hooker's headquarters almost as quickly as they were read by Lee's subordinates.

The plan Joe developed to take on Lee was complex and brilliant, perhaps one of the best-conceived operational plans attempted in the eastern theater throughout the war. He knew he outnumbered Lee by nearly three to one, with close to 120,000 troops, compared to little more than 40,000 for Lee. He'd leave a significant "demonstration" force behind, almost equal to the strength of Lee, under command of "Uncle John" Sedgwick. The rest of the force, under his own personal command, would swing right, cross the Rappahannock River fifteen miles upstream, and come crashing down onto Lee's left and rear. A third force, the cavalry, would swing wide to the right, then plunge due south and, finally, cut in across Lee's line of communications thirty miles to the rear.

Before the campaign even started, Lee was boxed. If he attempted to move on Hooker's advance, Sedgwick would tear into his rear. If he stayed in place, it would be Hooker crashing into his flank. Retreat was the only option open, and then superior numbers could run him down as he attempted to fall back on Richmond.

Hooker was realistic enough to not place too much hope in his cavalry. As for Uncle John, he knew that John had something of a reputation for being slow. But technology would overcome that concern. The observation balloon would be aloft from dawn to dusk, ready to relay information on any countermove by Lee. And telegraphy, at a tactical level of command, would come into play for the first time. As he advanced upstream and then crossed, a telegraph wagon would move with his headquarters, a team of trained men tacking glass insulators to trees and looping out the wire as they moved.

The moment Lee so much as sneezed, Joe Hooker would know and act accordingly.

And thus started the Chancellorsville campaign.

Any reader with even a passing familiarity with the Civil War knows the outcome, a total disastrous rout for Hooker, the result of General "Stonewall" Jackson's famed flanking march. It was a victory, however, that the South paid dearly for, with Jackson's death when he was shot by one of his own sentries.

And yet there is the fascinating story behind the story that explains why Hooker was defeated, and perhaps does remove a bit of the guilt from Joe's shoulders.

Just prior to the beginning of the campaign there was a startling leap in telegraph technology, the Beardslee Machine. It was as if the computer world was still operating with 386 computers using DOS, and suddenly a Pentium 4 with the latest version of Windows was dumped on the scene.

The Beardslee Machine was a rather complex box. If you ever visit the Fredericksburg battlefield park, be certain to visit Chatham House, where an original is on display.

The front of the box looks something like a clock face, with the letters of the alphabet, numbers, and even short phrases in a circle, all beautifully stamped in shiny brass. The clock dial is a pointer, and inside is a complex array of magnetos, magnets, and coils of wire.

The concept was delightful. Rather than having to use the cumbersome dots and dashes of Morse code, which took time to master, an operator at one end of the line would sit down before the machine and merely had to turn the dial and push it in at, say, the letter T. Instantly on the other end the dial of the receiver would turn to T, and a small bell would ding. Supposedly a good team could double the speed of sending and receiving, and, even better, if ever a rebel spy tapped into the line, the signals flying back and forth would be incomprehensible.

The War Department, enchanted with the machine, ordered it on the spot, and, just before the start of the campaign, the new wonder was incorporated into Hooker's headquarters.

So Joe Hooker set forth, his initial movement brilliant as he shifted the bulk of his army upstream without Lee getting a hint that anything was afoot. Hooker was so careful that even the pickets down on the river, who would openly boast and gossip back and forth with their opponents on the other side, were replaced with carefully drilled men who understood that if they leaked a word, they'd sit out the rest of the war on some remote island breaking rocks.

The telegraph team went bouncing along and crossed over the Rappahannock with Joe, stringing out wire as they went. The Union army was across, and into the tough stretch of woods known as the Wilderness, reaching a small clearing at the Chancellor House before Lee even began to stir.

The telegraphy team connected to the headquarters hooked up their wonder machines and punched out a message. The reply: pure gibberish.

Another try, again an incomprehensible mix of Zs, Q, and Xs. Another try and yet another try, the operator swearing, not even sure anymore if they were both trying to send to each other at the same time or not.

It was a wonderful machine—that had never been field-tested. One thinks that such follies only happen today, with high-tech weapons systems that suddenly run amok, firing missiles at an ally's ship or, rather than aiming at a target drone, suddenly swinging about and locking on to the stand full of observers.

The jostling, bouncing ride over twenty miles of typical nineteenth-century roads had knocked one of the machines out of alignment. No one had any idea, most likely not even the inventor, how to get it realigned, short of hauling it all the way back to where the other machine was located, placing them side by side, and getting them back in sync. Then they'd carry it back to the front, and by the time they got back, it would be out again.

Backup? No one had thought to bring along the old reliable traditional keys, and even if they had, how to let the other side know to switch over?

Joe was suddenly in the dark. High tech had failed and no one had thought to bring along low tech.

But there was still the balloon. From a thousand feet up, it could at least provide some reference, perhaps even a semaphore connection. And here as well, luck played out against Joe. Though the weather was clear, it was gusty with high winds. The tethered balloon bounced about at the end of its long leash and was laid flat almost to ground level, its operators finally forced to reel it back in and give up.

Here then was the origin of Joe's freezing up. He had flanked Lee, but throughout the careful months of planning he assumed that every step of the way he would know exactly where Lee was. Now he was in the dark, and at that moment his brain seized up and he froze.

Dig in.

Couriers were sent off, taking nearly a day to reach Uncle John Sedgwick before Fredericksburg and come back with a reply. Sedgwick, as well, did not help. Across the river, using pontoon bridges, he faced the same ground Burnside had assaulted back in December. Without a balloon behind him he had no idea if there were only five thousand troops in the trenches above (the real number), or twenty thousand, who could shred his attack, which was supposed to either hit Lee as he moved west or pin him in place and thus allow Hooker to swing down east. So General Sedgwick did what so many have done throughout history—he did nothing and just sat and waited.

Lee, caught by surprise, did not wait. Taking nearly all his available troops, he force-marched west, making contact with Hooker on May 1, 1863, just east of Chancellorsville. That evening Lee made the bold decision to split his divided army yet again. And thus began Jackson's famed flanking march.

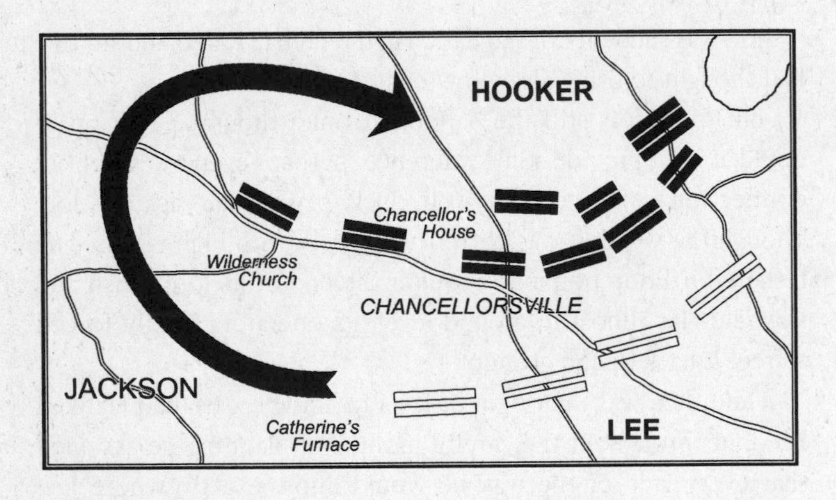

By the morning of May 3, 1863, Lee was gaining one of his greatest victories, but at a terrible cost. The evening before, Stonewall Jackson had been mortally wounded by "friendly fire"; when riding ahead of his advancing troops, he was gunned down by his own men in the darkness and confusion of the night battle crushing the Union right flank. Jeb Stuart was now in command of Jackson's corps, aggressively pushing forward to meet Lee, who was in direct command of the eastern wing of the army, attacking Hooker's other flank.

History always records the brilliance of this famed maneuver and yet, for a moment, one should perhaps turn the map around and look at it from the other side. Looked at in a different way, Hooker was in a superb position. He knew Lee's order of battle, and, by this stage, should have been aware that every single man available to Lee was committed to action.

Lee's army was not united. It was, in fact, divided into three distinct elements: Stuart, Lee, and the small force holding Fredericksburg.

Two of Hooker's corps had yet to even fire a shot, and in fact were actually deployed north of Jackson's men, poised on *their* flank, as if ready for a stunning counterblow.

Sedgwick, back in Fredericksburg, could now easily swat away the few troops facing him, and, at that moment, would actually be closer to Richmond than Lee. They could force Lee south, or turn and hit him squarely in the rear. Meade's Fifth Corps, poised north of Jackson's command, could catch him at a right angle and sweep him from the field.

And Joe Hooker froze.

Standing on the porch of the Chancellor House, he listened to the roar of battle sweeping closer from the west, and that roar drowned out all other thought. He was blind, and the damn telegraph did not yet work, which was made worse by the fact that, by now, the wonderful glass insulators had attracted the eyes of more than a few Union troops, who got a kick out of taking potshots at them.

On the porch of the Chancellor House, Hooker called a staff meeting. Every one of his corps commanders begged to be unleashed. "Look at it the other way, sir! They're still divided and we outnumber them!"

And at that moment a cannonball came winging in, striking

the front porch pillar that Hooker was leaning against. The pillar tumbled over, knocking the general unconscious.

It was a golden moment! Anyone with a touch of pro-Union sentiment wants to cry out to those corps commanders, "Now's your chance!" One can imagine Patton at such a moment, with Ike or Bradley knocked out cold in front of him. He'd have grabbed command with both hands and run with it, and most likely given his old commander a second knock on the head just to make sure.

But not these men. They all stood about, mouths gaping. There was some brief debate about "maybe we should do something," when Hooker groaned and groggily stood up, stuttering that he was still in command. It's almost a comic moment in a way, if not for the fact that thousands of good men were dying, a moment when someone should have quietly walked behind him and given his head another tap with a pistol butt or ball-peen hammer.

So they let him stay in command, though modern analysis clearly indicates he was suffering from a severe concussion.

The army folded up, retreated back across the river, and Lee had won his greatest victory. A tragic afternote was that of the cavalry and old Uncle John.

The cavalry wandered about aimlessly throughout the fight, was easily turned back, and accomplished nothing. As for Uncle John, he finally did charge the heights above Fredericksburg and knock the Confederates clean out of their position. Finally, he turned west, even as Hooker was fleeing the field. The following day, Lee pivoted back with nearly his entire force and encircled Sedgwick at Salem Church, five miles or so west of Fredericksburg. (John, true to form, had moved slowly yet again.)

Even at this late date, the situation could have been reversed. The more aggressive officers begged Hooker, who was dug into a defensive position, to sally forth and hit Lee in the rear even as he focused on John. But Hooker had had enough and left John to his fate. Only the failure by some of Lee's exhausted subordinates to properly coordinate an attack allowed John to disengage during the night and meekly slip back across the river.

Years later Hooker would admit that he had, in fact, defeated himself at Chancellorsville, first with his brain seizing up when he was rendered blind by high tech gone bad, then by an unlucky streak with the weather. Hooker seized up even more when he took a solid knock on the head. He should then have stayed down for the count.

GETTYSBURG: THE BEGINNING

The Vision Place of Souls: The Mythology of Lee

Pennsylvania, 1864

WILLIAM R. FORSTCHEN

Gettysburg is, without doubt, the most debated battle in American history. Attend any Civil War roundtable, sit by a campfire with reenactors, go to any college class on the Civil War, or just hang around with buffs, and sooner more likely than later the topic will come up: Could Lee have won at Gettysburg?

This single question is, in fact, a cottage industry. This author knows this well, having coauthored three best-selling books on the subject and written several articles as well.

It was, even before the last of the dead from the battle were buried, a point of controversy on both sides. Shortly after the death of Robert E. Lee in 1870, the controversy exploded into a bitter feud between "Pete" Longstreet, who said that Lee failed at Gettysburg, and the defenders of the "Marble Man," who could see no fault in their iconic hero of the "Lost Cause."

As the veterans gathered for the twenty-fifth, fiftieth, and the poignant sevety-fifth reunion, the bitterness subsided but the debate continued, to be picked up by scholars and popular writers. Even Faulkner weighed in, with his famous quote that in every Southern boy's heart there is a dream that it is again an early afternoon in July, the troops are arrayed, the artillery has fallen silent, and all things are still possible.

If your heart does lean toward the Southern cause, it is inevitable that when you visit Gettysburg, you will stand at the corner of the Angle, and there imagine the final surge forward to victory, or climb to the top of Little Round Top and dream that one more charge sweeps Joshua Chamberlain's men aside and then plunges into the Union rear.

Could he have won? Could Lee ever have won?

Absolutely yes.

The moments were there, the chances for *the* decisive blow that could have transformed a battle in southern Pennsylvania or northern Maryland into a stunning Confederate triumph. But could it have been on the field of Gettysburg itself? Perhaps on the first day, just perhaps, but after that . . . doubtful, and by the third day . . . impossible.

A battle is the climax of a campaign, the intricate ballet of the movement of troops, the ever-constant headache of supplies and logistical support, what the Romans so rightly called impedimenta, leading at last to the moment of contact with the enemy. In addition, there are the uncontrollable factors of weather, of a horse losing a nail, a lost order or a lost courier, the lag time of delivery of orders and their being acted upon correctly—what the military calls friction—to further complicate the headaches of command.

To analyze Gettysburg and the failure of Lee, it is best to view it as a campaign, and not just those three days forever carved into national memory and dreams.

• • •

On the evening of June 28, 1863, Gettysburg was but one small mark on a map, a crossroads like any other, like Westminster, Hanover, Chambersburg, or Carlisle. It was yet to be a word written in blood, a place name that, when whispered, would bring tears to so many eyes for so many long years after, and send a chill down the spine of so many, even today.

Today it seems as if that battle on that ground was an inevitable advancing fate. It was not. So engraved is this thought that park service personnel joke about questions from tourists, asking if the road signs and monuments had been damaged in the battle. As if, like Darius at Gaugamela, the battlefield had been constructed and paved before the battle had even been fought.

Gettysburg was but one place out of many where the fate of one nation or perhaps two nations would be decided, and on that evening of June 28, 1863, General Robert E. Lee, in command of seventy thousand—plus men, was headquartered at Chambersburg, Pennsylvania, approximately twenty-five miles to the west of Gettysburg. The road linked the two places, cutting through a pass in the South Mountain range, a range that Lee was using as a shield to conceal his movement northward.

Approximately forty miles to the south, General George Meade, with roughly ninety thousand men, was in Frederick, Maryland. He was at a distinct disadvantage in one sense. Lee had been in command of his army for over a year and had led that army on half a dozen fields of battle. George Meade had been in command for less than a day, having just replaced Joe Hooker, who had tangled with Secretary of War Edwin Stanton and overall commander General Halleck once too often and had been relieved. Seven months back, Meade was just a division commander, one of over twenty with the Army of the Potomac; he was promoted to command the Fifth Corps just prior to the

Chancellorsville campaign in May, and now, seven weeks later, he bore the lonely responsibility of fulfilling the orders given from Washington: to locate Lee, to defend Washington from attack, and to bring Lee to battle and expel him from Northern territory. These were contradictory orders, in fact, calling for defense while at the same time calling for a meeting engagement, with all the perils it might entail.

The two commanders of two armies were but forty miles apart, and neither was aware of the location of the other. A high-flying balloonist that day could easily have gazed down upon both, but, on the ground, neither was aware of the intentions or movements of the other.

The arm of service that should have been fulfilling that task, of scouting, of shielding, of probing and analyzing the cavalry, had failed—on both sides. All buffs of Gettysburg know that Jeb Stuart, commander of Lee's cavalry, had failed in his assigned task, wandering off on what became nothing more than a confusing romp behind Union lines, and was totally out of touch with Lee since the start of the campaign.

Less discussed is the equal failure of Union cavalry, who simply took after Stuart. Lee, for over two weeks, had completely slipped away from view, crossing over into the Shenandoah Valley, then marching on that broad, open avenue northward where the name changed to the Cumberland Valley, all the time the mountain range to his east acting as a shield. His location was as mysterious to the North as the Army of the Potomac's location was to Lee.

In short, both armies, their infantry, their artillery, their impedimenta, were within forty miles of each other, and neither knew it.

In the analysis of Lee in command, and his failure at Gettysburg, here is the point of departure for why he failed and how he could have won the battle, though some of the roots of failure can be traced back further into the past.

The Confederate triumph at Chancellorsville, fought early in May, had come at a terrible cost: the death of the legendary Stonewall Jackson. For nearly a year, Lee's army had been organized into two corps, of four or five divisions each. Jackson's corps tended to be the body of maneuver, while Longstreet's was the anvil, the heavier unit that held position while Jackson leapt to the flank. As Patton was to Bradley, so Jackson was to Lee. But Jackson was dead, and across the previous six months, many a good brigade and division commander had fallen as well.

Not just generals had fallen. Lee fought his battles with, at times, a near frightful, uncontrollable aggressive spirit. And it cost. From the Peninsula to Chancellorsville, the Army of Northern Virginia had sustained over eighty thousand battle killed, wounded, or captured. By the numbers, that is more than 100 percent losses. Granted, many of those listed were lightly wounded and exchanged prisoners—who rejoined the ranks, but far too many of Lee's best soldiers were buried somewhere between the James and the Potomac.

It was a loss rate that the South, with but one-fifth the white male population of the North, could not sustain much longer. On the Northern side, there was, as yet, no need for universal conscription; the losses of an Antietam or Cedar Mountain could be made up simply by recruiters standing at the docks as immigrant ships unloaded, and, thus far, the vast reserve of free African Americans in the North, and their yet-to-be-freed brothers in the South, had not been tapped.

Lee knew as he went into this campaign, which would finally be known as Gettysburg, that he had the manpower for one more good fight, a fight that must clearly resolve the conflict; otherwise, the bleeding out would reach an inevitable conclusion. Also, a victory, an overwhelming victory in the east, was needed to offset what was realized to be an inevitable defeat in the west at beleaguered Vicksburg.

With the death of Jackson, Lee decided to reorganize his army into three corps. The first corps would be Longstreet's. Pete was a known factor in command, perhaps given to the "slows" according to some, but well organized, methodical, and a master on any battlefield when directed by Lee. Next would come two new corps commanders, Richard "Dick" Ewell, and Ambrose P. Hill.

Dick had been a brilliant division commander under Jackson. He was one of the few men to serve with Jackson whom old "Stonewall" really trusted and would have recommended for such a command. Ewell, however, had lost a leg at Second Manassas, a wound that had nearly killed him, and he was slow to recover. Though obedient and subservient to Jackson, he could be testy with others, and more than one would observe that with his wounding, at least in the short term, something had gone out of his fighting spirit and his ability to command.

The other new corps commander was Hill. He was famed for his offensive spirit. His "light division" had saved the day at Antietam after force-marching at the double for nearly a dozen miles, and Lee expected that here indeed would be his new foot cavalry commander.

He had chosen wrong, tragically wrong. It would not come out until long years later, though within the good ol' boys' club of any military organization the truth must have been known. Hill was dying of syphilis, most likely a souvenir of his early days out west or in Mexico. Hill was beginning to slip into the tragic tertiary stage of the disease, which can be manifested in myriad ways, some of which include violent mood swings. By the middle of 1863, the brilliant division commander of 1862 was on the first steps of the final slope down. As the campaign began to move toward its climax, one-third of Lee's army would be under the command of a man who could barely keep the saddle. The history of that time is interestingly silent about Hill's role, or lack of a role, at Gettysburg. It was part of the Victorian code to not discuss such things. Hill was sick, and by mid-morning of the first day of battle he was excused from command.

He would fight again and die in battle in the last week of the war, not a battle casualty, some would say, but, rather, a suicide. When surrounded by Union soldiers and called upon to surrender, he grinned and tried to ride out of the trap, to be gunned down and thus gain honorable death and glory.

His impact, regardless of his illness, was indeed profound with Jackson and Lee, for on their deathbeds, in the final hours when, in their minds, they again were in the field, they both called out aloud for Hill "to come forward." But at Gettysburg he was a nonentity.

Thus, on that evening of June 28, 1863, General Lee had two corps commanders of infantry who would be of dubious worth, and a commander of a corps of cavalry who had simply disappeared and obviously failed in his mission to screen the army and keep it informed of Northern movements.

It was perhaps here, before the first shot at Gettysburg was fired, or the enemy even sighted, that Lee lost the battle.

A careful self-analysis, an assessment of resources to use modern terms, should have taken place. For, on that evening of June 28, there was the famous incident of the arrival of the amateur spy.

Little is known historically of the man called Harrison. He was an actor, a loyal Southerner, and was apparently contracted by Longstreet to go out and gather information at the start of the campaign. Why Pete felt the need to have him do so is a mystery. Regardless of the motivation, it did reveal a woeful lack in the Confederate Army, that of a well-organized intelligence-gathering system.

Up to very recent times, those who fight in uniform have something of a distaste for those who do not—the spy, the lurker, the man who serves by buying drinks at a bar for a drunk staff officer, or, as Harrison did, to act like a cuckolded husband searching for his runaway wife, and thus become an object of bemused scorn even as he counted flags and guns and noted down corps flags. In Victorian culture, Harrison would have been held in even lower regard because he was an actor. Today, such people, strangely, are considered by many as heroes above even Lincoln and Lee. In Victorian times, there was an instinctive mistrust of someone who could change who he was and playact at who he was not.

This actor-turned-spy, Harrison, was the one who brought to Longstreet and Lee word that the Army of the Potomac was not lingering in defensive positions near Washington but were, in fact, now force-marching north, well into Maryland, and, in another day, would have advance elements into Pennsylvania.

The news came as a shock to Lee. Just like before the Battle of Antietam, the Army of Northern Virginia was spread out wide across several thousand square miles of ground. Several divisions were far to the north and east, racing toward the Susquehanna River at Harrisburg and Wrightsville in a vain attempt to seize the bridges across that river. Other units were dispersed, foraging off the land in order to feed men who had marched on short rations for months, and fatten out their horses on the rich grass of summer.

If Harrison was right, the Army of the Potomac could come plowing into the middle, perhaps cut one or more divisions off, and destroy them before Lee could react. On the other side of the equation, however, there was the offensive consideration offered by Harrison. If the Army of the Potomac had indeed ventured out of the safety of the fortifications surrounding Washington, and were now sixty miles north of the city, here at last was a chance for a crushing defeat. If their opponent could be brought to battle and smashed, there would be no chance to run, as they had after First and Second Manassas, to the cover of fortifications. They had cowered at the end of the Peninsula campaign, withdrawing to the cover of ironclads on the James and waiting transport ships.

Defeat in Pennsylvania for the Army of the Potomac just might mean total defeat, the ideal, the holy grail sought after by generals across history, The Battle of Decision, or the Battle of Annihilation.

At West Point, where Lee had been the highest-ranking cadet of his class, and later returned as superintendent, this concept of the single battle of annihilation was held up to all as the supreme moment of command. Napoleon at Austerlitz had ended a war thus, the same as Wellington had at Waterloo. The Napoleonic school of thought, both in terms of tactics and strategy, held sway at West Point. The senior instructor there was a devotee of the French historian Jomini, whose works were considered the final word on how to fight a battle and how to win a war.

So, based upon the report of an amateur spy, orders were quickly passed that across the next three days, the Army of

Northern Virginia would rendezvous at Cashtown, an excellent tactical position just on the east side of the South Mountain range. Cashtown offered a superb defensive ground position as well, where the Confederate logistical train could remain on the far side of the mountain range in safety.

If the Army of Northern Virginia concentrated at Cashtown, they could then wait for Meade to come to battle, or make the next offensive move with confidence.

Cashtown is ten miles to the northwest of Gettysburg.

It was here, though, that there should have been the time of self-evaluation, or as my coauthor and I called it in our alternate history of Gettysburg, the moment of "Lee's Epiphany."

Why was there not the realization by this capable commander of the following:

1. He was moving his entire army based upon the report of one amateur spy. How could his command structure have failed so thoroughly as to force him to such a decision?
2. The second question automatically derives from the first. At Waterloo, Napoleon cried out, "Where is Grouchy?" Grouchy was his lost corps, who were sent to delay the Prussians, and who then should have arrived on the field to crush Wellington's left. Instead, it was the Prussians who arrived to crush Napoleon. Where was Stuart? At the very least, a dozen riders should have been sent out to track him down—in fact, to track him down days earlier, to recall, to demand an explanation, and, some maintain, to fire him.
3. Two of his three corps commanders were, at that moment, of doubtful quality. The illness of one . . . well, gentlemen did not talk of such things, but it still was impacting. The

other was already observed by some to be a bit shaky in the field, was new at his task, and would need careful guidance in his new command.

If there had been such an epiphany, it would have drawn Lee to a startling conclusion, one that any true general must at times face and then resolve: Am I truly in command of my army on the eve of battle?

A frank self-analysis by Lee at that moment would have resulted in a negative answer.

What could have been done, then, *before* the word "Gettysburg" would carry with it so much meaning? Perhaps a reorganization of the army then and there. Maybe not necessarily going back to two corps, or even relieving Hill or Ewell, but definitely a sharper and closer understanding of what would be expected should have been communicated by Lee to his direct subordinates.

There is a myth that has shrouded Lee for over 140 years, a myth that critics of my alternate history quickly run to and hold up as truth . . . the myth of Lee as the courtly commander in the field, the man who would always "suggest" rather than order, the man who was sensitive never to offend, even if by not offending a battle might be lost, a nation lost.

Rubbish.

Go back to eyewitness accounts of Lee in the heat of battle on so many other fields. At Antietam, he personally rallied fleeing individuals and drove them back into line, galloping from crisis to crisis that day, personally giving direct orders to plug the gaps in the lines. At Salem Church, he furiously raged at brigade commanders and his own staff for failure to carry out orders. At the Battle of the Wilderness, there was the famous incident of his facing Union fire and, by example, rallying the famed Texan Brigade. This, indeed, was a man who could, within the framework of his time, be a Patton if need be. No soft-spoken, gentle milksop could ever have commanded such an army, a tough, courageous, victorious army, if he was not made of steel.

Why Lee did not act more forcefully in the three days prior to battle we shall never really know. Some theorize heart disease; Shaara implies it in his novel *The Killer Angels*. Yes, Lee had suffered what appears to be a mild coronary in February 1863, but he fought at Chancellorsville with mad aggressive spirit only a few months later and would continue to do so for the rest of the war. If anything, there is constant reference to his inexhaustible energy and drive, right up to the last day of the war.

Perhaps the common "soldier's complaint" had laid him low. There were many accounts during the campaign of men cramping up and suffering diarrhea due to an overindulgence of peaches, cherries, and sweet corn not yet ripe. There is implication that Lee might have been suffering from this during the battle. And yet again, at any given moment in that war, in that age of questionable sanitation, a fair percentage of any army and its commanders were suffering from the "two steps," or far worse, dysentery or typhoid, and nearly all had worms, were lousy, and flea-bitten to boot, yet they did their duty with vigor.

Unless laid flat on his back, which he was not, he could have and should have continued command. And so he started his move toward Cashtown, but he did not truthfully ask of himself, "Am I ready for battle? Is this army ready for battle?"

GETTYSBURG: THE BATTLE

Pennsylvania, 1864

WILLIAM R. FORSTCHEN

Forty miles to the south of Lee, George Meade, the reins of command in his hands for little more than a day, made his first decision, and it was the right one. He retained Hooker's staff and Hooker's plan of march: the army broke down into three wings, advancing on a broad front that flanked on the left along the base of the South Mountains (with rebel forces just on the other side of that barrier), a central force ten miles to the east moving toward Taneytown, and his third wing covering the right flank ten miles farther east, near Westminster, Maryland. It presented a front twenty miles wide, now probing forward, seeking contact.

Its impedimenta of packs, cookware, and personal items would be dropped off at Westminster. Trace out the route of any Civil War campaign and you will always find the anchor point to be either a rail line or a navigable river. The vast amount of supplies required for nineteenth-century warfare could be moved no other way.

A rail line ran from Westminster straight back to Baltimore. It would be the anchor point for Meade, until his advance north carried him to contact with the enemy, or to the rail lines running along the Susquehanna River.

A day later Meade, considering the potential for battle, sent out two of his top men with an eye for "good ground," Generals Warren and Hunt. Hunt was commander of the Artillery Reserve. Their survey revealed an excellent defensive position directly to the front of the center and east wing of the Army of the Potomac, a position that would become a "what if" of history—the Pipe Creek Line.

Pipe Creek was then a meandering stream, so narrow at points that a boy could wade its few dozen feet and not get his knees wet. It supported a number of mills, each with a pond backed up behind it. An important military point in relationship to some of these mills was that they cut lumber, and, over the years, the slopes to either side of Pipe Creek had been denuded of trees and converted into broad, open pastureland.

It held the promise of a most excellent killing ground. Hills on the south side rose up a hundred feet, looking down on the floodplain of the creek, several hundred yards wide, then sloping up to hills on the far side, all open as well. It offered the potential of some of the best artillery ground of the war and, if occupied on the south bank by the Union army, could position them for the annihilation of Lee if he attempted to storm it.

The report back to Meade was quick and thorough. Here was the place for battle. A good killing ground across six miles or so of front, the right flank protected by sharp hills and rough terrain, the left flank by a folding back of the stream. As an added bonus, the main supply head for the army, the terminal at Westminster, was but six miles away.

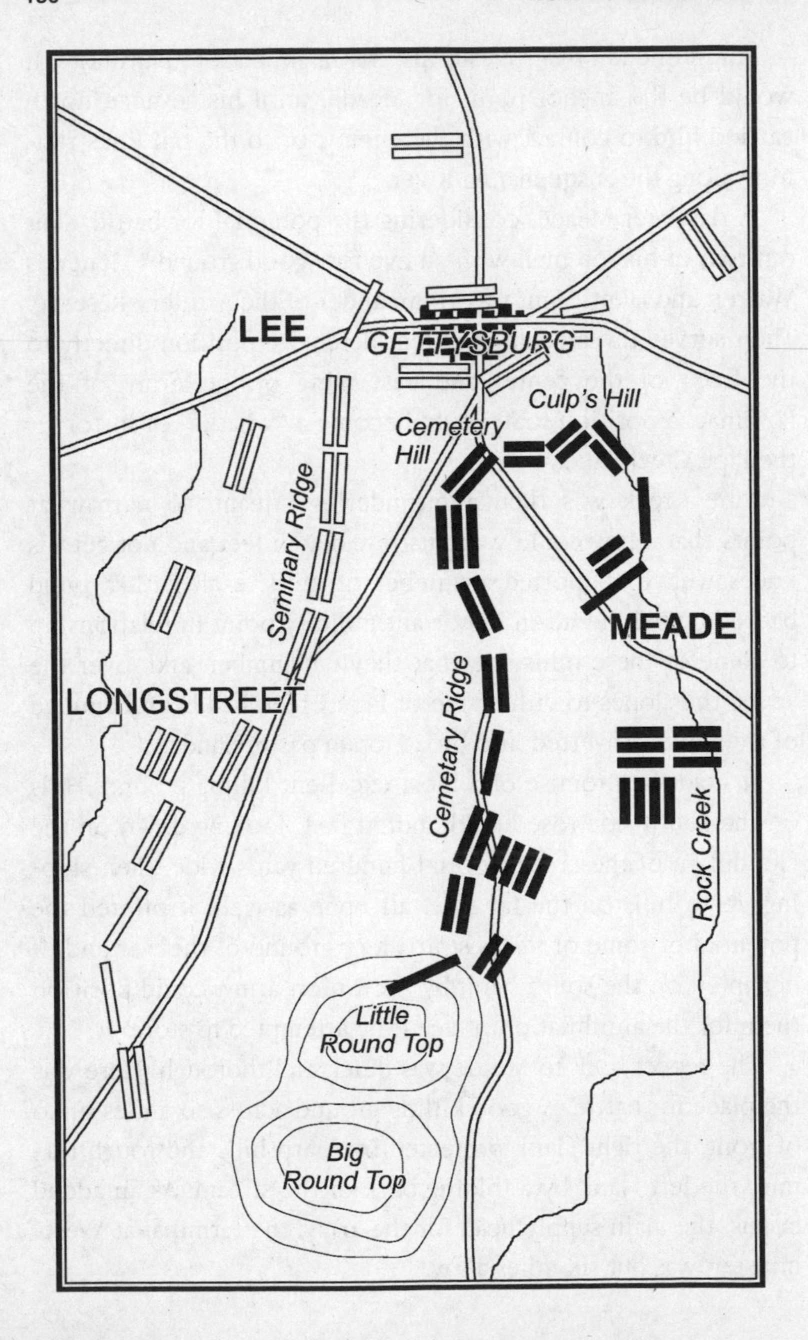
LEE
GETTYSBURG
Culp's Hill
Cemetery
Hill
Seminary Ridge
MEADE
LONGSTREET
Cemetary Ridge
Rock Creek
Little
Round Top
Big
Round Top

It was here that Meade chose his place for battle. It was twenty-five miles southeast of Gettysburg—and thirty-five miles southeast of where Lee had chosen his place for battle at Cashtown.

Here, at this moment, on the morning of June 30, 1863, all things were still possible. Both generals were concentrating their forces, both sensed that battle was imminent. Of the dozens of place names on the maps that both examined, places such as Heidelberg, Hanover Junction, Gettysburg, or Taneytown, none held more significance than the other, none yet had deeper meaning, linked forever to national destiny.

All paths were still open.

The ground between the two armies that morning was a no-man's-land. Both knew their opponent was somewhere "out there," in an area of roughly one thousand square miles. The question was, where? Both sides were racing to concentrate, both hoped that when battle was joined it would be on the ground they had chosen. The wishes of neither were answered.

We venture now back into what is so well known by so many, immortalized in thousands of histories, hundreds of novels, and one film, based primarily on fiction.

From the left wing, Meade sent a probe forward, a light division of cavalry led by John Buford. Arriving in Gettysburg late on the afternoon of June 30, they almost brushed with a brigade of Confederate infantry from North Carolina, led by James Pettigrew, who withdrew to just west of Gettysburg and sent a report back that he thought he had made contact with the enemy.

Contrary to the myth of Shaara's novel, on that evening of June 30, John Buford did not go around making deep and profound pronouncements about how here was the good ground, that here was the place to stand and die, holding 'til the last man until the lunkheads back at headquarters finally realized just how good this magical ground was and rushed forward to hold it.

His report was simple: "Have made contact with Confederate infantry, I am positioning to west and north of Gettysburg, expect a fight come dawn, awaiting orders."

The dawn engagement between John Buford's cavalry division and Harry Heth's division of veteran Confederate infantry started the battle of Gettysburg a mile to the west of town. This stage of the battle, however, was not a bloody, to-the-last-man, to-the-last-bullet stand by Union forces as portrayed in the movie *Gettysburg* or in Shaara's novel. In fact, Buford's command suffered less than 10 percent casualties overall, minor when compared with the horrific losses of other units during the three days of fighting, and indicative that though tough, the opening engagement to hold the ground west of town was not a do-or-die epic.

But at that moment, Gettysburg was like a vortex beginning to form. On the Confederate side, Pettigrew engaged first at the brigade level, only to discover that what he expected to be a light screen of a few cavalry regiments, backed up by militia, was a bit tougher. He sent back to division for support. Thus, up came Harry Heth, who, on his own, acting within the parameters of a division commander of a very aggressive army, decided to engage and sweep the resistance aside.

On the Union side, General Reynolds, commander of the left wing of the Union army, had set out with his gallant First Corps just after dawn. It was no mad dash, as legend implies, not a desperate, minute-by-minute rush to save the "good ground." They advanced to the sound of the guns, Reynolds rode ahead of his infantry to eyeball the ground, told John he'd take over, and that was that. Less than thirty minutes later, Reynolds died as he led his men into battle, the first of at least a dozen corps and division commanders to become casualties.

It is significant to note that, although John ordered up his own First Corps and the Eleventh Corps to Gettysburg, he ordered Dan Sickle's Third Corps to remain in place at Emmitsburg, ten miles to the southwest of Gettysburg. If this indeed had been a mad dash to save the "good ground," as novels and a film imply, certainly the Third Corps would have been ordered forward with all possible speed.

Why weren't they? Because John was not sure if he was just brushing against a wing of the Confederate army or not. Perhaps it was a feint to draw him northward, while the "real" attack came through the mountain pass to the west of Emmitsburg. If that was indeed the case and he, Reynolds, had "developed the situation," as it was then called (meaning contacted part of the Confederate army), it would be up to Meade to either pursue, hold, or fall back and lure Lee in against the Pipe Creek Line. Of those three scenarios, as late as midday Meade still leaned toward luring the rebels south against his chosen defensive line. Gettysburg was not the be-all and end-all of the universe, a place that Must Be Held, otherwise the war would be lost.

On the Confederate side the thinking was the same. Gettysburg, at mid-morning, was not the place that had to be taken. Lee was still thinking in terms of luring Meade farther north, toward Cashtown.

Nearly anyone with a passing knowledge of the battle knows the results of that first day. Heth was repulsed by Reynolds's First Corps. He called upon the next division up the road, Pender's, to come up and help out. By sheer coincidence, from the north and northeast more divisions were seemingly advancing toward Gettysburg. Far to the northeast was Early's veteran division; next to them was Rhodes's division. But their orders that morning were actually to move toward the concentration at Cashtown, by way of Gettysburg. But now, they were marching to the sound of the guns.

It was not a bitter, all-day struggle. After Heth was bloodied, there was a simmering down and, for a while, almost silence. The Union Eleventh Corps came in and moved north of town.

That sad, hard-luck unit. Routed at Chancellorsville, cursed as "those damn stupid Dutchmen," little was thought of them. The majority of men in these units were Germans actually, not Dutchmen, and in the mid-nineteenth century Germans had yet to acquire a reputation as warriors. They were shopkeepers, scholars, farmers, and beer drinkers. If you wanted a race of people who could fight, imitate the French, whose uniforms both sides did adopt throughout the war. In fact, the technical terms for most commands and maneuvers were in French. There were even jokes in the army about how Germans saluted, the joker then either raising both hands or showing his back. (It took a while for these societal attitudes on our part to change for the better!)

The position they were assigned was a broad, open plain, at a right angle to the better position held by the First Corps and a fundamental violation of tactical deployment: never present a salient, a right angle, to an opponent, for he can then strike it on two flanks in addition to head-on, thereby crushing the apex.

Why did the Union army deploy this way? Because this was still a meeting engagement, both sides probing, feeling out the other, not sure who was where and in what numbers. It was the chance of fate that Lee's army was superbly positioned, at that moment, to come in from both flanks and, in so doing, crush the apex of the right angle in the Union position.

The individual division commanders, Early and Rhodes, started to commit into the fight. Lee finally arrived at the edge of the action, realized that fate had indeed taken hold and that any hope of luring his opponent to attack him in a prepared position at Cashtown was finished. He then ordered all troops to commit.

Now battle was truly unleashed, not a daylong fight to the last man to hold the "good ground" and buy time for Meade to come up, but a vicious fight nevertheless. There was actually a moment of hesitation on both sides, neither sure, until Lee finally committed and then pushed in.

The apex at the point of the Union line, the junction between the First and Eleventh Corps, began to collapse. The right flank of the Eleventh Corps, hanging out in midair without any good defendable ground, was hit hard by Early and began to crumble, and then just broke apart. Last to give up, the fearless Iron Brigade absolutely savaged several brigades of Confederate troops before being overrun.

The survivors of the Union's First and Eleventh Corps fell back through Gettysburg and finally rallied on Cemetery Hill. Their losses—some were killed or wounded, but most were taken as prisoners—were approximately seven to nine thousand. Confederate losses to achieve this victory were at least five thousand, maybe as many as seven thousand. Gettysburg was off to a bloody start.

Now come the "what ifs." In the historical debate about Gettysburg, the argument started in the 1870s, with two great "what ifs" emerging. The debate was triggered by an increasingly acrimonious exchange of letters and public comments between Longstreet and what was identified as the pro-Lee group.

This debate reached firestorm proportions when, in the 1880s, *Century Magazine*, to commemorate the twentieth anniversary of the war, solicited articles from any and all participants from every campaign from 1861 to 1865.

Century Magazine was the *Life* magazine of the nineteenth century. Highly popular and well illustrated with engravings, this series about the war, published monthly across four years, would later be reprinted in four volumes as "Battles and Leaders of the Civil War." It was a brilliant marketing success. They are so popular, in fact, that the volumes are still in print today and are required on the bookshelf of any student of the Civil War.

The articles, ranging from the accounts of generals to privates, were printed on the anniversary of each battle, and were eagerly anticipated by all who had actually been there.

The history of the publication itself is fascinating to look at. It was, after all, but twenty years since the war. Memories were still fresh and, in many cases, still painful. With the United States barely reunited as a country, it is remarkable that a national magazine would publish accounts from both sides together.

There is a wonderful Victorian chivalry to many of the articles, whether they were written that way originally or edited, and often there are compliments to the bravery and nobility of opponents. In many ways, this series actually helped to heal the wounds of division, for what veteran could not nod and smile when an opposing general called him brave and chivalrous?

And yet there was a fascinating subtext, a subtle use of language, an oblique casting of blame when it came to supposed comrades on the same side.

When the "Gettysburg" issue came out, it would have been great fun to have simply sat in the corner of a post office in any town north or south. Veterans would come rushing in with their comrades from that day, their children and friends, eager to grab their subscription issues. Opening them they would start to read, and most likely within minutes the howls, the "damns," and the far darker curses (yes, the f-word was definitely around back then) would have exploded. It is a wonder that *Century Magazine* did not start a second Civil War, between "comrades" on the same side.

There for the South to read was the Longstreet thesis. Longstreet made the obligatory nod to the "Marble Man." But subtly, with very correct use of words, the unthinkable was said—that Lee fought the battle poorly and, by so doing, the man who might very well be sitting very close to the throne of God, had failed.

Here was mentioned the famous "go around the right" theory, and a countercharge as well that if only Ewell had followed "the old man's" orders that day and aggressively attacked Cemetery Hill, Gettysburg would have been won on July 1, without even a need for a "go around the right" on July 2.

Angry responses in print were flung back. Longstreet had been stubborn, slow, all but insubordinate, sulking and immature. He had bungled the attack of the second day, and was nearly in dereliction of duty on the third day. Lee had been master throughout; it was Longstreet who had failed, with his foot dragging, obstintely failing to correctly follow orders.

There was controversy enough for the Union side to swallow as well. General Sickles was right. If only Meade had listened to him, Longstreet's second-day attack would have been smashed apart before it began. Meade had failed miserably to pursue the enemy after his victory. Others bickered about the abject failure of the Eleventh Corps, and all tried to lay claim to the fact that it was their actions, or their unit's, which had won the battle and thus won the war.

Hovering over all of this storm and thunder in print was a golden shimmer of memory, that here was the summation of the war, and that at that moment, looking back across twenty years, all who were there did indeed know that here was the battle that would decide the war. Therefore every order, every maneuver, every step by every man, right down to the lowest private, carried with it the fate of the nation, the burden of history, of honor or dishonor to the latest generation.

Consider in contrast a modern analogy that has gone, as well, into the realm of legend: Omaha Beach. Hundreds of books, thousands of articles, and at least one darn good movie and television miniseries have been devoted to it. Yet, when it happened, when the assault landing craft, C-47s, or worse yet, gliders, were boarded, how many actually did think, "Here is the weight of the nation, the fate of the war, upon our shoulders. We are the 'happy few,' chosen by fate to be a band of brothers this day, and in so doing save the world"? There were indeed fleeting moments of such thoughts, especially when men witnessed the sheer size of the invasion force, the spectacle of thousands of ships and planes heading toward Normandy—but when the shock of battle came?

As has been analyzed time and again by historians, such as Keegan and others, at the moment of battle nearly all men are focused on that instant and care little or nothing for higher concepts and higher ideals, or their future place in history.

I must add that this is being written by an author who has helped to write a book about Omaha Beach with a veteran who was there, has stood on that beach and cemetery, and yes, wept.

At that moment, the focus narrows down to you, the individual, to how you shall survive the next thirty seconds. If well trained enough, for a leader the focus is the mission, the orders given from above, the need to move one's men forward or to hold ground. This by no means should ever be thought of as a denigration of heroes, for nearly all were heroes that day at Omaha, or that day long ago at Gettysburg, but to think that such men transcended the crisis, the tension, the terror of the moment and thought of lofty ideals is a stretch.

It is only later, far later, that the realization sets in of the significance of that day, and with it, the need to justify.

It is twenty years later, fifty years later, that the battle becomes legend. Then the loftiest of ideals can be spoken of, both by those who were there, and perhaps more important, by those of later generations who look to those who were there as men to be envied, as men who did indeed have their St. Crispin's Day.

So it was when *Century Magazine* came out. It was indeed in praise of brave men, fascinating since the accounts were, as historians call them, primary sources, articles written by the actual participants. But it was now twenty years later. Explanations had to be made, axes had to be grinded and swung, reputations had to be raised or sunk—and in some cases, the classic game of cover your posterior had to be played.

And in post offices and parlors across America, in 1883, there were howls of rage over what was published, floods of letters written to editors of *Century Magazine* and local newspapers . . . and at reunions, more than one fistfight and even lawsuits broke out.

For the Confederate side it came down to Lee. Did Lee indeed lose the Battle of Gettysburg, or did a higher fate dictate that "the Cause" was foredoomed to failure, and being foredoomed, the real issue became that the men who were involved faced their fate with honor?

This rather Calvinist view was indeed now dogma in the

South when it came to the war. Their cause had been right. They had lost. That, therefore, meant that God had ruled against them. But if their cause was just, why did they lose?

The answer was God must have a higher plan for America. Therefore, it was honorable to have lost, as long as each man had faced battle bravely, and thus proven his manhood and/or his leadership. This was the age of "Muscular Christianity," of real men being devout and yet tough. The war was thus justified as a testing of manhood, and as such was setting an example of honor and courage for generations to come.

Central to this thesis was Robert E. Lee.

Lee was the embodiment of the Lost Cause ideal. Therefore it was impossible that he had lost Gettysburg; rather, it was others who had lost it.

Now comes one of the great myths. Why did Lee lose? Because he was a gentleman. He *never* gave direct orders, some maintained—always it was a gentlemanly suggestion to a fellow gentleman. "May I suggest, General Ewell, that you consider taking that hill." Heaven forbid a Patton-like order: "Take that damn hill or I'll find some s.o.b. who can."

In contrast the most devout of all in the Confederate ranks, Jackson himself, was noted for his relentless, even vicious approach to battle and command. Heaven save any man who did not carry out his orders to the letter.

Lee's opponents in blue were eager to accept the theory that he lost because he was too much the gentleman. It created a noble enemy whom they had tested their manhood against.

Even though Lee had lost, that was no longer the issue, and any who dared to raise it were damned. It was almost a form of doublethink to argue that Lee never actually lost a battle. Gettysburg . . . well, even though he was in command, it must have been others who lost it for him.

So, to turn back at last to the original question, did Lee lose Gettysburg? Of course he did.

The usual definition of victory is that you prevent the enemy from fulfilling his plans, your army is intact, and your opponent is destroyed or forced to withdraw.

Therefore, Lee lost.

The next question then automatically surfaces. How and why? So much has been written on that subject alone that any attempt to catalog it all would be next to impossible. Every regimental history ever published claims somehow to be the point of decision. Every general, on both sides, if they survived, would somehow come to claim a crucial moment, when they knew the fate of the nation rested upon them, and they had decided.

One popular myth, so enshrined now that even this author hesitates to even raise an oblique challenge, is Chamberlain's charge at Little Round Top. All can describe in detail that incredible moment when, out of ammunition, Chamberlain realized there was but one thing left to do: to fix bayonets and charge, thus saving the left flank, the army, and, consequently, the Union on that second day.

Perhaps . . . dare I say it, having once been a member of the Twentieth Maine Volunteer Infantry reenactment regiment? Perhaps, just perhaps, with the rebels closing in and ammunition gone, Chamberlain shouted for bayonets. Confusingly, the order to present weapon after fixing bayonet is "charge bayonet." The bayonet is to be leveled at the enemy with lusty cheer from every man in the line. Some have suggested that "charge bayonet" was heard as "Charge!" The regiment bent back at a right angle, pivoted, began to sweep, and then every man raced pell-mell down the hill to everlasting glory.

But back to the main question, if Lee lost, *how* did he lose?

"The Ewell Thesis," for starters. This comes from the pro-

Longstreet crowd, who argue that if only the timid Ewell had been more forceful on the first day and had charged Cemetery Hill, as Lee "suggested" so politely, a suggestion that should have been understood as a command, the Union army would have been routed.

Again ridiculous. Yes, Lee did pass an order for Ewell to attack, if practical. Ewell would later argue, most likely correctly, that his men had force-marched fifteen miles to get into the fight, had fought a running battle through the town of Gettysburg, had overrun the Eleventh Corps, taking thousands of prisoners, and that there were no good positions to bring up supporting artillery. Plus, his men were "played out" with exhaustion.

A film about Gettysburg describes this moment, with an elderly general remonstrating Lee later that evening, denouncing Ewell as fainthearted, that but a single regiment could have taken "that damn hill."

Rubbish again.

"That damn hill" was indeed good ground. A brigade of Union infantry had, in fact, been held in reserve there since mid-morning and had been digging in like moles. At least forty artillery pieces ringed the crown as well. Behind those pieces, tough gunners all, was the best and most professional branch of the Union army. Forty guns would have shredded any attack up that open slope. It is, perhaps, a fitting coincidence that July 1, 1863, was exactly one year to the day after Malvern Hill, where Lee had sent in a series of uncoordinated attacks against a hill far less significant than Cemetery Hill, and had been absolutely torn apart by a hundred Union guns, losing over five thousand men.

No troops on that field, that evening, could have taken that hill as long as the artillery held. Across the entire war, it might very well have been the best artillery position ever occupied by the Army of the Potomac, made even better since the Confederates had no real position for their artillery to even begin an effective counter-barrage.

The Ewell Thesis is a dead end. And yet, there is a significant point. Lee did not go down into the town that evening to, perhaps, grab Ewell by the collar if he did indeed wish an attack. Instead, he remained at his established headquarters in a small house on Seminary Ridge.

Now comes the other great thesis—the Longstreet Thesis, the "go around their right" thesis.

Here is good ground for debate, but this author maintains the debate has always been on the wrong ground.

Shaara, in his novel *The Killer Angels*, and in the movie based on that novel, *Gettysburg*, has Longstreet talking about "going around the right." This does indeed connect back to some historical fact. There are no notes existing from any staff meeting that took place during the fight. After-action reports filed on the Confederate side were limited; the memory of "going around the right" was not mentioned until later, though, after the fact, some claimed Longstreet did speak of this during the battle.

The overriding question is, what does "going around the right" mean? Was Longstreet talking in a tactical sense, meaning to extend but a mile or two, or even just to sweep around Big Round Top and seize what were claimed to be all the Union supplies parked behind that hill?

Again absurd, if what was meant was tactical.

First off, due either to poor staff planning on Lee's part, Longstreet's part, or both, when the flanking march that resulted in the second day's battle set off, it was already toward mid-morning. The ground had been poorly surveyed. In fact, the entire column was forced to turn around and countermarch for miles because someone had not checked the road out to discover it was clearly visible from both round tops.

Second, the so-called holy grail of "all" the Union supplies parked just behind Round Top was a myth. These four hundred wagons held simply a few days' worth of tactical supplies in the field. In reality, the vast wagon train of supplies for the Union army, over *five thousand* wagons, were parked twenty-five miles away at Westminster, with several hundred of these to be rotated up each day as the army needed them.

Capturing the wagons by going a little bit farther round the right, as some maintain, supposedly leaving the Union coffers empty when it came to rations and more ammunition, would have changed nothing. The Union army was swimming in supplies.

Third, and by far the most important point: all those who dream on the Confederate side about sweeping around the Round Tops or going over them, and thus destroying the Union army, have always neglected one small detail. By four P.M. of the second day, the Sixth Corps, the largest corps in the Union army, after force-marching thirty miles up from beyond Westminster, were now filing into reserve positions behind the Round Tops, just as Longstreet's attack began.

Even if Longstreet had indeed gone around or over the Round Tops, even if Chamberlain had turned and run the other way, the Union army had fifteen thousand additional men in reserve. Tired, yes, but fighters all, and frustrated they had not yet had their moment of glory. (It is wonderful fun to read some of the monuments to the Sixth Corps on the field at Gettysburg. A few men were wounded in some regiments by stray rounds, but nevertheless the monuments declare that by their mere presence, the Sixth Corps, though never committed into the battle, helped to save the Union that day.)

Any tactical march around the right would have ultimately created the same results, a blunting and then a stopping of the Confederate advance, perhaps with far more casualties if they had indeed tangled with the Sixth Corps.

But what about a far broader sweep?

Let's look at the third day and the potential of the fourth day before analyzing what might have been with a broader sweep on the second day.

The third day at Gettysburg, from the Confederate side, is a fight that has gone out of control on Lee's part. Several historians correctly point out that Pickett's Charge was, in fact, a decision by compromise and, like most compromises with command decision in war, a terrible one.

At dawn on the third day, his fighting blood indeed up, Lee rode the line along Seminary Ridge with Longstreet and their staffs. Lee's initial proposal was a grand charge, every division from the far right to the far left advancing at once—an Austerlitz or Waterloo.

Longstreet argued vehemently against it, and with a more realistic eye. The three divisions that had attacked on the second day were absolutely shredded. Overall the attack force had sustained 50 percent casualties, one of the three division commanders was down, and most of the brigade and regimental officers were down as well.

So compromise came into play, and the grand assault devolved to a strike from the left by Ewell, to coordinate with an assault from the center with the remaining divisions, six divisions in total.

And then that derailed. For reasons that have never been adequately explained, Ewell went off half-cocked, attacking shortly after dawn against Culp's Hill, even as Lee discussed the day's plans with Longstreet.

Culp's Hill is, today, one of the forgotten parts of the battlefield. The standard auto tour of today ignores it completely, as it also ignores the line held by the Union Eleventh Corps. But it was the crucial anchor to the Union right flank and a superb defensive position, well fortified by the morning of the third day. Ewell, with this attack, rammed against a citadel and was soon fought out.

So, in the end, it came down to three divisions attacking the center. And then a vague statement by Lee of a follow-through with additional reserves, once the three assaulting divisions broke the center of the Union line.

Tragically for those involved, two of the three divisions detailed off for the attack had sustained horrific losses the first day. In any twentieth-century army, the two divisions would have been detailed off the line for rest, refitting, and reorganization. But Lee's army was down to what it had left in the field and no more. Every man, fought out or not, must try yet again. For example, one of the regiments in the first day's battle, the Twenty-sixth North Carolina, had lost well over five hundred of its eight hundred men. Of the three hundred remaining, less than a hundred would survive the final charge.

Here was the final failure of Lee at Gettysburg: a miscalculation of the factor of morale on both sides. For his own side, the assumption was made that his men could do whatever was ordered, regardless of loss. But, just as crucial, Lee misread his opponents, a sin that Sun Tzu, and so many other writers about the theories of war, point out can be the worst mistake of all: to misunderstand, miscalculate, or underestimate the morale and will of your enemy.

On nearly every field of battle, Lee and his men had seen the Yankees run when pushed hard enough. The Union army had been battered the first day, nearly pushed back the second day, and logic now whispered that one final grand assault, an assault as psychologically devastating as the Imperial Guard advancing at Austerlitz, would send the Yankees running.

But this was Pennsylvania, not Virginia. It is hard for an American reader today to fully grasp, at a visceral level, just how intense was the identification with one's state in 1863. Yes, we are proud of our home state, or if from New Jersey, as I am, joke about it. But to die for it? If called to die in battle, we will do so for America, for the *United States* of America. The blow we suffered on 9/11 was not a blow against New York City or even New York State—it was a blow against each and every one of us.

But in 1863, as troops formed, as they stood on the volley line, the cry would be, "For Virginia!" or "Forward Ohio, Forward!"

One example: as Union troops crossed the Mason-Dixon Line, leaving Maryland (which was technically a Southern state), and returned to Northern soil, to Pennsylvania, the old Keystone State, flags were unfurled, bands played, and regiments cheered, "Three times three for old Pennsylvania!" One officer, born and raised in Pennsylvania, wept, turned to a comrade, and said, "I can think of no better fate than to die on the soil of my own state, in defense of the Union." His wish for that fate would be fulfilled a day later.

Lining the wall at the Angle were men of New York, Maine, New Hampshire, New Jersey, and Pennsylvania. Long afterward they would recall—and, yes, the memories were most likely true—

that the night before the fight, they had talked about what the morning might bring, and all had agreed they would be damned before they would run from rebels while defending Northern soil.

Upon such sentiments, wars are won, and Lee should have sensed it, that on that day, July 3, 1863, the men lining the low stone wall sixteen hundred yards away would not run, and indeed they did not.

So Lee lost Gettysburg and with it, eventually, the war. But could he have won?

Yes, of course, he could have won Gettysburg, but the winning must take us far outside of Gettysburg and the minutiae that claims that if only this regiment had moved left instead of right, if only Ewell or Longstreet, if only. . . .

My coauthor and I, in a three-book series about an alternate Gettysburg, argue that Gettysburg was the one battle, fought by Lee, that reads like fiction. In other words, if ever there was a battle where Lee did not behave like Lee, it was there in southern Pennsylvania.

Forget the courtly Lee, forget the what-ifs, and go to a deeper sense of the fight and Lee's record before and after. Lee was a master of operational warfare, meaning the broader sweep beyond the tactical moment, the planning out of operations days in advance with bold sweeps of twenty, thirty, even fifty miles.

We maintained that Lee's greatest victory was not Chancellorsville, but rather it was Second Manassas. Chancellorsville opened with Lee caught totally off guard. Only circumstance, weather, a random shot by a cannonball, and a technological glitch saved Lee, far more than the gallantry and pluck of Jackson's flanking march.

Rather, it was Second Manassas that should be studied more. The order of battle for the Union side in that fight is confusing to many today. Lee was not facing just one army. In fact, he was facing two. General Pope, who had been sent to take command from Meade, never officially took over all of the Army of the Potomac; instead he commanded the Army of Virginia, formations that had stayed behind to guard Washington, or campaign in the Shenandoah Valley while McClellan fumbled around in the Peninsula. McClellan's forces were being recalled north, were forming up and were to combine with Pope. Lee knew he must act quickly to prevent this junction and the creation of a combined command.

Lee launched Jackson on the most daring march of the war. Over fifty miles in two days, under a scorching August sun. Weaving through a mountain pass, dodging between the two armies of the Union, Jackson fell on the Northern supply head at Manassas Junction, looted it clean, burned what was left, and for fun smashed up every locomotive his men could lay their hands on. Then they simply disappeared, hiding away in a forgotten railroad cut while waiting for Longstreet, the "diversionary force" in front of Pope, to disengage, and follow the same route Jackson had taken.

Thoroughly befuddled, Pope fumbled about, at last stumbled into Jackson, engaged, and then was torn apart when Longstreet came booming in on his exposed flank and rear.

It was brilliance at its best, and the mind that conceived it seemed to have gone asleep at Gettysburg.

The first-day victory for Lee at Gettysburg had been the lucky accident of troops originally converging on a different point, then stumbling into two exposed corps of the Union army and taking them apart. But the cost had been the near total destruction of half a dozen brigades on the Confederate side.

The first day ended with the Union falling back from a marginally defensive position to a superbly defensive one.

It is a wonder Lee did not see this on the evening of the first day. It is a wonder that Lee did not see, as well, that he was not in control of the battle, and worse, not really in control of his subordinates either.

A "Lee-like" battle at that moment would have been to step back, to think, to become operational, to take Longstreet's suggestion of "around the right," but then to expand it to another Manassas. A wide sweep of thirty miles, a taxing one-day march but doable for those veterans, in a day and a half would have taken Lee and his men far around the Union left flank, and into their operational rear, while at that same moment every available Union soldier was pouring into Gettysburg. He should have easily surmised at this point that the Union supply head would be Westminster, the nearest rail junction still operational, and there at Westminster would be the holy grail of all the Union supplies, the same as at Manassas Junction.

And beyond that, he would be between the Union army and Washington, the great terror of terrors that had haunted every general of the Army of the Potomac since the start of the war. In such a position the Union would have to attack frontally to try to batter a way back through. Gettysburg should have been the bait and switch, a first contact, a fight and then a "suckering in," even as Lee swung wide and then plowed into the vulnerable rear. It was clear to Lee by late in the evening of July 1, 1863, that the surviving troops of the Army of the Potomac's First and Eleventh Corps were digging in. It could be seen and heard. That could only mean the rest of the army was now coming up, as indeed they were. By moving wide to the right, Lee would have won the Gettysburg campaign.

Could Lee have then won the war after a victory at Gettysburg, or Westminster? Perhaps another essay, or perhaps a series of books, might answer that.

But history is history. Lee did not swing wide and he went down to a tragic defeat, a defeat that eviscerated forever his ability to wage an offensive battle.

His failure: command and control. There should have been a clear recognition when forced to rely upon an amateur spy for intelligence, when his cavalry corps had simply disappeared, when two of his three corps commanders needed firmer guidance, that something was fundamentally wrong with his army on the eve of battle, while there was still time to rectify it.

Dare I say it? His failure was one of arrogance. Not an arrogance of ego, or of personality, but rather an overestimation of what his army could achieve if he ordered it to do so. This sin was indeed recognized the evening after Pickett's Charge, when he lamented that he had asked his men to do the impossible—because he had come to believe they could do the impossible.

Failure of control on the battlefield is obvious. Except for the lucky chance of troop movements on the first day, his attacks on the second and third days were abysmal failures of coordination.

And, finally, the narrowing of focus. The hill, that hill, the ridge that sloped southward, linking to another hill anchoring the left flank of the Union line, became an obsession. It was indeed the good ground, good ground for the Union. Ground he should have walked away from but instead continued to attack and attack again until it bled out.

A postscript: Of the nearly 2 million who visit Gettysburg each year, the vast majority are Southerners. It is indeed ironic in one sense. One would think a place of great triumph, Chancellorsville, Manassas, Chickamauga, would be the place of pilgrimage to the Lost Cause. Instead, it is to the place of defeat, the place where a dream died.

If you can be a quiet observer, dispassionate, stand at the Angle, the High Water Mark, and watch who comes there, who looks across the field with tears in their eyes, who might whisper to a son or daughter, "Here is where your great-great-grandfather died in Pickett's Charge."

Victory and defeat blend together at Gettysburg into one, a struggle in which we all now feel united, where our ancestors were indeed a band of brothers, our St. Crispin's Day.

Some years back, I spoke with a park guide, who shared a story. He had taken an Asian couple around the field and they had soaked it in with awe, asking questions, the questions revealing a serious study of the battle before they arrived. Curious at the end of their drive around the battlefield, the guide asked them, "Why are you so interested in Gettysburg?"

They smiled proudly. "We are new American citizens. This is our history now."

Joshua Chamberlain was right. Gettysburg is the vision place of souls.

THE CRATER: THE MINE

Petersburg, near Richmond, Virginia, July 30, 1864

WILLIAM R. FORSTCHEN

It was the morning of July 30, 1864, and the potential for that day was the ending of the siege of Petersburg, Virginia, and with it, the end of the Civil War. At least, it should have been. . . .

A tunnel, just over four hundred feet long, had been dug from the Union lines under a crucial Confederate position that guarded the main road into Petersburg. Four tons of powder had been packed under the fort and the fuse was lit. Everything was in place—for what turned into one of the most bungled tragedies of the war.

Two months earlier, in May 1864, Union general Ulysses S. Grant initiated the spring campaign in Virginia, with the goal of destroying Robert E. Lee's Army of Northern Virginia and then taking Richmond. What ensued during the next forty-five days was the bloodiest campaign in American military history, with the Union army sustaining more than seventy thousand casualties. Unable to take Richmond by direct assault, Grant swung south of the city in a vain attempt to take Petersburg, a main rail junction, twenty miles south of the Confederate capital.

Petersburg was the back door to Richmond. Four main railroad lines from the Deep South joined in Petersburg, along with several turnpikes and plank roads. Nearly all supplies to Lee's army and to Richmond funneled in through this bottleneck. If Petersburg fell, defending Richmond would be impossible. The result would then most likely have been political collapse.

The assault on Petersburg between June 15 and 17 was bungled, and in the last week of June, Grant called a halt to offensive operations. The Army of the Potomac had been bled out, and the opposing sides settled down to a siege.

The rings of Confederate fortifications surrounding Petersburg had been built in 1862 and strengthened for over two years. The position was impregnable to frontal assault. Except for the lack of barbed wire, photographs of the fortifications look remarkably like the western front of World War One.

Lee's army was stretched thin, having to defend nearly forty miles of front, from north of Richmond down to Petersburg and then westward for half a dozen miles. He had no real reserves, and the only thing preventing Grant from breaking through was the simple fact that one man inside a well-built earthen fort or trench could stop half a dozen attacking opponents. What Grant needed was a way to either get around, over, or under the fortifications. Airborne, of course, was still a long way off, and he did not yet have enough men to try to flank out farther to the west.

The Ninth Corps with the Army of the Potomac had always been viewed as "outsiders" by the old veterans of the Army of the Potomac. The Ninth Corps was something of a wanderer, having fought in North Carolina, Kentucky, Tennessee, and even at the siege of Vicksburg, while their comrades in the east had faced Lee at Gettysburg.

The commander of the Ninth Corps, however, was not unknown to the men of the Army of the Potomac—and was thoroughly despised by the rest of the army. General Ambrose Burnside. A rather eccentric character, Burnside was tall, rotund, with huge sideburns (urban legend maintains that the reversal of his name gave these whiskers their name), his balding head always crowned with a tall round hat.

He was a man who could show flashes of genius. His campaign in eastern Tennessee around Knoxville during the winter of 1863 had stalled and finally turned back the veteran troops of General "Pete" Longstreet. But to the Army of the Potomac, Burnside's name was always associated with three debacles: the infamous "Burnside's Bridge" at Antietam, the suicidal assaults before Fredericksburg in December of 1862, and the tragic "Mud March" of the following month.

At Antietam, Burnside's Ninth Corps had joined in with the Army of the Potomac and occupied the left flank that day. Ordered to advance by General George McClellan, Burnside had wasted the better part of the day hesitating, focusing on a narrow stone arch bridge and then attacking it head-on. Less than a thousand Confederates had blocked his entire corps of approximately twelve thousand men for hours until the bridge was finally taken. The delay was the final blow to a terrible day, allowing Lee to bring up his last reserves and turn Burnside back once he had crossed Antietam Creek, a stream his corps could have easily waded at half a dozen places.

Ironically, as if failure was a guarantee of success, a month later Burnside was elevated to commander of the Army of the Potomac after Lincoln fired McClellan. But unlike some commanders, Burnside was fully aware of his own shortcomings and actually tried to turn the promotion down, but Lincoln insisted.

The result—the disaster at Fredericksburg.

In December 1862, the Confederate army was well dug in along the heights above the colonial town of Fredericksburg. Burnside ordered a daylong series of uncoordinated assaults that accomplished nothing, other than to add twelve thousand more names to the Union casualties' lists.

A minor but significant point to this failure, which might very well have played a crucial role in a disaster yet to come: one of the Union division commanders that day was George Meade. His division alone was able to penetrate the Confederate defenses. He sent back desperate appeals for reinforcements, which Burnside denied. Meade bitterly complained afterward that if Burnside had backed him up, he could very well have turned the Confederate right flank. That is doubtful, but the key fact here is that Meade believed it.

Burnside was finally removed when, in January 1863, he decided to initiate the risky venture of a winter campaign. The weather had been dry and warm for several weeks, the dirt roads now able to withstand the movement of over a hundred thousand men and their supplies.

Winter campaigns prior to modern motorized equipment and paved roads were risky ventures. Snow or several days of icy rain could paralyze an army. Just look at Napoleon in Russia. Even a modern army can be overwhelmed by winter weather, as the Germans learned in 1941.

Burnside's incredible luck played true to form. He gave orders for his troops to tear down their winter quarters before setting out on what he planned to be a flanking march similar to what Joe Hooker would try four months later in the Chancellorsville campaign.

Winter quarters for both armies were usually small log cabins, roughly eight by ten feet square, canvas-roofed, with chimneys made out of cracker boxes and empty ammunition cases. They could be amazingly snug and warm, with enough room for four to six men. Tearing their cabins down was supposed to be a positive morale signal to the men that they were setting off on their final campaign to victory.

Reports show that quite literally, just as the men finished the destruction, packed up their gear, formed ranks, and started out on the first day of march, the heavens darkened and within a couple of hours an icy rain began to fall, a rain that would turn into a four-day deluge.

By the end of the first day, the roads were rivers of mud; the nights were a frozen hell. The men, thoroughly soaked, huddled together in the woods and fields under shelter halves, even the most experienced unable to get a smoldering fire going.

By the second day, artillery pieces were sinking up to their barrels in the mud, with fifty to a hundred men working to pull each piece out of the freezing soup, only to watch it sink back in again after an advance of a few dozen feet.

What made it even more bitter was the hilarious humor of their Confederate opponents on the other side of the Rappahannock River. Rebels made up big signs out of bedsheets, "Burnside, stuck in the mud!" and posted them along the riverbank. The Yankees were too disgusted with the truth of it to even respond.

Horses by the hundreds collapsed and died from exposure and exhaustion, blocking the roads with the wagons and artillery pieces they had been pulling. Men staggered through the freezing rain, completely soaked and out of food.

Burnside finally abandoned the campaign, ordered his men to turn about and stagger back to their camps—the ones they had destroyed before leaving. It almost would have been comic, if not for the human tragedy. Hundreds died from exhaustion, disease and exposure, and veterans would later recall that this indeed was the low point of the war for them, with desertions soaring and the army all but disintegrating.

Burnside was removed from command of the Army of the Potomac and transferred, along with his Ninth Corps, to other fields of action, to finally return to rejoin the Army of the Potomac in May 1864.

And yet . . . there must have been something right about the man. Until their dying day, the veterans of the Ninth adored him. Years later, at reunions, they were ready to defend his name with their fists (or canes), claiming that though luck had played against him, there were times when he was a genius and, above all else, truly cared for his men.

It is reported that when a name would be presented to Napoleon for promotion to general, his question was always the same, "Is he lucky?" Burnside never would have made it in that army.

So in June of 1864, Burnside and his men were back with the Army of the Potomac, stuck in the trenches before Petersburg, along one of the most dangerous stretches of the line. An earthen rebel fort just one hundred yards away dominated a sloping ridge above the Union position. Any incautious peek over the top would usually result in a minié ball between the eyes.

Life in the trenches was hell. It was late June, the heat and humidity typical of southern Virginia was stifling. When it didn't rain, everyone choked on the dust. When it did rain, everyone laid in the mud. The stench must have been unbearable, given the sanitation habits of these ninteenth-century boys-turned-soldiers.

One of the regiments with Burnside's command was the Forty-sixth Pennsylvania Volunteers. The regiment was primarily made up of "coal crackers," miners from Schuylkill County.

In the trenches for a couple of weeks, and disgusted with the entire affair, these men were indulging in that undeniable right of soldiers, to gripe, and one of them offhandedly made the comment, "Why don't we just dig a tunnel under that damn fort and blow it to hell?"

A captain overheard the comment, and kicked the idea around with a few of his men, who claimed it would be a cinch to do the job, given the right tools. The captain went to the regimental commander, Colonel Pleasanton, who needed no persuading, and, before the day was out, he was standing before Burnside, explaining the proposal, pointing out that if there was a regiment in the Union army that could do the job, it was his.

Right here we see a positive side of Burnside. Pleasanton was a mere colonel of a regiment, one of over thirty under Burnside, and yet within a few hours, Burnside was hearing him out.

Burnside saw the wisdom of it and immediately ordered Pleasanton to draw up a plan and requisition order for equipment while he carried the proposal up the ladder.

A few days later, Burnside went to see General George Meade. Meade, as you will recall, had been a division commander under Burnside at Fredericksburg, and now the roles were reversed; there was no love lost between the two.

Meade's role in this army was largely that of fifth wheel. On paper, he was actually in command of the Army of the Potomac, but in reality he was not, because the overall commander of all Union forces in the war, General Grant, had established his headquarters with Meade's army in Virginia. In every action, from the Wilderness to Petersburg, Grant took direct command, with

Meade simply passing the orders along. Here would be one of many breakdowns in the scenario to come.

Meade had one of his military engineers present at the meeting, who immediately dismissed Burnside's proposal as absurd, since everyone knew a military tunnel could not be longer than approximately three hundred feet, due to lack of ventilation.

Burnside countered that these men were professional miners, had sunk shafts of hundreds of yards in the coalfields of Pennsylvania, and knew their business. If they said they could run the tunnel four hundred feet, they could indeed do it. In fact, he had already authorized them to begin preliminary work.

Meade hit that one hard—how dare Burnside order such work without his prior approval? Burnside was stunned, assuming Meade would have immediately grabbed hold of his plan and complimented him for his initiative. He covered himself then with the counter that at the very least it was keeping the men busy.

Meade announced he'd have to pass the proposal up the chain of command, meaning Grant, and at last gave grudging permission for the Forty-sixth to continue digging, but none of the requested supplies would be forthcoming from army command.

Frustrated, Burnside left the meeting, but encouraged his men to start work in earnest. Shovels and picks were fashioned out of bayonets and hunks of scrap metal. Shoring was constructed out of cracker boxes and bits of lumber. The excavated earth was carefully carried out at night and concealed in a ravine. The ventilation problem was solved right from the start. Complex to describe, it was actually very simple. An airtight door was constructed across the mine entrance, except for a "pipe" made out of cracker boxes with their ends removed, and then caulked together end to end. This pipe extended from its hole through the airtight door to the face of the mine, where the men were digging. On the other side of the door, out in the open, an airtight wood stove was constructed and a roaring fire built within. Its only air intake was through a flue pipe that penetrated the door. Therefore, the fire sucked its air supply from inside the mine, the displaced air replaced by fresh air being rushing down the cracker-box pipe to where the men were working.

So much for the pronouncements of experts serving as military engineers with the Union army.

In short order, the mine was leaping forward ten to fifteen feet a day, with the promise of being under the Confederate fort by the latter part of July.

The distance to be dug, and the bearing the tunnel had to follow, was crucial. Nothing would be more embarrassing than to fall twenty feet short, or to one side of the fort or the other. The problem was to get the observations, the triangulations, which actually just required simple plane geometry that any junior engineer could accomplish, given the right tools.

Burnside requested a theodolite from army command and was promptly refused. Such an instrument was too precious to be risked at the front line. Not to be outflanked, Burnside dispatched an officer to an instrument maker in Washington, D.C., to obtain the necessary tools and, above all else, to keep his mouth shut, not only to keep Meade in the dark, but the ever-lurking Confederate spies as well.

The officer returned with the precious instrument, and, with great caution, it was edged up out of the forward trench and the angles taken, with one man being killed by an alert rebel sharpshooter in the process. The tunnel was moving dead on, straight toward its target, and had only a couple of hundred feet to go.

With the obvious potential success of the tunnel, Burnside forced Meade's hand. A recommendation was finally passed up to Grant to support an offensive operation built around the detonation of the mine. Grant gave his approval, but the approval had some serious limitations "suggested" by Meade. Meade would maintain "tactical" control of the battle, and Burnside would only command his own corps in the attack. Burnside had requested control of two reserve corps, a request often given to the leader of an offensive action, to bring up reserves as he saw fit, rather than having to send off couriers in all directions to get permission in a moment of crisis.

Now came the time to actually plan the attack. This battle stands as unique among nearly all the actions of the Civil War. It was an offensive planned weeks in advance, the ground was well examined and known, and the disposition of the enemy was known; in many ways it "reads" more like a battle in World War One or World War Two, with the attacking forces heavily trained and ready.

Burnside's corps had four divisions. The Fourth Division of the Ninth Corps was unique. It was the first division of African-American troops to be assigned directly to the Army of the Potomac.

The men of this division were volunteer recruits who had joined the USCTs, the United States Colored Troops. Many today assume, because of the splendid movie *Glory*, that the Fifty-fourth Massachusetts was the "first" black regiment in the army, the first to go into action, and also that it was composed primarily of escaped slaves.

Those assumptions are wrong on all points. Other black units had been formed earlier than the Fifty-fourth, one seeing action in the fall of 1862, and in actuality, most of the recruits were free men of color living in the North when the war started.

A typical regiment of this Fourth Division was the Twenty-eighth USCTs. They had been recruited out of Indiana during the winter and spring of 1864. The vast majority were free men prior to the war, and a high percentage were literate. Their officers had gone through an OCS program to be trained to lead the USCTs. The qualifications for the officers were top-notch. Candidates had to be well-seasoned combat veterans with top recommendations from their commanding officers in their old regiments, and they had to submit to a rigorous exam and training before being posted.

The USCTs were unique in other ways. By late 1863, the pool of white volunteers for the army had dried up. With casualty rates averaging two thousand a day by the spring of 1864, the war was increasingly unpopular. Bounties of up to $1,000 were being offered (in 1864 money, the equivalent of roughly $100,000 today), and there were few takers. Those who did take it were usually bounty jumpers, men who would get their initial payment of a hundred to two hundred on signing, then leap off the train as it took them to the front. Recruiters finally took to locking the men into boxcars under armed guards to get them up to the battle lines. And usually, as soon as they were turned over, they were gone, or would definitely run at the first chance, head back North, and sign up again in another state.

The old line regiments, made up primarily of patriotic volunteers from 1861 and 1862, loathed these men and claimed they were worse than useless, which in fact they were.

In contrast, the fighting potential of the African-American volunteers was far superior, if they could only get onto the field of battle. These were men who had been literally begging to get into the fight since the first day of the war, seeing it not just as a war to save the Union, but as a war of liberation, and as Frederick Douglass so eloquently proclaimed, a means of recognition of full citizenship. For how could that citizenship be denied once a man had put on a uniform, picked up a rifle, and carried on his hip a cartridge box stamped "U.S."?

And yet, few commanders in the field wanted these men. It would finally take a showing of courage and blood to change that attitude. As for the average white soldier in the ranks, there was a vast array of attitudes, ranging from glad acceptance to outright hatred and threats—until these men went into battle and showed their grit, and the realization finally sunk in with their white comrades that these were indeed soldiers.

It is one of the good sides of Burnside that he took the Fourth Division, gladly accepting it to his command, but tragically assigning a less-than-competent division commander, Edward Ferrero.

For that matter, all of Burnside's division commanders were less than adequate, the worst of the lot being James Ledlie, but more about him later. Another of Burnside's good qualities, but also a fault when it came to higher command, was his profound sense of loyalty to his men. Most of his brigade and division commanders had been with him since the start of the war, and thus he tended to back them up, always ready to offer another chance, even when they proved to be failures.

Burnside now started to lay out the plans for the assault once the mine was detonated. It was brilliant.

The fort to be destroyed occupied one of the most crucial positions in Lee's defensive line. Six hundred yards behind the fort to the west was the Jerusalem Plank Road, an essential highway that served as the connector into the town of Petersburg for Lee's defensive front. If the road should be severed, all Confederate infantry to the south of the point of rupture would be cut off from their primary line of supplies, and retreat.

A couple of hundred yards "up" this road, heading in toward Petersburg, was a colonial-era church and cemetery on a low rise. Control of that ground with several batteries of artillery would render Petersburg defenseless, and, in fact, from that churchyard it was only a half-mile dash into the very center of town and the rail yards that converged from across the Confederacy. From that junction, a single line led north, twenty miles, to Richmond.

In short, take the road. After taking the road, take the churchyard. Once that falls, Petersburg is indefensible and must be abandoned. Once Petersburg falls, Richmond is doomed, all but cut off logistically from the rest of the South. And, as discussed above, if the town of Petersburg should be immediately occupied, all Confederate troops south of the town would no longer have a line of retreat and would be in the bag. Lee's army would then disintegrate.

It was fair to say that a successful attack might very well mean an end to the war within a month.

Burnside picked his Fourth Division, the USCTs, to lead the assault.

The choice was a logical one, which Burnside clearly explained, and was, in fact, a decision based upon nearly three years of combat experience. Increasingly, veteran troops were reluctant to engage in the mad dash of a charge—they had too often seen the results. Green troops that had yet to "see the elephant" would go forward with élan, especially if they felt they had something to prove. For the African-American soldiers, there was a definite need to prove something.

Besides, the other three divisions in Burnside's command had been bled out by the previous three months of campaigning, having suffered over 50 percent losses, but the USCTs were new to the front, rested, and aggressive in spirit. Their choice was logical from a military standpoint, and also shows yet another positive side of Burnside. When queried about the color of the men assigned to lead the attack, he replied that it meant absolutely no difference to him whatsoever. They were soldiers and he knew they would do their duty, a fairly unique attitude for a nineteeth-century general, North or South. He would then also add that he had additional confidence in these men because they were well trained and, above all else, did indeed have something to prove.

The plan laid out by Burnside was that once the mine was detonated, an hour before dawn, the two brigades of the USCTs were to rise up from their jump-off position, just behind the forward Union trench, rush the hundred and fifty yards up the slope to the Confederate lines, and they were not to stop.

This was to be a classic breakthrough assault. Burnside assumed, and correctly so, that with the detonation of the mine, Confederate troops to either flank of the explosion would be in shock or outright panic for several minutes, perhaps as long as fifteen to thirty minutes, after the shattering explosion.

Those in the first assault wave were to push on, one brigade swinging around the left flank of the crater created by the explosion, the other to the right flank. A single regiment from each brigade would "peel off" from the attack columns and push out at a right angle from the crater, broadening the hole in the Confederate line and keeping it open.

The remaining regiments were to then rush forward at the double, crossing the six hundred yards of open ground to the Jerusalem Plank Road. Once the road was seized, the left flanking brigade was to secure the road on the south side of the breakthrough. The right-flanking brigade was to turn and dash hell-bent toward Petersburg, seize the churchyard, and, if possible, continue to storm straight into Petersburg. Estimated elapsed time from detonation to securing the road, fifteen minutes. The push into Petersburg, fifteen to twenty minutes more.

Behind the Fourth Division, Burnside's three other divisions, formed up in columns, were to storm in directly on the coattails of their black comrades, keep the breech open, storm forward to the road, and press into Petersburg as well. And finally, behind them were to come two more entire corps, six additional divisions to roll up the Confederate army to either flank of the breakthrough along with battalions of artillery.

It was aggressive, it was brilliantly conceived, and it would forever shatter the Army of Northern Virginia.

What happened across the next two weeks is reminiscent of classic films about World War Two, where the heroes are given an impossible mission and then drill, and drill, and drill again until they finally go in. This was an opportunity unheard of during the Civil War, with its far more typical "meeting engagements," where battles tended to unfold minute by minute, with little if any chance for elaborate preplanning.

This author located documentation for his dissertation that proved that the Fourth Division was specially trained for the mission. Two miles to the rear, there was an outer line of Confederate forts that had been seized in the first days of the siege, and were now abandoned—and out of sight of the existing Confederate line. The Fourth Division was ordered back to this position and repeatedly drilled in how to assault the line. One participant recorded that a vast circle, roughly a hundred yards across, was laid out with stakes and strips of cloth. The men were told to go nowhere near this circle when they did charge, but rather to make sure they went around it and then charge toward the road beyond.

More than a few began to figure out that there would be some sort of massive explosion to herald the start of the attack, since rumors were circulating about the mysterious doings of the Forty-sixth Pennsylvania Regiment, and how that unit was made up of coal miners, and their section of the trench was sealed off from any prying eyes or visitors from other regiments. It didn't take much for these soldiers to put two and two together.

Finally, toward the end of their training, they were told what the mission would be, the size of the explosion, and that they were to push forward the instant the mine detonated, regardless of the debris and confusion such an explosion would create. Above all else, they were told, go nowhere near the "crater." They were to push on to the road and the city beyond.

Several days before the planned attack, brigade and regimental officers were taken into a ravine just behind the front line and shown their places of deployment prior to the attack, and the approaches to their assigned positions, which they would then have to find in the dark. On the night before the attack, once it was dark, staff officers would tape out the approaches and guides would be posted for every unit to lead them to their places. Ladders, actually rough-made wooden footbridges about ten feet long, were constructed as well. These were to be thrown across the tops of their own trenches to act as pathways as they went in. In addition, once darkness settled, pioneer troops would secretly go out between the lines to remove the barriers of stakes in front of the Union line so the attack could go forward unimpeded.

The one drawback to the jump-off position was that it was clearly visible from the Confederate side. Therefore, absolutely no lights were to be shown, anything that might rattle, such as tin cups and backpacks, were to be left behind, canteens were to be filled, and strict silence enforced.

THE CRATER: FAILURE

Petersburg, near Richmond, Virginia, July 30, 1864

WILLIAM R. FORSTCHEN

Everything was ready. Morale with the USCTs was sky-high. They sensed the importance of their mission, and the word within the units was they would die, if need be, to get it done and prove their fighting worth.

Then Meade stepped in and everything went to hell.

Once Burnside had gained Meade's grudging assent to go ahead with the mine and Meade had authorized a plan of attack, Burnside had placed a requisition for twenty thousand pounds of black powder to be used. As the tunnel finally reached the middle of the Confederate fort, roughly thirty feet underground, the miners hollowed out two chambers for the placement of the powder.

Meade flatly refused the request for twenty thousand pounds, claiming that his own people told him eight thousand was sufficient. Burnside argued that amount would cause an explosion that could indeed render damage, but that the additional twelve thousand pounds, which the Union had no shortage of, would double the effect of the blast and have a far more devastating impact on the morale of the Confederate survivors. Meade refused.

To detonate the mine, Burnside placed a standard request for a galvanic battery detonator, already in wide use in mining operations, and as backup, six hundred feet of quick fuse. With less than two days to go, the supplies arrived—eight thousand pounds of powder, loose in barrels, and rather than the battery and quick fuse, the miners of the Forty-sixth received "slow fuse" in ten-foot lengths with no backup system. This meant that the men had to create approximately fifty splices for the fuses in order to have a five-hundred-foot length, and had to unpack the powder and haul it loose up to the explosive chambers and there repack it—a highly risky operation, to say the least.

They forged ahead and did their task anyhow.

With less than sixteen hours to go before the assault, Meade ordered Burnside to report. At this juncture, Meade announced that he was changing the order of battle.

The black troops would not lead the assault.

Stunned, Burnside could barely reply, finally stuttering out that these were the men assigned to the task nearly a month ago, that they had trained relentlessly, that they knew their tasks, and that if any troops would bring victory the following morning, it would be them.

Meade offered a vague excuse that if the troops were slaughtered (a not-so-subtle declaration that he expected the attack to fail), abolitionists in the North would complain. Burnside fired back that it would indeed fail if the men best trained for the job were pulled off the line, but Meade was adamant, finally falling back on the position that he had talked it over with Grant, who supported the change of plans.

An analogy is most definitely appropriate here. This would be the equivalent of the First and Twenty-ninth Divisions, waiting in port on June 4, 1944, to go into Omaha Beach, men who had trained for this assault for months, being pulled out of the order of battle, with Ike telling Bradley to replace them with troops untrained for the assault. One can imagine the debacle that would have ensued in what everyone knew already would be a tough fight.

The suspicion is there that besides the subconscious desire of Meade to screw up Burnside's plan, there was a more overt reason—namely, that if the attack did succeed, he wanted white troops to carry the honor of leading the charge that won the war. His statement that abolitionists would be upset carries little weight. It was not a concern when the Fifth-fourth led the suicidal assault at Battery Wagner, or during other desperate attacks in the last year of the war. In nearly every action so far involving black troops, they had been praised for their valor.

Horrified, Burnside returned to his headquarters and broke the news that the black division was out of the attack and would be placed in reserve. At this point, the man who could alternate between genius and folly broke down. He turned to the commanders and asked for one of them to volunteer to lead the assault. The response had an almost Monty Python quality to it, with all three of them silent and avoiding eye contact.

What happened next was a continuation of this madness. Burnside took three straws and asked the men to draw. Ledlie drew the short straw. This would be one of the most bizarre command decisions of the war, and also one that set the nightmare in full motion.

One would think that Ledlie, upon drawing the short straw, would have been out of the headquarters, called for his staff, convened them before dark, and, in a damn good hurry, explained what would be done and where the men were to deploy.

Instead, he immediately retired to his command post, a bombproof bunker behind the lines, called in his brigade commanders, vaguely told them that their division would now lead the attack, and then dismissed them. The brigade commanders would later report that he was already drunk.

There were no directives, no orders of march, no word as to where to deploy, and, worst of all, no word on what to do when "one helluva big explosion" would mark the start of the attack.

Burnside, the variable genius, was nearly as bad. His master plan crushed, he withdrew to his own headquarters, eight hundred yards to the rear, a position that would give him at least a partial view of the field, and waited out the night without doing anything more to ensure success. Meade had crushed him and he simply gave up.

Shortly after midnight, the white troops of the three divisions broke camp and started to filter down to what was supposed to be their jump-off positions. But now, with the change in the order of battle, Ledlie's men were to occupy Ferrero's position, while another division was to occupy Ledlie's, and chaos ensued. There was so much confusion and noise that pickets along the front were anxious as hell, rebel sentries starting to shout over and ask what all the ruckus was about.

To make it worse, Lee, with a fighter's instinct, had come to the conclusion that something "was up." Grant had tried to lure some of Lee's reserves up toward Richmond a few days earlier, and on that evening Lee smelled an impending attack. He had received reports as well that something strange was going on in front of the Jerusalem Plank Road, perhaps even a tunnel under the fort guarding the line. Men reported subterranean sounds, and the old trick of placing a saucer of water on the ground, with all men in the fort then remaining stock-still, had paid off. The water in the pan vibrated, meaning something was going on underneath. A few attempts at countershafts had been attempted, but, as yet, they had not found anything.

During the night Lee started to shift some reserves back to the Jerusalem Plank Road . . . just in case.

The mine was scheduled to detonate between 3:30 and 3:45 A.M. At that time of year, and before standard time and daylight savings time, it was approximately a few minutes before the first glow of dawn.

The slow fuse was lit by one of the men of the Forty-sixth Pennsylvania, sandbags were thrown across the entrance, and everyone hunkered down and waited . . . and waited . . . and waited.

First light began to break in the east, meaning behind the Union lines. By 4:15 A.M., it was bright enough to read a newspaper headline. The assault force was flat down on their stomachs behind the Union front lines, and, at this point, the only thing that protected them from being spotted was their dark blue uniforms. In the early morning glow, they could easily see the Confederate fort above them. In a few more minutes, a blind man would be able to see them from the other side.

In frustration, Burnside sent a message down to the miners, asking what the hell had gone wrong. But they already knew. With fifty splices on the old fuse, somewhere it was bound to have winked out. Two men now volunteered to crawl into the tunnel, carrying a lantern, and find out what was wrong, truly two of the bravest volunteers of the Civil War.

They had to crawl nearly the entire length of the tunnel, four hundred feet. The fire had gone out where the last of the slow fuse connected in a T junction to the fast fuse, which would race into the explosive chambers to the left and right of the tunnel.

They respliced it, took a deep breath, lit the short end of the slow fuse, and scrambled like hell to get out, leaping out of the tunnel's exit just seconds ahead of the explosion, which took place at approximately 4:45 A.M.

Those who saw it go off describe the explosion not so much as an explosion like we see today with material like C-4, but rather as a dull rumble at first, a shock wave beneath one's feet, and then a vast mushroom-like cloud of dirt that soared heavenward, lit within by bolts of fire and boiling yellow-gray smoke. Pieces of hard-packed red clay, the size of small houses, raced upward, mingled with men, parts of men, rifles, scorched bits of uniform, and the artillery guns from within the fort, all of it soaring upward and outward in a spreading cloud.

The men of Ledlie's division had been in no way prepared for this, especially as they looked straight up and saw hunks of debris raining down. Some broke in panic and headed to the rear. Amazingly, one Confederate soldier from within the fort survived the blast, thrown over a hundred yards and landing naked, just in front of the Union entrenchments. Sympathetic Yankees dragged him in and offered him a drink.

The blast spread out, debris rained down. Torn into the Confederate line was a crater over two hundred and fifty feet long, in places nearly sixty feet wide, and over thirty feet deep. If Burnside's original request had been followed, the damage would most likely have been half again as great, perhaps rendering a gap four hundred feet wide in the Confederate lines.

To either flank, in spite of what the veterans in gray might have said years later, there was pandemonium. Some observers claimed a hole over a quarter mile wide opened in the Confederate line within a few minutes of the explosion as the survivors ran for their lives. One must remember that this was 1864. The heavy weaponry of World War One and World War Two, with thousand-pound bombs and one-ton shells, was something totally beyond the experience of any Civil War soldier. The detonation of four tons of powder less than a hundred yards away must have been a terrifying experience then. Frankly, it would be even now for even the most hardened veteran.

But on the Union side nothing happened!

Ledlie's men had been given no clear orders, other than to go forward once the explosion took place and occupy the line. Stunned by the blast they had not been trained to expect, they just stood up. Reports indicate it was a good ten minutes or more before they moved past their own entrenchments and started up the slope.

The footbridges that were supposed to be in place so they could go over their own trenches were nowhere to be found, and the obstacles in front of their lines were still in place. To advance, they had to climb down into their own trenches, climb up the other side, weave their way through the entanglements of sharpened stakes, and then at least *reach* no-man's-land. All semblance of military order disintegrated immediately.

They wandered up the slope in small groups, command and control all but gone because the units had been jumbled together in the confusion of the night and moved to a strange position. Officers ran back and forth, looking for their lost commands and extolling the men to advance.

The noise was becoming deafening as well. It wasn't just the explosion. Burnside had requested and received agreement from General Hunt, commander of all Union artillery, to position a massive array of guns to support the attack, over 140 pieces, including huge heavy mortars. The artillery's purpose was to pin down the edge of the flanks and then blow open a hole in the Confederate line. They set to their work, but the fire and smoke just added to the confusion.

Ledlie's men made it up the slope and took one look at the huge crater, and the collective opinion of that already worn-out division was that the smoking crater looked like a fine place to hunker down, look for souvenirs, and see what happened next. Almost to a man they piled in. One cannot blame them. They were veterans. Standing out in the open was dangerous, and, with the waste of precious time, Confederate fire was beginning to come in from the flanks, dropping a man here and there, and they knew that was just a portent of things to come. The crater, for the moment, was the safest place to be.

Urgent appeals from Ledlie's brigade commanders were sent back for additional orders. Traditionally, a division commander was expected to go forward with his men, not necessarily out in the front, though many did, but most definitely between the first and second wave of an advance. Ledlie was dead drunk, a quarter mile to the rear in his bombproof shelter, joined there now by the other division commanders.

The next division in line now went forward and exactly imitated Ledlie's men. The flanking fire was growing hotter, though some did try to push behind the lip of the crater and move toward the road.

On the Confederate side, General Mahone, in direct command on the spot, hurried to patch the massive hole. He ordered a few hundred Virginians to rush forward, with shovels and picks, and start digging an emergency reserve line halfway between the point of the explosion and the road, while at the same time sending out a desperate plea to Lee for any and all reserves.

Now the third division of white troops went in, the vast majority of them piling into the crater as well, though some of these did try to broaden the front, occupying short stretches of trenches to either side of the crater.

But there was not one man on that field at that moment who truly grasped the full plan, or that the golden opportunity to turn this into the war-winning punch was melting away under the boiling July heat.

The two brigade commanders of the black division did know, and they waited in agonized frustration at the reserve jump-off position. There were no orders from Ferrero or Burnside. From their position a quarter mile to the rear of the fight, they could see the debacle unfolding, but what to do?

Over nine thousand Union troops were jammed into a cauldron not more than two hundred yards across, with the crater in the middle. A determined punch, even now, might still win the day. For a few minutes, they actually considered saying the hell with higher command and going in on their own. But the rigid command and control of the Army of the Potomac played out yet again that day. It was a rare man in that army who would seize the moment and go in, and the hell with waiting for orders. Neither brigade commander, though good soldiers, were made of that far sterner stuff.

One went to the rear to beg to be released, and, of all people, he ran into General Grant, who was watching the fight. He begged to go in and then, uncharacteristically, Grant himself hesitated, most likely doing so because of the misgivings that Meade had communicated about this entire operation and his mistrust of Burnside. He ordered the brigade commander to wait for orders through proper channels, turned around and rode off, stopping only long enough at Meade's headquarters to tell him that he was in direct command now, since the presence of the supreme commander was required at a conference in Washington. Grant pointedly told Meade that he was also authorized to convene a court of inquiry if he so wished. Then he rode away from the field, got on a boat at City Point, and was gone.

What took place next between Meade and Burnside was, in this author's opinion, one of the most disgusting acts of commander failure, childishness, and cowardice of the entire war.

Burnside's headquarters overlooked the ravine where the troops had deployed during the night and up the slope to where the smoking crater was located. His range of vision did not extend beyond that. Any communication with the front would require at least a half-hour round trip by a courier across increasingly dangerous ground, as Confederate infantry began to push in to seal off the breach and isolate the men in the crater.

One wishes it were possible to reach across time and scream some advice. At Gettysburg, General Hancock was on the front line when Pickett's Charge came in. General Dan Sickles, much maligned by many, nevertheless stood alongside his men at Gettysburg as well, and lost a leg doing it. If only Burnside had gone forward and seized direct control, he might have reversed all that was going wrong.

He did not.

Meade's headquarters was barely a half mile away from Burnside, farther back from the front. The two were connected by telegraph, and the transcripts of their communications across the next several hours are in the Official Records of the War of the Rebellion.

Meade started to tauntingly ask Burnside why his troops were not advancing, to which Burnside replied that it was now time to release the reserve corps, which could still push through in spite of the confusion. Meade fired back he would not release the reserves, since reports were coming to him that Burnside's men were already broken. Burnside took exception to this and an argument ensued between the two, both trading veiled insults, demands of apologies, and finally a threat by Meade to relieve Burnside of command.

It is almost comic when read, except for the fact that good men were dying while their generals traded demands for apologies.

One can only imagine a Patton, or a Sherman, walking in on such a scene and what would have ensued.

Burnside did, at last, authorize his Fourth Division to go in. This author estimates that the time was approximately eight A.M., though accounts vary widely from as early as seven to as late as ten.

It was a forlorn hope, but they valiantly went forward anyhow. The Confederate general Mahone had worked brilliantly to contain the breach. Confederate infantry were reclaiming the trenches to either side of the crater and establishing a perimeter behind the breach as well.

As the two brigades of USCTs, still committed to their original plan of sweeping to either side of the crater, crossed into the open field between their own lines and their objective, a devastating enfilading fire cut into their exposed flanks. The breach, which should have been a couple of hundred yards wide to either side of the explosion, was now hemmed in. The men tried to herd through the narrow openings to either side of the crater and push forward to the primary objective, their officers shouting for the troops now hunkered down inside the crater to get the hell up and join them in the charge. Few responded. The charge of the black troops, caught up by pressure on the flanks, trying to make their way up and over the rabbit warren of Confederate entrenchments while under fire, began to collapse.

Yet again, the analogy to World War One is appropriate. Men would pour into a trench, turn a corner, and there be confronted by rebels pouring back into the fight.

The battle now turned vicious. In the close quarters of trench warfare, where opponents turn a corner and there is the enemy only a few feet away, chances are there will be no prisoners. Studies by many military historians have shown that in such a situation, the moment of fight or flight, there is no room to run, no time left for a man to throw down his gun and ask for quarter, no opportunity for a chivalrous foe to shout to a distant enemy to "give it up." It is up close, it is near panic on both sides, and the tendency is to shoot first and ask questions later. In this fight the situation was made far worse because of the racial tensions already existing. The flag bearer of the Twenty-eighth, trying to climb out of the trench along with his colonel to rally the men to a charge on the road, was blown backward, his arm nearly torn off by a canister round, the soldier then impaled on the bayonet of a broken rifle lying in the trench. Hand-to-hand fighting surged around him and the flag was lost.

The charge staggered forward, suffering horrific casualties, then stalled, the thousands of men behind them in the crater refusing to join in. The black troops were driven back and sought the dubious shelter of the crater as well.

What ensued for the next three hours was one of the most hellish fights of the war.

The air temperature approached a hundred degrees. Down in the smoking crater, packed side to side with men, the heat was trapped. It's estimated the temperature might have stood at 120 degrees or more.

The Confederates moved up several light mortars, only needing an ounce or two of powder to lift the twenty-four-pound ball out, arcing it a few dozen yards down into the packed Union infantry.

Rebels picked up broken and dropped muskets and hurled them like spears, while others, driven to battle madness, would leap up to the lip of the crater and fire down into it as rapidly as they could, their comrades passing up loaded rifles to the shooter until somebody dropped him.

In desperation, a few officers tried to organize their men to start clawing a trench on the west side of the crater back to their own lines, but the effort was obviously doomed.

A terrible, dark rumor swept through the trapped white troops that if they were caught alongside colored troops they would be summarily executed. It's believed that dozens of black troops might have been murdered by their *supposed* comrades, and some of the white troops were killed as well.

The crater became the lower depths of hell.

Meanwhile, Burnside continued to beg Meade to at least send in a relief force to try to open a corridor to extract his corps, but Meade refused.

Finally, shortly after one in the afternoon, a determined push by Mahone took his men up to the lip of the crater. The next few minutes were nothing short of slaughter. Hundreds of rebels, driven mad by the terror of the explosion, the heat, the close proximity of the enemy, and the fact that many of them were black, poured devasting fire down into panic-stricken troops in the crater.

A mass breakout was now attempted, thousands of men crawling up the west slope of the hole, tossing aside their weapons and making a mad dash for the safety of their own lines. It was a shooting gallery, and hundreds fell.

At last the battle was over, and the surviving prisoners were herded out and taken to the rear. Reports are conflicting. There are some claims of executions of black soldiers, and yet other reports of fairly humane treatment, General Lee ordering that all prisoners were to be treated the same regardless of race.

Many of the white officers taken prisoner were terrified of execution. Mahone witnessed the preliminary interrogation of about thirty officers, lined up and being asked what unit they commanded. Some did indeed command white units, but more than a few had quickly torn off their unit insignias and tried to claim their men were white. The rebel interrogator turned from each of them with disgust and finally came to a man still wearing the insignia of a USCT regiment. When asked who he commanded, his reply was, "The Twenty-ninth USCTs, you damn rebel. And if you want to shoot me, go ahead. . . ."

Mahone, deeply moved, stepped forward and shook the officer's hand, saying it was good to see at least one man with courage, and promised him fair treatment.

There was one more final tragedy to play out that day. Late in the afternoon, Burnside, on his own initiative, sent over a flag of truce to Mahone, asking for a cease-fire so that the wounded between the lines could be tended to, an offer that Lee readily agreed to. The asking for truce was a time-honored ritual, but the key element was that by tradition, the defeated general was to ask for it.

When Meade found out, he hit the roof, sent a scathing memo to Burnside that he had no authority to ask for a local truce on the line, and demanded that a message be sent to Lee withdrawing the request. Hostilities were to resume, and Burnside would most likely face additional charges for overstepping his authority.

Lee was stunned by the callousness of this retraction; firing reopened, and several hundred men died between the lines as a result.

Per Grant's suggestion, Meade immediately ordered and then convened a formal court of inquiry into the debacle of July 30, 1864, chaired by the ailing General Winfield Scott Hancock.

Two sacrificial goats were offered up over the next two weeks of testimony. Obviously the first was Burnside. Under examination, Meade tore him apart, placing full and sole blame for the disaster on the eccentric general.

There is a very telling conversation Burnside had, outside the courtroom, that reveals much of the man. Colonel Pleasanton, the man whose regiment first conceived the idea and then dug the tunnel, was overwhelmed with grief over the failure of the plan. He wished to testify before the court of inquiry regarding the complete lack of cooperation by Meade, the near-sabotage when it came to the tools, powder, and equipment—especially the fuses—and the change in the assault plans.

Burnside ordered Pleasanton to go on temporary leave. His reason: "There is nothing you can do for me now. They've already made the decision regarding my fate and I can not let you throw your own career away in a futile cause." He ordered Pleasanton home on leave until after the furor had died away.

Upon the completion of the inquisition of Burnside, he was ordered to take leave. He was never called back to the army, and quietly retired early the following year. General Parker was ordered to take command.

The other scapegoat: the USCTs. Within two days of the battle, anti-administration and anti-abolitionist papers in the North were already bannering headlines that the "colored had run like cowards"—a blatant lie, which, tragically, has endured in some texts of the battle to this day. The failure of the white divisions was glossed over and blame was laid squarely on the black troops, who had indeed moved forward. It was a convenient lie as well, because it provided cover for so many officers who had failed to do their duty that day, without doubt right up to Meade, and in many ways, Grant as well. Their excuse was that Burnside screwed it up and the black troops capped off the disaster.

One noted testimony from an officer with a white regiment challenged the lie, claiming that if the blacks had failed, why had so many of them died, and why did their bodies lie farthest forward. This officer bitterly declared that if the original plan had been followed, the day would have been the crowning victory of the war.

But too many careers were invested in following the argument set forth by Meade. There was the simple fact, as well, of a deep-seated prejudice, and the sense that the old club of the Army of the Potomac had to be protected and in the end would win the war without the help of others. Meade simply had too many political allies in the ranks. His version of events held.

From the court of inquiry, only one officer was directly tossed out of the service. Ferrero received a reprimand and was transferred to another command. The USCT division was pulled from the front line and relegated to rear-line service, finally to be transferred out of the Army of the Potomac and into the Army of the James, where a corps of African-American troops was created.

Ironically, it was these same men, nine months later, who swarmed out of the trenches before Richmond, on the night of April 3, 1865, and were some of the first Union soldiers into the Confederate capital, gaining the glory, long overdue, of taking the rebel capital.

Their postwar service is another of the forgotten chapters of history. While white regiments, by the hundreds, demobilized immediately after Appomattox, the USCT corps was detailed off to Texas as occupation troops, to present a viable threat to the French troops occupying Mexico. They endured a horrific summer of Texas heat, polluted water, and bad food. Scurvy decimated their ranks, and nearly as many men were felled by disease as were killed before the crater. Finally, in late 1865 and early 1866, they were the last of the volunteer regiments to demobilize and be sent home, having earned their right of citizenship with blood.

A follow-up inquiry regarding the crater was held by Congress in the last months of the war. It was even more of a whitewash than the original inquiry because, by this point, Grant and Meade were on the edge of victory, and Burnside was a forgotten relic back home in Rhode Island.

The battle was a classic example of the collapse of command and control, the absurd dangers of rivalries within the high command, and the failure of concentration of force. Even as late as eight A.M. on that fateful day, if the African-American regiments had been backed up by well-led troops from the two supporting corps that Meade refused to commit, the day could have been won.

The crater has been one of the most misrepresented and least understood battles of the Civil War. It truly looks more like a twentieth-century battle, and within its failure are clear demonstrations of military folly and a failure to adhere to so many of the basic principles of war, especially unity of command.

George Bernard Shaw, in a wonderful play set during our Revolution called *The Devil's Disciple*, has an outraged officer cry out upon hearing that the British army will go down to defeat at Saratoga, "Good God, sir, what will history say?" To which his friend replies, "It will tell lies, sir, as it always has."

For nearly 130 years, standard scholarship on the Battle of the Crater has declared that a major trigger of the debacle in the later stages of the fight was panic, and, some stated, the craven cowardice of the black troops.

This convenient excuse covers the far broader failures of high command and division commanders, right down the line to the infantry of the white divisions.

A more modern study of the fight now shows, without doubt, that if allowed to go in first, the USCTs would have carried the day without question. And even when committed, far too late, into a hopeless fight, they fought with valor.

They were men of war, men far better than those who claimed to have led them.

BATTLE OF ISANDHLWANA

The Anglo-Zulu War

January 22, 1879

BRIAN THOMSEN

Because of the huge success of the famous Michael Caine–Stanley Baker film directed by Cy Endfield, the very word "Zulu" calls to mind the valiant defense of a grossly outnumbered British garrison of 140 men against a force of 4,000 Zulu warriors at Rorke's Drift in South Africa. Despite no fewer than six breaches of the compounded entrenchments by the native warriors, the British fought them off for two days, at which point the warriors respectfully ceased combat and moved on to another objective. Zulu casualties: 350 dead; British casualties: 17 dead, 10 wounded.

As a result of that heroic stand, eleven Victoria Crosses were awarded, a record for a single British battle.

Their successful stand was a result of careful and quick planning, the fruits of exemplary training, strict discipline, and courage in the face of battle.

It was a shining moment for the British army.

What it wasn't was a victory. (The Zulus voluntarily withdrawing makes it a draw at best.) More important, it lacked military/strategic significance, and it wasn't the entire Anglo-Zulu War.

Moreover, it occurred on the heels of a devastating defeat that didn't have to end the way it did.

The Anglo-Zulu War was a direct result of British expansionism at the end of the nineteenth century, when, through the annexation of new foreign territories (such as the Transvaal in Africa, to which they laid claim after its local authority went bankrupt), they also acquired any problems, prejudices, or threats that had been incurred by the previous government administration. As Africa became more and more an object of the land- and resource-grabbing interests of Europe, old tribal rivalries between indigenous peoples such as the Zulus and others were temporarily replaced by animosity toward the thieving invaders with the lighter-colored skin. The Zulu nation in particular felt that they had been wronged by the previous administration under the Boers (the descendants of Dutch settlers and not "native" Africans) concerning certain land dealings with them, as well as with other factions, such as the Swazis and the Kaffirs.

Upon the death of his father, the warrior Cetshwayo proclaimed himself absolute ruler of the entire Zulu nation, militarizing his warriors using methods he had learned from his uncle Shaka, updating them slightly to take into account the firearms of these new interlopers, even training them in their use should they become available through dealings with other factions or as the spoils of war.

Cetshwayo ruled with an iron hand, and was considered by some to be a barbaric tyrant (it was alleged that he had slaughtered a large number of young females of his tribe who had married men other than those he had chosen for them), but nonetheless proved to be successful in uniting his people against the common invader and a skilled military leader.

The Zulu king was presented with an ultimatum to disarm and go home by the British on December 11, 1878. He turned it down. A state war was declared.

The British, under the command of Frederick Augustus Thesiger, the Second Baron of Chelmsford, moved their force in South Africa from Pietermaritzburg to a forward camp past Greytown, then, by January 9, 1879, on to Rorke's Drift, and two days later on to the heart of Zululand itself.

Garrison was made at Isandhlwana Hill.

Rather than taking the time to properly fortify the base camp, tents were set up on the crest of the hill to make do, and Thesiger split his forces, leaving fourteen hundred behind at base camp while he led the rest in search of their intended Zulu prey, leaving the camp at four A.M. on the morning of January 22. Those who were left behind were placed under the command of Colonel Anthony Durnford.

Four hours later, the garrison was attacked by a force of approximately twenty thousand spear-wielding Zulu foot warriors.

The camp was ill prepared for the attack, and Durnford's lack of leadership and, indeed, his distraction hastened the end of all of the soldiers under his command, as his forces were quickly overrun by the Zulu onslaught.

A few men did escape the slaughter (Victoria Crosses were awarded to Lieutenants Melville and Coghill, who managed to save the Queen's Colours of their regimental battalions), but most met with slaughter at the tips of Zulu spears.

When the battle was over, and it really didn't take very long, 1,329 of the 1,400 British combatants were dead.

Three thousand of the twenty-two thousand Zulu warriors

were also killed. Though this did not affect the outcome of either this battle or the stand at Rorke's Drift, it nonetheless did weaken the Zulu force over the long term of their campaign. Indeed, Cestshwayo likened these casualties to a spear thrust to the belly of all of the Zulu people.

When Thesiger returned with his men on the night of January 22, he and his men were forced to bivouac among the dead, whose bodies had been eviscerated by the warriors out of consideration, to allow the escape of their spirits to the lands of the dead.

So what went wrong?

First, Thesiger had picked an extremely poor place to set up garrison. There was very little natural cover and even less means of fortification. The ground was sun-baked and hard, and the lack of proper digging tools made further entrenchment difficult at best. Moreover, the size of his force precluded the use of their wagons (which, by placing them in a circle called a laager, would have provided a last line of defense and fortification) to set an organized and defendable perimeter for their camp.

Moreover, Thesiger had not directed his men to do a full reconnaissance of the area, and, as a result, they were disadvantaged in terms of sight lines for sentries, and were therefore unable to provide a full assessment, before it was too late, of any threat that was approaching.

In addition, Thesiger had not compensated for the mixed nature of his force. Though it was made up of mounted regiments, infantry, and auxiliaries, it also had supply wagons drawn by oxen, which were ill suited for traveling off road, and as a result slowed down any action taken by the force.

Furthermore, Thesiger had not secured the garrison with a plan of defense before he divided his army and went off to find the Zulus. Had he done this, the Isandhlwana garrison might have done a better job of holding off the warrior force in the manner that would soon be used at Rorke's Drift.

Thesiger's lack of experience with the terrain prevented him from being able to observe what was happening back at the camp, apparently causing him to disregard at least two reports of the attack, since he couldn't see any evidence that things were amiss.

Durnford was also to blame (and indeed paid for it with his life). In addition to splitting his forces by sending men to engage the Zulu warriors in skirmishes before they hit the camp, thus spreading an already thin force farther apart, he also failed to marshal his base camp into an easily defensible square formation that could take advantage of a fire-step skirmish line with access to ammunition (which had yet to be unloaded and was not readily accessible to the men at hand).

Other recent theories on this engagement also conjecture that Durnford set his skirmish line too diffusely. Where they should have been shoulder to shoulder, they were instead spread out to seemingly try to cover a larger expanse of land. Or perhaps Durnford had ordered his men to retreat, thus emboldening the Zulu warriors, who would have considered that to have been an act of cowardice.

Finally, and most important, both Thesiger and Durnford had grossly underestimated the number of warriors in the attacking force, not realizing that they were outnumbered by almost twenty to one, and moreover that *they* were willing to take casualties in the name of dissolving the perimeter so they could overrun the inferior force and slaughter them in hand-to-spear conflict.

The lack of a defensive plan and the discipline to enforce it made this force into fourteen hundred sitting ducks ripe for their Zululand executioners.

As Rorke's Drift would later prove, one could indeed hold off an enemy of superior numbers, particularly when one had superior firepower available. At Isandhlwana, the forces did not run out of ammunition, they just couldn't get to it in time.

Poor planning and placement.

Both Thesiger and Durnford had made the natural assumption that they were better prepared for the enemy than they really were.

They assumed they had the upper hand in terms of number and technology and tactics, and, as the battle on the day after proved, they could have had they been ready for it.

The guns don't shoot themselves, and it shouldn't have been done every man for himself.

It was a gross lack of leadership, and all who had the ill luck to be garrisoned at Isandhlwana Hill paid the price. Thc eleven Victoria Crosses and the valiant men who fought their hearts out on the following day defending the honor of empire and Crown against overwhelming odds can never change that fact.

THE BATTLE OF MAJUBA HILL

Boered to Death

The First Boer War, South Africa, February 26, 1881

BRIAN THOMSEN

The Boers (also called Afrikaners or Voortrekkers) were the descendents of Dutch settlers in South Africa, who found themselves unhappily under British rule when Sir Theophilus Shepstone annexed the South African Republic for the British in 1877. This happened after the Anglo-Zulu War in 1877, when the republic went bankrupt and was basically foreclosed upon. There were actually two independent Boer republics left, the Orange Free State and the Transvaal Republics. Their independence was initially recognized, at least temporarily, by the British in the early 1850s. The British hedged this generosity by publicly stating that both areas would eventually be ripe for easy annexation by peaceful means within a few years. They were wrong.

Instead of being inspired to join the empire, the Boers of the South African Republic repetitioned Parliament for the return and recognition of their independence. This was denied. They protested the denial, but to no avail. So, in 1880, the Boers revolted and quickly formed commando units, with a total of perhaps seven thousand mounted rifleman irregulars, and began a guerrilla war.

Major General Sir George Colley, the recently appointed governor of Natal, which also oversaw the area of Transvaal, was charged with putting down this rebellion. He got conflicting advice about the tact he should pursue. As a learned, successful, and revered military tactician with many victories in other campaigns to his credit, he pursued the military option and set off with a force of roughly a thousand men under him to squash what he saw as an ill-armed and rustic rebellion.

After less-than-successful altercations with the enemy at Laing's Nek and at Ini gogo River, Colley set his sights on Majuba Hill. This was where the Boers had to make a stand, as the hill gave an exceptional vantage point from which they could dominate the major pass between Natal and Transvaal territories. Having conquered half the world in the last two centuries, there was not a glimmer of doubt of an easy victory in a straight-up battle by the experienced British soldiers.

On February 26, Colley led a detachment of 350 men from his total forces on a night march up the steep precipice. Colley planned that under the cover of darkness his men would be able to easily take the high ground, without being detected by the Boers until they had taken the summit. Once the British were on the summit, the Boers would have to attack dug-in troops and be slaughtered or accept the splitting of their rebellion. The movement did go undetected, despite the exceptionally steep and arduous terrain. As a result, Colley and his men had only barely achieved the summit by dawn, having battled the treacherous slope all night.

The British soldiers were exhausted, but Colley was rewarded with a clear view of the Boer camp below.

The goal had been attained.

They were at the summit.

The first part of the mission had been accomplished.

Colley announced that all who had taken part deserved a rest, including Colley himself.

Two of his junior officers, Hamilton and Macgregor, thought that other matters should be attended to first. Perhaps a more thorough reconnaissance of the area and ridges around the summit should be conducted before camp was actually made? Perhaps there were routes available other than the ones they had used, which might have provided better and more varied access to their position, and perhaps these routes would be more visible by daylight?

Another strong suggestion that the two officers made was that the men should entrench their forces, readying themselves for assault and attack, while protecting them from the eventual sniper fire they had previously experienced from their enemy.

Moreover, the reserve ammunition and supplies that were at the rear of the column that had made the ascent should be brought up to the summit and centralized so that in the case of a retreat from any direction on the periphery it would be available for resupplying the force.

Colley vetoed all of the suggestions. His arguments seemed persuasive, to himself at least.

The hard stone of the summit would make it hard to dig trenches.

There would be time for that later.

The men were exhausted.

He was exhausted.

He could plainly see the enemy encamped far below. No attack seemed to be forming.

Surely no harm would come from taking a breather for a while and getting some well-earned rest.

After all, it had taken him and his men all night to get there.

Any assault from below would take time, and by the time it got organized they would be well rested, dug in, and ready.

With the dawn's early light the Boers below could see the British forces at the top of Majuba Hill, and a force was dispatched to displace them.

Knowing the terrain reasonably well, the Boers remained under cover as they climbed the steep slope with much greater ease than their nocturnal predecessors, and occasionally took the opportunity to take a shot at Colley's forces along the way, usually with deadly accuracy, picking off their opponents from a distance one at a time.

When the Boers reached the crest they immediately made their presence known with rapid and well-aimed fire that raised such a cloud of smoke that the British could barely see their firing opponents as they rallied toward them.

The response from the British was confusion, followed by an inclination to retreat, which was countermanded by actual events and turned into a rout.

This was not what they had expected, no, not at all.

How could these ill-equipped and ill-trained rebels achieve the summit so easily, while all along picking off the Crown's own well-trained soldiers?

The dispatches from Colley's men tell the tale:

9:30 A.M. "All very comfortable. Boers wasting ammunition."

11:00 A.M. "Boers still firing heavily . . . and begin to move away."

Midday "Firing kept up incessantly by Boers. . . . Expect to be here two days at least. . . . Boers cannot possibly take position from us. . . . Certainly the Boers' losses are heavier than ours."

2:35 P.M. "Our men driven from the hill . . . many, officers, some of high rank, killed and wounded."

4:00 P.M. (From a press correspondent on nearby Mount Prospect) ". . . the slaughter was fearful . . . the battle is all but over. The Boers triumphed at almost every point, firing with deadly effect, knocking down our men on all hands. . . . The loss must be something fearful."

Colley, despite the sporadic fire that had commenced since their presence had been observed from below, was asleep when the actual assault occurred . . . but immediately sprang into action and began barking orders to try to make up for lost time. He died almost immediately thereafter, when his forehead stopped a slug from the barrel of a Boer sharpshooter's rifle.

Macdonald, who had advised him on the entrenchment issue earlier, commanded a force of twenty men trying to hold back an oncoming force on the west side of the hill, fighting valiantly. His men were picked off one by one until only he and his lance corporal remained. When they ran out of ammunition they continued to try to forestall the inevitable, hurling rocks at Boers and eventually even pummeling them with their fists when the rocks were no longer available.

When it was all over British casualties were 93 killed, 133 wounded, and 58 taken prisoner, out of only 350 men. The entire force had been wiped out in a few hours. Among those captured was the valiant Second Lieutenant Macdonald, who was finally subdued only after losing his pistol and sword, and then was held only by the enforced restraint of four armed Boers.

Boer losses were recorded as one killed, five wounded.

The attack itself had lasted an hour, but this was only after the Boers had successfully sniped at Colley's unentrenched forces for hours.

So what went wrong?

Colley was overconfident (despite previous defeats) and disregarded the suggestions of his junior officers. True, he was an extraordinary military tactician with numerous strategic victories in his past, but it only takes one truly stupid mistake to bring a brilliant career and an honored life to an end. This was such a defeat.

Had the men been entrenched, they might have been able to defend themselves, but such was not the case. As a result, they were sitting ducks out in the open, to be picked off by the eagle-eyed sharpshooters from below.

Moreover, by not taking a full lay of the land and getting to know the terrain at hand once the summit had been achieved, he had failed to organize his forces into the most defensible position.

Colley simply did not foresee that they would need a defensible position. They had taken the summit to turn it into an offensive position from which they could attack the camp below.

Colley didn't foresee the situation that would come to pass and had disregarded the more cautious advice of his junior officers . . . and wound up paying for his bullheadedness with his life. Moreover, once the assault had already begun, Colley refused to believe that they were at risk until it was way too late to mount an adequate response.

Throughout the entire First Boer War, the forces of the

Crown underestimated the Boer warriors. The Brits had assumed that because they were fighting fellows of European descent, they would obviously fight like Europeans.

The Boers had other ideas.

To begin with, they dressed in earth-tone khaki clothes that blended into the landscape. They had learned this made hunting easier against indigenous wild game, and it proved to be equally beneficial when hunting a more dangerous target—namely, the infestation of lobster-backed limey, also known as the British army. Their nonuniform dress also made it easier for the warriors to blend in with the seemingly uninvolved Boer citizenry.

It was also the end of the era of mass fire as the key weapon of war. Rifles were more accurate, and their effective range was ten times that at the start of the century. The Boers were excellent marksmen and were content to snipe at the British from hidden places, rather than restricting themselves to battlefield clashes on the field of honor. This was publicly and loudly stated as being very unsporting of them, and definitely un-European. There was also a prevailing arrogance that in almost a century, excepting at Isandhlwana, no group of badly dressed locals could defeat the regular army. It simply didn't enter into consideration.

This sort of pigheaded arrogance on the part of the British high-level officers led to the mind-set that allowed Colley to so underestimate his adversaries. Not only did he fail to entrench his forces, he limited his camp to the summit, cutting off all possibility for cover, retreat, and escape. He had led his men to a position where they were sitting ducks, sure enough and ripe for sniping by the unsportsmanlike Boer marksmen.

The real mistake Colley made was that the rules of war had changed, and he had failed to accept this. He did not learn from his mistakes, and this led to one defeat after another for Her Majesty's soldiers.

The scruffy fighters had made their point, and in August of 1881 Parliament under Prime Minster Gladstone re-recognized the independence of the Transvaal Republic, though subject to oversight by the Crown, whose influence and opinions were decidedly disadvantaged by the lack of performance of Her Majesty's services during the war.

GORDON AND THE SIEGE OF KHARTOUM

Sudan, January 26, 1885

BRIAN THOMSEN

On January 26, 1885, after close to a nine-month standoff, with no relief column in sight and the stronghold's defensive perimeter weakened by the seasonally receding waters of the Nile, the city of Khartoum, under the command of Governor General Charles George Gordon, fell to the forces of the Mahdi Muhammad Ahmad.

Their conflict was by no means personal.

Indeed, they probably would have gotten along if they weren't confronting each other on the battlefield.

But one was a jihadist answering to a higher power.

The other was under orders from the Crown to perform a mission honorably, despite his disagreement as to what that mission was, and his lack of support to accomplish it.

Charles George "Chinese" Gordon was the closet thing Victorian England had to a military superstar celebrity. A veteran of the Crimean War and the second Opium War, and the subsequent victories over the Taipings (the campaign from whence he received his moniker of "Chinese" Gordon), he also waged a semi-successful campaign to suppress the slave trade in the Sudan.

He was outspoken and believed in efficiency, and as a result managed to step on many toes both in the military and in the government, never quite willing to spend the time to do the political thing for those back home.

He was a man of action who didn't always take the time to put his position in the proper words or, indeed, to listen to those words from his superiors.

The people in the street at home didn't care, nor did those who were serving under him.

The politicians in England and Prime Minster Gladstone, however, were less than pleased, and, when given the opportunity to shut him up by sending him off to evacuate Khartoum, they did.

They would show him who was boss. He would be the face of their retreat.

Gordon, however, had other ideas.

The Mahdi was Muhammad Ahmad, formerly a carpenter and boat builder who was divinely inspired to lead his people in jihad against the infidel Egyptian authorities, laying claim to the Sudan in the name of Islam. Without formal Western training, he managed to amass an army that was capable of overrunning the Egyptian militias and confronting the European forces on an even keel.

Moreover, he established an intelligence network that kept the foreigners off base and managed to undercut their dominance in the area.

When given the choice between following a group of foreigners who looked upon you as second-class citizens and serfs, and one of your own who claimed to be following the will of a powerful and vengeful god, the Mahdi's arguments for the latter were considered quite persuasive, and soon his force was both dominant and swift, quickly sweeping forward and evicting the infidel in its wake.

Khartoum was in his path, and that was the location that Gordon had been sent to evacuate before the Mahdi could lay claim to it with his superior force.

Within a month of Gordon's arrival at Khartoum, he found the city to be virtually blockaded by the forces of the Mahdi, thus hampering any major effort to continue the evacuation that was supposedly his immediate orders. As a result, the legendary warrior and defender of the Crown decided to dig in and prepare for a stand by utilizing the natural defenses that were afforded the city on two sides by the White and Blue Nile Rivers, and fortifying the land-bound part of the perimeter against any direct assault from the Mahdi's forces.

Both leaders then just sat back and waited for close to six months. During this time, Gordon pretty much abandoned any plans (if he ever had any) for evacuation, instead using the rivers and several barges and steamers he had at his disposal to carry messages down the river, launch attacks against enemy installations, and restock his supplies as available through foraging raids. He reasoned that, eventually, Gladstone and his cronies would come to their senses and send a larger and better-equipped force (either over ground or on the river) to help him secure the stronghold against the forces of the holy warrior he was confronting.

Likewise, the Mahdi sat back and waited, directing forces against other targets for the time being, perhaps assuming that the Queen's man of action in the stronghold would eventually seize the opportunity and evacuate the place peaceably. As jihadists go, he was more concerned with killing infidel and disloyal Egyptians. The foreigners would be fine if they just went away.

There was rumor of correspondence between the two leaders that bespoke a mutual admiration—Gordon supposedly had tried to convince the Mahdi to forgo jihad, while the Mahdi had tried to convert Gordon to embrace Islam.

Around September, the Mahdi's men became more aggressive, having already seized the nearest garrison, which was in Berber, thus further isolating Gordon's stronghold and effectively stopping any ground-based gaps in the stronghold blockade, leaving only the rivers as a means of egress from Khartoum.

By mid-November, the Mahdi's forces began to concentrate on attacks on the steamships that Gordon had been utilizing (Gordon's only mobile artillery/firepower, and also one of his few means of escape downriver). Gordon was down to only two steamers by this point, the others having gone downriver earlier, with their status at that point unknown to Khartoum. Gordon lost one of his remaining steamers through these sieges, and the level of the Nile kept dropping as the dry season continued. Soon the other steamer would not be able to navigate, and the Mahdi's forces would be able to cross the Nile on foot, completely encircling Khartoum.

By mid-December Gordon had sent his last steamer downstream. The Mahdi had agreed to let the steamer through, but it was to be the last. Gordon stayed behind, sure that reinforcements would arrive, completely disregarding his orders and all reports to the contrary.

Khartoum was surrounded.

There was no longer a way to resupply.

There was no access for reinforcements.

They were cut off.

The siege began in earnest, and daily rations of food became smaller and smaller.

Reinforcements reached El-Metemmah on January 14, rendezvousing with the four steamers Gordon sent down the river over one hundred days before.

But they were too late.

The Nile was now shallow enough near Khartoum to cross on foot.

The Mahdi's force could now attack on all sides, and they did.

The drop in the water level of the river left one portion of the city unprotected by wall, ditch, rampart, or water. The Mahdi's forces lay siege at this breach, and on the morning of January 26, the city was overrun and Gordon was killed (allegedly pistols blazing from each hand).

So what went wrong?

It is not fair and too simple to say that reinforcement just didn't arrive on time, or that traitors and turncoats managed to subvert the defense of the city and Gordon's forces, or that the change of tides and their weakening of the defense of the perimeter was inevitable, or that the Mahdi's forces were both more motivated and of sufficiently larger strength.

Though Gordon was immediately lionized in the press as a heroic martyr, there is little doubt that his not-to-be-envied fate, with his head on a pikestaff, was largely his own fault, his having defied direct orders to evacuate Khartoum at one of the numerous opportunities prior to the final stages of the siege.

Indeed, if the greatest tragedy of the fall of Khartoum was the death of Gordon, it should also be remembered that the Mahdi had ordered that he be captured alive; his death therefore winds up being more of a mistake than a tragedy.

In addition, it must be remembered that Gordon's primary orders, indeed the reason why he was sent to Khartoum, was to evacuate the city and not to defend it. His superiors in England had weighed the facts at hand and taken politics and expenditures into account and had settled on that course of action. The fact that he believed he lacked a sufficient amount of boats to do the job, and that the dire threat of attack during the journey to a safe haven was too great, might have been accurate, but, given the alternative (which occurred), it does seem to point to a lapse in command judgment.

This is not to discount the culpability of the various anti-Gordon factions back in England, who, despite public outcry and the alleged personal intercessions of the Queen, dragged their feet in regard to sending him the required reinforcements. Whether it was due to Gladstone's habitual dithering or just a general dislike of Gordon, for whom many sought failure for his mission (and disgrace for the man), it is clear that help was not dispatched in a timely manner. It was all the more tragic that it arrived only two days too late.

And as to England's dominion in Africa, the Mahdi, and the general aftermath?

Well, according to Lytton Strachey in his volume *Eminent Victorians*, "And yet it was not with the Mahdi that the future lay. Before six months were out, in the plenitude of his power, he died, and the Khalifa Abdullahi reigned in his stead. The future lay with Major Kitchener and his Maxim-Nordenfeldt guns. Thirteen years later the Mahdi's empire was abolished for ever in the gigantic hecatomb of Omdurman; after which it was thought proper that a religious ceremony in honor of General Gordon should be held at the Palace at Khartoum. The service was conducted by four chaplains—of the Catholic, Anglican, Presbyterian, and Methodist persuasions—and concluded with a performance of 'Abide with me'—the General's favorite hymn—by a select company of Sudanese buglers. Everyone agreed that General Gordon had been avenged at last. Who could doubt it? General Gordon himself, possibly, fluttering, in some remote Nirvana, the pages of a phantasmal Bible, might have ventured a satirical remark. But General Gordon had always been a contradictious person—even a little off his head, perhaps, though still a hero; and besides, he was no longer there to contradict. . . . At any rate it had all ended very happily—in a glorious slaughter of twenty thousand Arabs, a vast addition to the British Empire, and a step in the Peerage for Sir Evelyn Baring."

One can't help but wonder if the power brokers back in London got their most favored outcome anyway, snatching a pointless victory out of the blood of the enemy, and ridding themselves of their own inconvenient leaders as well.

THE PHILIPPINES THEATER

Spanish-American War

Manila, August 13th, 1898

BRIAN THOMSEN

A fatal bit of miscommunication can sometimes snatch defeat out of the jaws of victory, or, more precisely, senseless death and destruction out of the jaws of peaceful surrender and compromise.

The Spanish-American War had afforded America a chance to do some empire building on their own, and the Spanish influence in the Philippines proved to be a tempting bonus that could easily be secured on the other side of the war while war was waged on the shores of Cuba and elsewhere.

Admiral George Dewey was already a recognized American war hero before he ever ventured into Manila Bay in the Philippines. He served valiantly with the U.S. Navy in the Battles of New Orleans and Port Hudson during the Civil War. (Though the Civil War is not normally looked upon as a naval war, numerous battles between the Union and the Confederate forces resulted in altercations across the high seas during the years of the war, and also provided both sides with key experience in the effective utilization of naval blockades.) In the years following the war, he made his way up the ranks of service before docking in Washington, D.C., in the 1890s, with a political appointment as president of both the Lighthouse Board and the Board of Inspection and Survey.

In 1897, he accepted an appointment set up by then Assistant Secretary of the Navy Theodore Roosevelt as the new commander of the Asiatic Squadron based in the Far East. This put him in place for action when the Spanish-American War began in April of 1898, with the sequence of events set in motion by the supposed sinking of the *Maine* by forces sympathetic to the Spanish in Cuba.

The United States forces had planned in advance for the war with Spain, and Dewey had been briefed that the objective for the Asiatic Squadron under his command, on the occasion of war, was to martial an assault on the Philippines, the Spanish holding in the Pacific that the United States had been eyeing for annexation.

So, on May 1, 1898, Dewey proudly led his force into Manila Bay, fearless of reports of mines in the harbor entrance and other martial threats, to confront the local Spanish enemy.

In less than a day, the rust-bucket Spanish squadron on-site was destroyed and Manila Bay was blockaded.

The campaign in this part of the Pacific was over almost as soon as it had begun, and without the loss of a single American life.

Dewey was victorious.

All that now had to be done was to arrange a peaceful surrender and wait for American occupying forces to arrive.

Unfortunately, those forces did not come through for at least three months. Four detachments finally arrived, allowing Dewey at last to push for a formalization of the capitulation of the Spanish forces since, though they had been contained by Dewey's naval show of force, no formal surrender had ever been mounted.

On August 7, acting on orders from Washington, D.C., Dewey sent an ultimatum to the Spanish commander that a bombardment followed by a frontal assault would commence unless the port capitulated. (A forty-eight-hour delay was also included to allow for the peaceful removal of civilian noncombatants.)

The Spanish commander seemed to be agreeable, but pointed out that Dewey's own forces blocked the peaceful relocation of the civilians, who indeed had nowhere else to go.

This set the timetable back an additional twenty-four hours, followed by a further delay of three days due to matters that slowed down the arrival of the occupying American troops, who had to be in place on land before the surrender could actually occur.

All of these delays allowed enough time for Dewey and his Spanish counterpart to come to a meeting of the minds on how the surrender could be exercised with the least loss of life and property possible. The plan was that Dewey's forces would direct a bombardment on Malate Fort (which had already been heavily bombarded and then abandoned in their previous altercation, now three months in the past) for about an hour as a new and proximate show of force by the Americans, which would provide the Spanish governor with a necessary reason to surrender. He would then hoist a white flag from the fort to signal all of his forces to stand down and allow the American troops to enter town and peacefully begin the occupation without any further loss of life on either side, and without embarrassment to the leaders of the Spanish forces on-site.

Dewey was quite proud of himself.

The delay between his initial victorious attack and its now-several-months-delayed resolution had not engendered any new casualties or wear and tear on his forces.

Just a little show of force, followed by the waving of a white flag, and then all would be welcome to some dancing in the streets of Manila.

Everything started according to plan.

The ships were targeted on the fort for bombardment.

The American troops were in readiness to peacefully enter the city.

The Spanish governor was ready to run the white flag up the pole and initiate the surrender.

Dewey was confident, nay, even cocky, and ready to pat himself on the back, so let the bombardment begin!

And it did.

After the prescribed amount of time, it stopped.

Signals were given and the governor raised the white flag of surrender as previously agreed.

Unfortunately, Dewey and his men in the harbor didn't see it.

The governor had indeed raised the flag, but the wind caused it to fly at an angle where it disappeared against the background of the surrounding white wall, rendering it virtually invisible to the ships at sea.

After what he considered an acceptable interval, Dewey grew impatient and opened fire again, hoping to nudge things along. Only then did he see the white flag against the background of the newly wrought smoke, fire, and rubble caused by round two of the bombardment. Immediately, he ordered his ships to cease fire.

However, these actions only caused further confusion for the forces on the shore. The American troops who had started to enter the city after the cessation of the first bombardment were taken aback by the resumption of fire, and wound up in a skirmish with the equally confused Spanish troops, resulting in sixteen American deaths and over thirty wounded.

Moreover, insurgents on the ground who had been massing against the Spanish forces during the period of the blockade, planning to assist the Americans in the final assault (but who had obviously not been taken into confidence by the American forces and therefore had no idea of the plan that was in place), launched their own attack on the Spanish outpost, not realizing that it had quickly already fallen into American hands.

So what went wrong?

First, even a "play" show of force has to be taken seriously, and all of its ramifications considered in advance. You are still using live ammo, and people can still get hurt (in this case resulting in the only American casualties in the Philippines theater for this little war).

Second, no matter how good the plan (or smart the planner), always have a backup plan ready, and, more important, a means to make sure that all sides are always on the same page.

Third, Dewey could have used the elapsed time between the initial assault and the arrival of occupation forces to more fully plan the implementation of the occupation so that he would not have been confronted by the delays in the surrender schedule caused by not having a practical plan for civilian evacuation and the timely placement of occupying troops into places of readiness.

Fourth, keep all involved parties in the loop—the insurgent

factor should have been taken into consideration and dealt with in advance. They thought they were there to help. Just because they were not regular army didn't mean that they needed to be left out in the cold.

Indeed, the Pottery Barn rule was in effect even back then ("you break it, you buy it"), thus leaving the occupying force of American troops with the job of restoring order to Manila and eventually the entire Philippines, and enforcing a semblance of peace on the ground. In many cases, this involved suppressing and restraining the insurgent forces, who had initially just wanted to assist the attacks on the Spanish, but now wished to be part of the power grab that goes hand in hand with the conquest of an oppressed nation.

Our high-tech troop deployment methods of today effectively eliminate such a delay between victory and occupation. What happens afterward, though, appears to be an ever-present bedevilment of non-forward-thinking American commanders.

Even given the limitations of his time, three months was a long wait, and the easily obtained victory in battle yesterday can still cause casualties in the peace that can't be signed until tomorrow.

SAMOA

April 1, 1899

BRIAN THOMSEN

In the late nineteenth century, the conflicts of U.S. versus European expansionism led to many close calls (skirmishes or little wars) in far-off lands that had been attracting the acquisitive interests of the then-major powers.

The Samoan Islands were a point of contention between Germany and the United States in the 1880s, as both nations looked to expand their empires into the Pacific.

The United States had diplomatically secured a coaling station in Pago Pago in exchange for protection against hostile (read non-American) interlopers. Unfortunately, Germany had designs in the area too, and wished to secure a hold on nearby Apia Harbor, resulting in a confrontation with American forces in 1888, when German ships shelled Apia—and an alliance of U.S. and British warships docked there.

Congress got into the act and ordered the fleet to retaliate to protect U.S. interests in the region, which they did, but actual war was put on hold until a conference between the three powers could occur in Berlin.

While waiting for that to happen, on March 16, 1889, a hurricane settled the matter, destroying the three American warships and the three German warships that were at a standoff in Apia.

The three powers decided not to press their luck, Mother Nature having already expressed her opinion and meteorologically advocating arbitration, and divided Samoa in three among themselves.

Unfortunately, nobody bothered to check with the Samoans, and in a matter of time civil war broke out among the puppet chiefs of the various powers, and local insurgency reared its ugly head.

In 1899, the German puppet tribal chief rose to the top, nominally uniting Samoa and diplomatically violating the tripartite treaty that had been negotiated.

The United States and Britain were incensed and formed an alliance to put Germany back into its place, or, as they claimed at the time, reestablish order in Samoa.

The combined force under a shared command successfully utilized their seagoing firepower to bombard the opposition into submission. Nominally, this was directed at the Samoan insurgents still carrying out the civil war, though the fact that they also managed to take out both the German consulate and a German gunboat was probably not coincidental.

Tribal order was reestablished with the help of the allied show of force, and Malietoa Tanu was crowned king of Samoa with the blessing of the U.S.-British alliance, at which point the German-backed rival for the throne and his allies opened fire on the new ruling coalition.

The alliance had had great success with quelling these forces before, through the use of the bombardment from sea, but their egos were bruised from being surprised on shore, so they instead elected to send a party into the brush after the insurgents.

They knew that they were no longer fighting the Germans.

This was just a small native force.

A little bit of inland peacekeeping and order would soon be restored.

Or at least so they thought.

On April 1, 1899, a combined force of 122 British and American soldiers supplemented by 100 native irregulars entered the brush under the command of Lieutenant Freeman of the Royal Navy.

Once they had proceeded far enough into the brush that they could no longer be observed from the ships offshore (and therefore were at least temporarily cut off from the immediate assistance of reinforcements or a bombardment cover fire), they were ambushed by the recalcitrant rebels and their chief, who opened fire on the party from well-positioned placements in the tall grass, which provided them both a superior vantage point for shooting as well as obscuring cover for protection.

Now, up to this point the Anglo-American forces had made a habit of basically frightening off their native opposition with superior firepower. Their weapon of choice at the time was the machine gun: noisy, fast, and quite effective.

Quickly, they set up their rapid-fire weapon and prepared themselves for it to do its stuff, but instead of the reassuring *rat tat tat tat tat* of bullets flying from the barrel and into the brush, all they heard was a single ominous *click*.

The gun had jammed. The rebels seized the moment and increased their fire, slicing through the formerly advancing column.

Thinking quickly, Freeman ordered his forces to retreat back to the safety of the shore, where covering fire from the sea-bound gunships saved them from a complete massacre.

Still, not all of their party had made it back safely.

Two American and one British officer were discovered the next day, their heads severed from their bodies, and their ears missing, probably taken as souvenirs by the erstwhile pseudo-chief.

So what went wrong?

To begin with, the three major powers (United States, Great Britain, and Germany) never looked at their conflict as being anything more than a conflict of their national interests. The actual subject—Samoa, and more precisely the Samoans—were really minor concerns, and none of the parties involved had spent enough time to examine their interests and possible reactions to the conflict that was at first happening around them, and then happening *to* them.

As is often the case, some people resent when you play war in their backyard rather than your own.

This led to a degree of cockiness whereby they never really considered the Samoans to be a threat, and thus, when the cake-walk into the bush turned into a turkey shoot, with the allied forces as the gobblers, the commanders in charge had to do some quick thinking to get out of there with their plumage intact.

Moreover, the cocky reliance on the machine gun to scare off the opposition was lazy at best, and fatally derelict in practice.

Everything was fine when they played under European rules with big guns and big boats shooting at each other off the coast, but when it came to man-to-man fighting in the brush against the people (or rather, as the allies saw it, the *natives*) who lived there, it shouldn't have taken an idiot to tell them that they might have been both outnumbered and outmatched, particularly when the great equalizer, the machine gun, failed to do its duty for Queen and country, and jammed, and the big guns offshore were unavailable to save the day until the actual time they were able to realize that the day needed saving.

Another conference settled the skirmish and Samoa was once again redivided, this time between the United States and Germany, with Great Britain accepting considerations in another area of the world.

Interestingly, the United States has managed to maintain its interest there, and American Samoa is still a part of the American empire.

THE BOXER REBELLION

The Seymour Expedition

China, June 1900

BRIAN THOMSEN

It's a funny thing—sometimes other people's countries don't take kindly to major influxes of foreign interests taking control of their fate.

They resent the loss of territories to other powers, and the breakdown of central and established authority in the name of the new generation of modernization.

And sometimes the old guard raises its head again and tries to retake control and get things back on the old track, when things were better.

Such was the case in China in 1898, when the dowager empress Tz'u-hsi returned herself to power as regent, wrestling control back from the young emperor, who was overly sympathetic to (one might say under the thumb of) European interests, and advocated a return to the ways of the good old days.

From her active encouragement, a secret cultural society dubbed "the Fists of Righteous Harmony" came into being, promoting a xenophobic, anti-Christian agenda that blamed all of the woes of China on the foreign devils, and advocated a mix of traditional and mystical Chinese values that would overcome the taint of the Westerners and neutralize their technologies and weapons. They were known to the Europeans as the Boxers, a loose translation of their original Chinese name that evoked their ritualistic practice of shadowboxing.

Though they were not necessarily a sanctioned organization of the reestablished ancien régime, they nonetheless assisted its delicate return to the old ways by performing terrorist attacks on foreign interests (such as the railroads) within China proper, more precisely in the northeastern region of China, where the Europeans had been pressing for and been granted territorial, railroad, and mining concessions that basically rendered these outside interests as autonomous to local authorities. Initially, the Boxer attacks were directed at Chinese Christians, whose conversions were seen as an act of collaboration with the foreign devils, and usually took the form of arson directed at their homes and businesses.

Things really began to heat up on December 30, 1899, when the Boxers were blamed for the death of a British missionary, which immediately drew strong protests from the British and German governments (the sovereigns of each being distant relatives), and resulted in the arrest and execution of certain suspects believed to have been responsible and involved with the Boxer cause.

What was not offered was any condemnation from the dowager empress of the actual act or those involved in the Boxer cause, an omission that was looked upon as a tacit endorsement of the activities of this secret society.

The Boxers continued to make their presence felt, and on

May 29, 1900, two British missionaries were attacked, one being killed. A twenty-four-hour ultimatum was issued by the British foreign ministers demanding that this so-called Boxer Rebellion be condemned and quelled immediately. The Boxers upped their attacks on foreign interests, sabotaging the railroads and cutting telegraph lines; as a result, the foreign legations in Peking sent for help and reinforcements to defend their nationals and their national interests from these rabble-rousing terrorists.

Given the apparent sympathies the Chinese government had with these rebels, an eight-nation alliance of outside interests (the United States, Great Britain, Austro-Hungary, France, Germany, Italy, Russia, and Japan) was formed under the moniker the China Relief Expedition, whose public persona and mission was solely the protection and rescue of their own nationals and national interests within China.

On June 9, the foreign delegation in Peking requested further reinforcements for their own protection from the Boxer factions that were ruling the streets—right before the telegraph lines out of the city were cut.

The alliance responded immediately, and a combined force drawn from ships off the mouth of the Pei Ho River, totaling a little over two thousand men in contingents ranging in size from twenty-five Austrian seamen to eight hundred British marines, were placed under the command of British Vice-Admiral Sir Edward Seymour and were dispatched for Peking on June 10.

The so-called Seymour Expedition (also sometimes known as the Seymour Relief Expedition) planned to advance from Tien Tsin to Peking as soon as possible. The relief column was made up of several trains, since the rail route was the most direct as well as the most expeditious. As the trains moved fast and no delays were expected, minimal supplies were carried so as not to overburden and possibly slow down the expedition.

The objective was to get there fast, secure the interests, and do the job.

Nice and simple.

Unfortunately, things did not proceed quite so quickly or easily.

From the minute they left Tien Tsin, they met with Boxer opposition, which slowed them down and diverted them into skirmishes that drained their supplies.

According to U.S. documents chronicling the expedition:

> *From the report of Secretary of the Navy John D. Long 11/17/1900*
>
> *"On the night of June 9, Admiral Seymour of the British navy, the ranking naval officer, received a telegram from the British minister at Peking, advising him that 'unless those at Peking were relieved soon, it would be too late.' At 9:30 the next morning a relief column, under command of Admiral Seymour, started for the Chinese capital by train, the expedition consisting of 915 British officers, seamen and marines, 450 German, 312 Russian, 158 French, 112 American, 54 Japanese, 40 Italian, and 25 Austrian, a total of 2,066. Finding at Langfang that the railway had been so much damaged as to render it useless as a means of advance, this column, after ten days' fighting in a difficult country, without the transportation, ammunition, or supplies necessary to an extended campaign, encumbered by wounded to the number of 230, and entirely cut off from communication front and rear was obliged, June 20, to fall back, and having on their return march captured the imperial armory near Hsiku, a few miles above Tien Tsin, there awaited reinforcements. Of the part borne in this hazardous expedition by the American sailors, honorable mention is made in all reports.*
>
> *"In the meantime the foreign settlement in Tien Tsin itself was*

subjected to attack, and communication between that city and Taku was interrupted. On the 19th of June a detachment of 8 officers and 132 enlisted men, chiefly from the first regiment of marines dispatched from Cavite by the Newark *and* Nashville, *arrived at Taku. Instructions were immediately given that this force should take part in the forward movement for the relief of the besieged at Tien Tsin. This force, aggregating a little more than 500 men, was, however, too small to accomplish its object, and was speedily driven back by overwhelming numbers.*

"The following day, June 22, British, Russian, German, Italian, and Japanese reinforcements arrived, making a combined force of about 2,000 men. The foreign city of Tien Tsin was entered and the siege raised. On Sunday morning, June 25, an advance was made to the relief of Admiral Seymour's command, who were entrenched at a point about 8 miles from Tien Tsin. This movement was accomplished with little opposition, and early on the morning of July 14 the walled city of Tien Tsin was captured by the allied forces."

As a result, the Seymour Expedition never reached Peking, having had to abandon the railways on June 19, twenty-five miles outside of their besieged objective, and retreat back to whence they came.

Unfortunately, the Boxers had indeed fallen in behind them and set a skirmish line between them and Tien Tsin.

Seymour's men were forced to take refuge in a fortified Chinese government building, which after the fact turned out to be the Hsiku Arsenal, where they were able to temporarily restore their depleted supplies from stocks of rice that were there, and settle down to hold off further attacks by the Boxers until reinforcements arrived so they could continue to fight their way back home.

Newly rested and reoutfitted and seizing an opportunity to continue their "strategic retreat," Seymour's men departed their temporary refuge, destroying any supplies they left behind to keep them from falling into the hands of the scavenging Boxers.

On June 26, they were right back where they started, having failed to relieve Peking, with casualties of 295 officers and men amassed from the day they had originally set out.

So what went wrong?

The first thing a relief expedition needs to do is secure the means to get to their destination.

Seymour rightly realized that the railroads were the most expeditious means, but overlooked the fact that they had already proven to be targets of the Boxers, and, as a result, his men spent more time repairing the means to their end than getting to their end. Indeed, one of the U.S. Naval seamen in the company turned out to be the most invaluable members, as he was the only one out of the more than two thousand strong who "could set out a fishplate and spike down a rail," making the very necessary repairs along the way.

Soon, it was commonplace for the rails in front and behind them to be sabotaged, forcing great gaps between the trains of the column and slowing their advance to a crawl.

Moreover, the minimal supplies began to run thin as the unexpected delays ate into the less-than-adequate reserves at hand.

A destroyed bridge turned out to be the final straw that curtailed their advance, and necessitated the abandonment of their mission, and their subsequent retreat.

Also, Seymour's preliminary reconnaissance before setting out did not adequately report the extent of the Boxers' influence in the area through which they had to pass. It was no longer a mere gang or criminal problem; it was a well-stocked insurgency that had been joined by members of the imperial army assisting them, with the possible blessing of the dowager empress herself.

Seymour had fooled himself into believing that their mission was indeed a humanitarian one, supported by the Chinese rank and file. Sadly, no one checked with the Chinese rank and file first.

Seymour and his men had grown dependent on the modern technology they had brought to China, the telegraph lines, the trains, the rapid-fire weaponry, and so on, but when they were deprived of the means to sustain these advantages, they quickly found themselves at the mercy of an indigenous force that wanted them to leave.

The rescuers became rescuees who only barely escaped, their mission failed, their egos bruised, and their empire embarrassed.

THE SCHLIEFFEN PLAN

Belgium and France, 1914

BILL FAWCETT

The German General Staff has been famous for its organizational and technical expertise since it was founded during the Napoleonic Wars. It has less often earned any renown for its imagination, with the notable exception of the Ardennes offensive in 1939. The beginning of World War One and the eventual stalemate were a direct result of this lack of imagination and originality.

It all began with the Schlieffen Plan. The German General Staff viewed the Schlieffen Plan as a blueprint for defeating France in six weeks or less. This would allow the German army to redeploy against Russia before that nation could bring its massive resources and call up their millions of reservists and conscripts. The problem was that when Count Alfred von Schlieffen wrote his plan for this invasion, it was merely a theoretical exercise. Also, it assumed the German army was twenty full divisions larger than its actual size in both 1905 and 1914. This first version of the plan had widespread implications because of the requirements it set on the soldiers who were to carry the plan out. In addition, his plan was really intended to demonstrate to the kaiser the need to add twenty divisions to the army for Germany to be strong enough to win a widespread European war. But the plan's message was quickly forgotten, especially after the count died. What was remembered was the promise of a six-week defeat of France and a short, victorious war.

The Schlieffen Plan was to take advantage of the fact that one section of the French border was much more lightly defended than the rest. This was the western portion that ran adjacent to Belgium, which was a French ally. It was decided that attacking through Belgium, which they assumed would capitulate quickly, would provide an avenue into France that would not only allow the German divisions to roll up the French defenses along the rest of the border, but also would provide a relatively clear route to Paris. It was concluded that the collapse of France after Paris surrendered in the Franco-Prussian War forty years earlier indicated that a similar coup would result from Count von Schlieffen's plan. So the plan had over half the German army rushing through Belgian and smashing through the relatively soft Franco-Belgian border.

That was the plan. It was an admirable document, which justified fully the addition of twenty divisions to the German army—which was exactly what Alfred von Schlieffen intended. What would have shocked him was that for the more than a decade the plan was studied before World War One, not a single alternative plan was even considered. To the General Staff, it was The Plan, and their efforts were all aimed at perfecting and refining it. The problem was that, in those ten years, the political structure of Europe had shifted. For example, England went from being a traditional rival to being an ally of France.

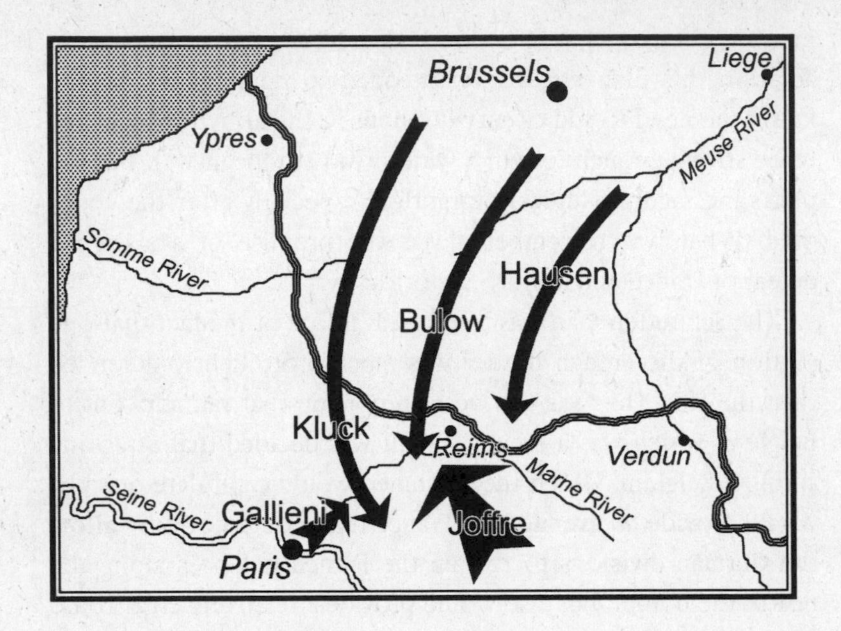

There was another problem with the Schlieffen Plan. It was one plan, not a series of variants. There were no alternatives, no if-then provisions, nothing to reflect what is called the fog of war. Because it was created to demonstrate the need for more troops, not to be the sole plan of action for the largest war in Germany's history, there was no need for flexibility, none at all. And the lack of flexibility doomed it from the start.

That said, it is a tribute to the German soldiers, mostly men recently called up from their civilian jobs, that the Schlieffen Plan came so close to working, despite its flaws. So what went wrong? How did France manage to stop the plan's flanking attack and four hard years later win the war?

The French cooperated as much as they could. While the German General Staff planned to flank them, the French plan was to take advantage of the élan of their soldiers to drive the

Germans out of the disputed provinces of Alsace and Lorraine, and then continue into Germany, forcing a peace. It has to be remembered that it had been only a little more than forty years since those provinces were lost from France to Germany at the end of the Franco-Prussian War. This was the expected French war plan, and pursuing it actually contributed to what little success the Schlieffen Plan had.

But that was as far as it went. The real flaw in the Schlieffen Plan was that not only was it nearly impossible to fulfill, but that it had no room for error. The planner of the General Staff assumed that every German soldier would march the maximum projected distance every day, brushing aside all opposition. After all, they knew the members of the staff would do this. The problem was that no matter how much pressure they put on the field commanders to stay on schedule, it just wasn't going to happen. The average German soldier had a few weeks earlier been a civilian who was called up for service. It had been perhaps years since they were trained and put in reserve. There was no time for conditioning, because the ability to muster the reserves faster than anyone else was one of Germany's real advantages, and this advantage could not be squandered by wasting time doing exercises and marches. Once called up, the troops had to be committed quickly. These recent civilians were then ordered to carry a basic load weighing sixty-five pounds. This included weapon and ammunition, tools, a heavy coat, and rations. There was even a liquor ration, which was inspected nightly to ensure it was not drunk before the order was given. Officers were also expected to inspect more than two hundred feet each night to make sure blisters and other problems were quickly treated. But most of the officers had also been store clerks and salesmen a month earlier, and most were too exhausted to inspect *anything* after a long day's march. The bottom line of all this was that the German army was simply unable to march at the speeds demanded by the General Staff.

Yet another problem was logistics. This was a horse-drawn army, with trucks being an unreliable novelty. There were not enough trains to carry all the supplies needed for a 2-million-man army to the borders. In hostile territory, the only way to move supplies was in wagons. And the use of horses brings its own problem. A horse eats, and eats a *lot*, when working. With over four thousand tons of food and fodder needed every day just to feed men and horses, half the wagons had to carry food. There simply were not enough wagons for everything. So, many times a little decision-making drama was carried out: What to load? Ammunition and cannon shells, or two days' food for the horses pulling the wagons? The choice that war dictates was often ammunition, not fodder or food. But hungry horses simply moved more slowly, as do hungry men. And since the horses had on or in the wagons behind them all of the food and ammunition, the whole German army slowed with them. Instead of the constantly demanded twenty-five miles a day in the plan, the real rate of march was almost half that. But in the war games used to refine the Schlieffen Plan, supplies had not been a problem, and the faster rate of march was vital to the plan's success.

As the war started, it was soon realized that nothing could be allowed to slow things any further. So with a most unfortunate set of long-range consequences, nothing did. Almost.

Since the key element of the plan was for the army to punch through and then sweep across the flank and rear of the French army, it is surprising how little time was allocated to the complete occupation of Belgium. This was viewed as basically just a march, and scheduled at a speed that was nearly the same as would be used to cross friendly, German territory. But the Belgian army inconsiderately took a few days to defeat, holding out stubbornly in some forts. This caused even more pressure, which continued to flow down the ranks of the officers, demanding that nothing further hold up the movement. This pressure led to a series of "atrocities," as men torn from civilian life reacted with overwhelming force (sometimes in random directions) to anything that even *seemed* to threaten to slow them down. A stray shot, often from someone in the German ranks, could inspire every man in a unit to fire at any nearby building that might hide "the sniper." Hundreds of unarmed Belgians died, and the image of the barbaric hun was created. This propaganda nightmare was the result of trying to maintain the schedule. There is an irony to this, considering that the basis of it was a plan that began as a PR document itself. This perception certainly contributed greatly to the United States entering the war on the Allied side, and may have cost Germany a victory.

Then there was another small problem, not included in the Schlieffen Plan. When it was written, the political situation between England and France had been strained. After all, the two nations had a history of hundreds of years of war between them. But by 1914, the two governments had realized that they needed each other in order to have a chance against the kaiser's army. So rather than meeting a few French units that had been relegated to a friendly border, the Germans advancing down the coast closest to Britain ran into the British Expeditionary Force, the BEF. More time was lost, movement was slowed by hard combat, and the angle of German attack swung inland away from the British (and toward Paris) earlier than planned. Someone forgot to tell the British that, in the Schlieffen Plan, it was supposed to take them two months, not less than a week, to bring a significant force across the channel. The Germans never expected there to be more than a few British in France, which seems strange, since they were invading neutral Belgium, just across the channel from its closest ally, Britain, and the largest navy in the world. But even if they came, the General Staff dismissed the "contemptible" little army of Britain and joked that, if the British did interfere, they would send "some policemen" to arrest them. In reality, nearly a dozen divisions of the First Army on the far right of the advance found the BEF a tough opponent. So, with troops tied up facing the British Expeditionary Force, even fewer men were now available to roll up the French flank.

Two more factors intervened to stop the rapid destruction of France, both being completely the fault of the General Staff and its decisions. The twenty divisions Schlieffen wanted were never added. This meant manpower was critical. But knowing the French were going to attack in the center and invade German territory unless stopped, divisions originally intended to be part of the right (Belgian) force were transferred to other parts of the line, where the French were expected. These did help to stop the French assaults within a few days, but had the swing around the French army succeeded, any lost territory would have been easily recovered. Instead, these divisions were not at the point of decision. The other mistake was that, just as the war started, someone got worried about the Russians, who were moving with very un-Russian speed. So two corps were loaded into trains and sent east. They almost got there when they received word that Falkenberg had already defeated two much larger Russian armies without them. These same divisions, a total of nearly 100,000 men, were simply turned around and sent back to the western front, where they arrived too late to take part in the critical phases of the battle.

The German army did push into France from Belgium, but, rather than moving south and then swinging due west to Paris, time and resistance forced it to move diagonally toward its goal. The whole movement still took too much time, and the French were able to reorganize and create a new army, which met the exhausted and now poorly supplied German army at the Marne River less than a hundred miles north of Paris and stopped them. With no alternate plans, that was it. The German army dug in and four years of trench warfare followed.

Frighteningly, it might have worked, if the German army had gotten those twenty divisions Count Alfred von Schlieffen created his plan to convince the kaiser to raise. If those and the division "touring Germany," racing uselessly from front to front, had actually been part of the German First Army, history may also have been very different. So it appears the plan failed on almost every level, because the German General Staff clung to and stuck with an unworkable plan, whose original purpose was simply to show that a larger army was needed to win the war quickly, or exactly what did happen would happen.

So why did the Schlieffen Plan fail? The key factor from the beginning had to be a lack of flexibility. When you combine this with unrealistic movement rates and expectations, an inability for logistics to keep up, insufficient forces allocated to the breakthrough, and an unnecessary division of forces, then the Schlieffen Plan's failure was assured.

THE EASTER RISING

Dublin, April 24–30, 1916

BRIAN THOMSEN

On Easter Monday, April 1916, an insurrection began in Dublin that has gone down in the history of Irish independence under a variety of monikers, ranging from the Easter Rebellion to the Easter Rising, or, more simply, the Rising of 1916.

It was meant to be a demonstration of force by the Irish Republican Brotherhood (IRB) that would set the stage for a show of popular support for Irish independence and nationalism by a literal who's who in the story of Irish independence, including a future president and prime minister. There was also the founder of the Irish Republican Army and head of the Irish Free State. By securing control of the geographic seat of power for the Crown on the Emerald Isle, coupled with the display of solidarity that would be evident from simultaneous anti-Crown uprisings in the surrounding areas, a message would be sent, not just across the channel, but to the rest of the world that the time for Irish independence had indeed arrived.

Instead, it was a show of disorganization that resulted in the execution of fifteen Irish republican leaders. (Eamon de Valera, soon to be head of the political wing of the IRA, Sinn Fein, and later to become prime minister of the Emerald Isle, was spared, largely due to his American citizenship, which resulted in a delaying of his sentencing until the passions had subsided enough to curtail the executions.) It was also a further crackdown by British authorities, who wished to quell the rebellion once and for all.

The quest for Irish independence had begun many years before, almost as far back as the first spawn of an English king in the days of the Norman Conquests, when they tainted the lands of the Emerald Isle for the first time, and had included such hare-brained schemes as helping the French to invade, and even more so, the plot by several Irish expatriates who hoped to invade Canada and trade it to the Crown for Irish independence. But despite the efforts of such great men as Lord Edward Fitzgerald, Robert Emmet, Charles Parnell, and Arthur Griffith, the people of Ireland were still held firmly under the oppressive thumb of the British monarchy.

Having already survived the various penal laws that had stripped families of their legacies and the potential for prosperity, the Irish were unwilling to tolerate further coercive actions by the Crown and their landowning lackeys. The year 1913 brought with it the latest in enforced indignities, what has become known as the Dublin Lockout, whereby twenty thousand laborers who were trying to unionize were excluded from work by their employers. This lockout hit hard men who barely had enough to live on when working. It resulted in the suffering of their entire families from cold and malnutrition. Eventually the hope of having a union had to be abandoned out of the sheer necessity of the need to work and support one's family, even at a subsistence level.

As a result, the rank-and-file working class of the Emerald Isle realized that their lot would never be improved—that is, they would never achieve the same comfort and status as Protestants and other citizens loyal to the Crown.

A change at home was just not possible.

Perhaps it would be better to seek greener pastures in the land of opportunity, America. But the true rebels were not about to give up.

Ireland would be ruled by the Irish, or they would surely continue to die trying for as long as those invaders from across the sea refused to leave.

The Supreme Council of the Irish Republican Brotherhood had set in motion various plans to take advantage of England's preoccupation with World War One, including the consideration of military actions to be executed by the Irish Volunteers, who, though they shared many members, were considered a separate and distinct group from the IRB, and possessed its own chain of command. They realized that protests and requests for reform through legal means were going to get them nowhere.

They were not just disgruntled employees and the victims of prejudice. They were a captured and oppressed people, forced to live under foreign rule that was enforced by illegitimate occupiers, and though it was an occupation, no surrender had ever been sounded. The war was still going on, and the IRB fancied that it was about time they started approaching the situation as a martial one. A war required military planning, and a willingness to fight force with force, no matter what the course.

The immediate objective for the IRB was to seize control of the seat of government in Ireland, and force the British to grant the Irish home rule and their own independence from the Crown. The plan, as worked out by IRB leader Joseph Plunkett (and remarkably similar to one that had been drawn up by James Connolly of the Irish Citizen Army, yet another rebel group), was to seize the municipal center of Dublin and cordon off the city center from the inevitable forces of the Crown who would come to reclaim it. Though their numbers were obviously smaller than those of the Brits in charge, the IRB felt that they could distract the British forces with other risings in the area, allowing themselves to become entrenched at the Dublin seat of government, thus commanding a position of strength from which they could make their demands heard while the whole world watched the unseated forces of the Crown. The seat of government, the courts, and the central post office would be under their control, and they were not going to give them up.

Moreover, the IRB knew that though their number was dwarfed by the British forces, the other rebel groups would be more than willing to pitch in and swell their numbers with additional warriors willing to fight for Irish solidarity, from the ranks of such groups as the Irish Citizen Army, the Irish Volunteers, and even a burgeoning socialist party. The number of anti-Crown groups (and their members) was staggering, which was wonderful for the cause, but also set up numerous problems.

First, there was a jockeying for command. Which group would make the plan and lead the way? Given the numbers (and overlapping memberships), the actual assault was to be carried out by the Irish Volunteers under the planning of the IRB, but since great minds sometimes think alike, they immediately faced a new problem: What if another group, perhaps less organized, with an inferior plan, attacked first? And an old and ever-present problem of the Irish resistance: What if someone tipped off the forces of the Crown (whether it was a Crown sympathizer or a rival faction leader, such as the Irish Volunteers' own leader, Eoin MacNeil, who preferred negotiation and bargaining to acts of rebellion)? Either one would lead to disaster.

As a result, Padraig Pearse, a schoolteacher and organization director under MacNeil in alliance with the head of the Irish Citizen Army (who had also been planning a similar attack), put their plan into action while also creating diversions to all the rebels. Pearse announced that there would be parades and maneuvers done for Easter Sunday, thus seemingly preempting this time for rebellion. In actuality, Pearse's message had a double meaning to those who were also IRB members, clueing them that the time for rebellion was at hand.

On Easter Monday, five rebel battalions moved into position—four under IRB control, one a composite of others under Pearse. This fifth battalion also included such rebel luminaries as Joseph Plunkett, James Connolly, and a young officer by the name of Michael Collins.

The first battalion, armed and ready, seized the undefended Four Courts in the northwest, barricading it from British police/military intervention, the second took the south, the third (under Eamon de Valera) the east, and the fourth the southwest, while the fifth seized and made headquarters at the general post office. Positions manned, they awaited opposition and negotiation. Connolly, an ardent socialist who believed that the Irish rebellion was merely part of the whole world socialist revolution against the capitalist system embraced by England and other world powers, had convinced the others that the Crown would never use artillery against what they saw as their own state property, which would have to be viewed as an assault on their own capitalistic system—a belief proved wrong quite shortly thereafter.

The British forces moved in with an overwhelming number (four times that of the rebels, since Pearse's diversionary announcements had short-circuited and, indeed, preempted the other revolts around the city and countryside, which would have diverted the forces of the Crown to matters away from the city center) and isolated the headquarters at the general post office from the other battalions, which were soon attacked and shelled with Her Majesty's artillery. Once these forces were subdued or dispersed, they turned their attention to the isolated headquarters itself and battered it with Her Majesty's firepower.

On Saturday, April 29, Pearse issued the orders for all companies to surrender.

So what went wrong? Pretty much everything.

Distrust led to a fatal lack of communication and coordination. The fear of informers and the need for disinformation led to miscommunications, which disrupted the diversionary rebellions that were necessary to thin the available forces of the Crown away from the city center.

Connolly's firm socialist beliefs undermined his commonsense regarding the Crown's use of force against their own structures, and all of the rebels' firebrand beliefs blinded them to the reality of the lack of active support by the rank-and-file citizens of Dublin (who really only became agitated *after* the Rising, and looked upon most of the rebels as little more than troublemakers), which led to an unanticipated lack of supplies and manpower, resulting in their forces being dwarfed by those they sought to oppose.

Finally, by placing their headquarters at the center of the action, they made themselves easier to cut off from everyone else, stymieing communication and coordination, and eliminating a way and means to escape.

Pearse, Plunkett, and Connolly were executed by the Crown

for their errors and the ineptitude of the event. De Valera went to prison. Young Collins lucked out, and managed to blend into the crowd, so that he would live to fight another day (which came shortly thereafter, when he formed what we now refer to as the IRA, the Irish Republican Army).

But even the inept make ripe martyrs, and their missteps were equally matched by the resultant acts of the British oppressors, whose actions lionized new nationalists and galvanized support for the movement and the cause. The Dubliners who shied away from joining in on that Easter Monday soon had more than enough immediate reasons to assist the rebellion with the ham-fisted actions taken in response to the rebellion. Moreover, the ineptitude that allowed de Valera and Collins to continue being active players in the rebellion also led to a rigid point of view for dealing with the rebels, one that allowed the Crown to fully repeat all of the mistakes that they had made during the First Boer War.

Sometimes, even the victors continue to forget to learn from their mistakes.

EUROPEAN SIBERIAN INVASION

Romanovka, Siberia, 1919

BRIAN THOMSEN

Not all of the Doughboys got to go home at the end of World War One.

In 1918, the revolution in Russia had led to widespread instability on the global front, with the threat of a Japanese occupation of Siberia causing great consternation to American business interests located there.

The American president Woodrow Wilson had no desire to interfere with the civil war (it was not yet recognized as a revolution, Bolshevik or otherwise), but the collateral damage from internal military strife, and the rampant lawlessness of a society in turmoil, necessitated an armed intervention that reflected complete neutrality in Russian politics and matters of territorial integrity. Or, as Secretary of State Newton D. Baker summed it up in a statement to Major General William S. Graves, who was assigned to lead U.S. forces in Siberia, "Watch your step; you will be walking on eggs loaded with dynamite."

In addition to the nonideological objectives of the mission, several pragmatic tasks were also charged to Graves's men:

- Rescue a Czech legion that had been isolated from the West due to the war.
- Prevent the Japanese from occupying and laying claim to territories in Siberia that held American interests.
- Hunt down and capture German and Austro-Hungarian soldiers who had fled eastward to avoid captivity as prisoners of war.

Unfortunately, by the time they arrived on the scene:

- The Czech legion no longer needed rescuing.
- The Japanese had seventy-two thousand troops spread out over the region.
- The German and Austro-Hungarian soldiers were more than happy to surrender in exchange for the privileges of being POWs—namely, food and shelter.

As Graves's men waited in the freezing cold of a Siberian winter, Washington debated what their new mission would be.

By spring, it was decided that the allied military forces should protect the Trans-Siberian Railway from guerrilla attacks, as well as trying to keep the communication lines (telegraph lines) secure, or, as Graves related to his troops, "Our aim is to be of real assistance to all Russians in protecting necessary traffic movements within the sectors of the railroad assigned to us. . . . All will be equally benefited, and we will treat all factions alike."

Unfortunately, the locals were not necessarily supportive of their mission, and Cossack warlords, in a grab for power, formed guerrilla bands to bedevil the locals and plague the interlopers, whose presence was deemed both unwelcome and unwise. This was coupled with the work of Bolshevik partisans, who were steadily gaining power as unrest and anarchy continued to spread across Russia. The partisans had gained the sympathies of the locals, and their main objectives were to sabotage the transportation and communications systems and make the outsiders less welcome in the name of the new Russian nationalism, making the lives of the American support force a living, frigid hell of frostbite, malnutrition, and constant death threats.

It soon became apparent that the Cossacks were being financed by the Japanese, leading to bitter relations between the two interloping parties.

Moreover, a coal strike backed by the Bolsheviks (and rousing the ranks of the workers) led to a fuel shortage on the railroads that were manned by the anti-Bolsheviks, and the apolitical stance of Graves and his men did nothing to improve their standing with either party.

Graves just continued to move his now ill-used men around without a clear mission, resulting in numerous unfortunate altercations and no progress in their position.

A particularly egregious situation occurred near Romanovka on June 25, 1919.

Lieutenant Lawrence Butler had just taken command of Company A of the Thirty-first Infantry Regiment, and had bivouacked his men at the base of a hill near an important spur of the railroad that connected the Suchan Valley to Vladivostok. He ordered a guard to be posted at the top of the hill for the night, with orders to return to camp at daybreak—which he did.

He arrived back at camp followed by several hundred partisans.

Sharpshooters had taken positions on the high ground, picking off the U.S. soldiers in the camp below as they groggily tried to wake from a deep night's sleep.

Butler tried to rally his men from this surprise attack, but they were outnumbered three or four to one, and, when the smoke cleared (the attack interrupted by the arrival of reinforcements from a passing train, causing the partisan forces to withdraw back into the wilderness), thirty Americans were dead and twenty were wounded—and this was not an isolated case.

So what went wrong?

In terms of the incident at Romanovka, several things.

The novice officer Butler did not know that the sun rose in Siberia at four A.M., hours before reveille. As a result, the camp was unguarded during the final hours of the men's hard-earned, long night's rest, making them easy pickings for the assassins.

Likewise, the placement of the camp at the base of the hill allowed an easy vantage point for their attackers to pick them off while shooting from the high ground.

Finally, Butler and his men were still looking at this as a civil support service and never really attained a level of "wartime" self-preservation. Men did not sleep with their guns at their sides, and battle readiness had faded with the Armistice.

Their lack of preparedness and recognition of the dangers involved, as well as the mistakes of time and place, sealed their fates.

In terms of the overall Siberian campaign, it is fairly safe to say that the mistake was in getting involved in the first place. Where a certain amount of mission creep occurs in any campaign, the Siberian expedition was more a victim of "mission meander." It never had an applicable, clear objective from day one. Wilson's objective of keeping peace was not pragmatic, and the practical objective of protecting American interests (read industrial interests) was never adequately supported to the extent that the situation required.

There were never enough troops on hand to maintain order or rival the Japanese forces. The apolitical spirit/directive of the mission resulted in the force being at odds with both sides, and the lack of coordination with the other foreign powers involved (many suffering from hard feelings left over from the previous World War) neutralized any effectiveness they might have been able to achieve.

In the end, American interests in Russia evaporated, and the last of Graves's troops left on April 1, 1920.

A total of 353 American soldiers had been killed in the Siberian theater in the period commencing with the Armistice and concluding with their embarrassed exodus.

Years later, during the Cold War, the Soviet Union often pointed to this ill-conceived "intervention" as an example of imperialist American greed trying to make a landgrab on the weakened post-czar empire in ruins.

They could have also used it more precisely as a clear example of ineptitude.

A CLASH OF EAGLES

Reichsmarshal Goering's Blunders in the Battle of Britain

Southern England, Summer/Fall 1940

DOUGLAS NILES

You are Hermann Goering, the undisputed commander of the most powerful, modern, and effective air force that the world has ever seen. Your fighter forces, led by the reliable and high-performance Messerschmidt ME-109, can battle for air superiority wherever they can fly; thus far, they have never lost a fight. Your dive bombers, the redoubtable Stukas, have shattered enemy ground forces and sent many ships to the bottom. And your bombers, while not exceptionally large or long-ranged, are fast and deadly, flown by veteran pilots and capable of delivering lethal loads onto targets on land or sea.

But your pride has been stung by those pesky Englishmen of the Royal Air Force. When the German army, the Wehrmacht, had the British bottled up in Dunkirk, ripe for annihilation, you prevailed upon Hitler to allow you and your Luftwaffe to have the honor of the victory. Your planes would bomb them into oblivion! At least, that was the plan. But those enemy fighters flew across from England, and kept your bombers from doing much damage to the evacuating army. That Spitfire, in particular, proved a surprisingly good match for your ME-109s. In the end, the British lifted off a third of a million men in their spectacular evacuation, and you were left to bomb an empty beachhead.

But now those British are trapped over there, across the English Channel on their little island. They no longer have any place to run. It is the Luftwaffe's hour to shine.

The Battle of Britain was the first battle of major strategic import fought entirely in the air, for the control of that same arena. It matched up the two most modern air forces in the world of 1940. And, in the end, it was the first time the aggressive ambitions of the Nazi state were thwarted—though not without considerable cost to the defenders, who were stretched nearly to the breaking point.

Although the battle was of profound significance, control of the air in its own right was not the primary German objective in waging war against Britain during the summer and early autumn of 1940. In fact, the air battle was intended only as a preliminary step, a setup to the great amphibious invasion of southern England: Operation Sealion. This massive offensive had been in the planning stages since late 1939, as Hitler had anticipated the need to strike a knockout blow against the only one of the Allies he could not simply invade with his all-powerful Wehrmacht.

As an amphibious operation, of course, Sealion required the coordination of all three military arms—air, land, and sea. It is notable that, from the beginning, both the German army and the navy (the Kriegsmarine) were notably unenthusiastic about the plan. Even as the panzers swept through the Low Countries and France, winning shockingly quick victories over those countries in May and early June of 1940, most German military commanders sought to avoid the need for a full invasion of Britain. Hitler himself predicted that the English would collapse and sue for peace, after the sudden conquest of all of their continental-based allies. By the end of June, however, it became clear that the United Kingdom, under its pugnacious new prime minister, Winston Churchill, was determined to fight on. In July, Hitler ordered Operation Sealion into effect, with a scheduled date of September 15 for the actual invasion.

Despite their unchanging opposition, the Wehrmacht and Kriegsmarine had no choice but to do their führer's bidding. The plan called for a crossing of the English Channel, rather than the more challenging—if less thoroughly defended—route across the North Sea. So the army began to gather strength in northern France, with Army Group A contributing ten divisions that would embark from Le Havre, Boulogne, Calais, Dunkirk, and ports in Belgium; and Army Group B sending three more divisions on the far left flank, sailing from the port of Cherbourg at the tip of the Cotentin Peninsula. The navy began to gather landing barges from all across occupied Europe, shipping them overland or by river to the embarkation ports in northern France.

Of course, the British Royal Navy was still intact, and still presented a formidable threat to any German shipping in the vicinity of England. Although the Kriegsmarine possessed some fast, modern battle cruisers, it lacked any fleet capable of going toe-to-toe with the English in a duel of battleships. The mighty *Bismarck*, which would cause so much havoc a year later, had yet to be rendered operational. And even had she been available, she would have been no match for the combined gunnery of the determined British fleet.

Thus, control of the sea—essential for any amphibious

operation—would have to be gained by control of the air. In this endeavor, the Germans had one commander who was unfailingly confident, even to the point of bluster, in the ability of his forces to accomplish the requisite objective. Reichsmarshal Hermann Goering had been a fighter pilot during World War One, and he was a loyal Nazi who had been an enthusiastic supporter of Adolf Hitler since the party's early days. These two qualifications were enough to cause the führer to give him complete control of the most powerful air force the world had ever known—one of several Hitler blunders for which the free world may be eternally thankful.

Goering was an incompetent blowhard, and was recognized as such by many of the men who had to serve under his command. Impulsive and vain, he was given to making grand pronouncements of his Luftwaffe's capabilities to Hitler, only to find that the very capable men and machines under his command were not able to fulfill his extravagant promises. The first of these failures was the inability to wipe out the Dunkirk beachhead from the air. The next would be proven over the skies of southern England, though not before the Royal Air Force was very nearly brought to its knees.

In fact, the Luftwaffe had been designed to complement the German ground forces in the new, and strikingly successful, tactic known as the blitzkrieg—"Lightning War." Against the armies of Poland, Belgium, the Netherlands, and France, German dive bombers had terrorized the defending troops, shattering morale and crushing strong points, so the panzers could roll through on their lethal, penetrating attacks. Light and medium bombers had supported these thrusts, as well as disrupting Allied supply lines and hitting air bases and other installations. The Dutch city of Rotterdam had been savagely bombed in a successful attempt to compel the nation's surrender; at the time, the world professed great shock at this barbarity, though in subsequent years Allied heavy bombers would inflict damage that would eclipse the attacks on Rotterdam by several orders of magnitude.

But the Luftwaffe was not designed for the kind of mission required in the Battle of Britain. The frontline fighter, the ME-109, was a splendid aircraft, but could not carry enough fuel to linger long over England. The second-tier fighter, the two-seater and twin-engine ME-110, would prove to be utterly incapable of competing against Britain's modern single-engine craft. The Stuka dive bombers, while they could attack with great accuracy, were slow and very vulnerable to determined defenders. The largest bombers in the German arsenal were twin-engine Heinkels and Dorniers, which were barely capable of carrying medium bomber loads, in comparison with the four-engine aircraft already employed by the British and Americans.

Still, Goering was not a man to let a few inconvenient facts get in the way of his ambitions. And, in fact, he possessed some significant advantages. He could send about twenty-eight hundred aircraft into the battle, while the British could meet him with only about six hundred fifty fighters. He could attack from a multitude of bases, since the Germans had conquered France and the Low Countries, as well as Norway and Denmark. The latter countries were too far away for fighters, but the threat of bombers based there forced the British to defend the coast and countryside as far north as Scotland. The Luftwaffe was organized into three great air fleets (Luftflotte) for the battle. Luftflotte Five would attack from the Scandinavian countries; Luftflotte Two was based in Belgium and northeast France; Luftflotte Three would fly from northern and northwest France.

Against this array of air power, the British would resist with

Fighter Command, under the leadership of Air Chief Marshal Sir Hugh Dowding. His fighters were organized into some fifty squadrons, based across much of the English countryside, with the greatest concentration of them in southeast England, between London, the channel, and the North Sea coasts. The majority of the British fighters were Hawker Hurricanes, reasonably modern aircraft that could not quite match up to the ME-109 in speed and maneuverability, though the Hurricanes would prove more than a match for the Stukas, ME-110s, and other German aircraft. The best fighter in the British arsenal—and in fact in any non-German air force at the time—was the Supermarine Spitfire. These sleek fighters could match the 109 in most combat categories. Though they had a slightly smaller range than the German fighters, the Spitfires had the advantage of fighting above their own bases, so they did not have to fly as far to reach the battle, and, consequently, could spend more time engaged in combat.

Another key British advantage was two-pronged, and applied to the areas of intelligence, command, and control. Fighter Command was a centrally controlled operation, with a large plotting board and active staff capable of sending the British fighters where they would do the most good. This control was made effective by the unprecedented use of radar, which gave the RAF up-to-the-minute information on where the German air formations were, how large they were, and where they seemed to be heading.

While this level of control was exceptionally useful, the implementation needed refinement as the battle progressed. As the Germans were sending over large groups of aircraft flying together, Dowding felt that the British fighters should muster several squadrons into a “Big Wing” formation capable of meeting the attackers with large numbers of defenders. In practice, however, this gathering of strength often resulted in a waste of time, so the Germans could be intercepted only after they had already dropped their bombs and were heading for home. At the urging of his subcommanders, Dowding eventually relented, allowing the British squadrons to fly to the attack as soon as they could get airborne. This tactic resulted in significantly greater disruptions of the German bombing formations.

After a month of preliminary raids, primarily directed against the ports of southern England, the Battle of Britain was joined in earnest on August 8, 1940. During that day the Luftwaffe flew some fifteen hundred sorties (each sortie is one mission by one plane), with airbases and ports targeted. The objective was to draw the British fighters into the air, where they could be destroyed. For ten days, savage air battles raged across much of England. Aided by the crucial radar, the British were able to direct their fighters where they were most needed, and though both sides suffered heavy losses, the RAF was able to retain control of the aerial battlefield.

During this part of the battle, the Germans directed some of their efforts against the radar towers themselves, but the spindly looking contraptions proved remarkably difficult to destroy. As the towers required pinpoint accuracy on the part of attackers, the Stuka dive bombers were at first employed in these strikes, but the lumbering planes with their fixed landing gear were subjected to wholesale slaughter by the RAF. The faster medium bombers, attacking from higher altitude, had more survivability but lacked the accuracy to knock out the towers, and so these efforts were, for the most part, abandoned early in the battle.

Almost immediately, another key element of strategic air battle began to come into play. Flying a fighter in combat was dangerous work, of course, and both sides suffered significant losses. About half of the pilots whose planes were shot down were either killed or badly wounded. The other half, however, managed to survive, either by parachuting or crash-landing. In the case of the British pilots, these men could return to the battle, often as soon as the next day. Every German pilot who came down, however, was destined to spend the rest of the war in captivity—that is, he was permanently removed from the Luftwaffe's roster. British factories continued to produce airplanes, and though they could not entirely keep up with combat losses, the RAF remained able to maintain its strength. The Germans, on the other hand, faced a level of attrition that, in the end, would prove insurmountable.

After the first ten days of intense but inconclusive combat, Goering could see that his forces were not attaining the air superiority judged crucial for all future operations. Within another week, he authorized a change in tactics that moved the battle into its second phase. On August 24, the targeting was shifted to the larger RAF bases, which were farther inland than the primarily coastal installations that had been attacked at the start of the battle. The attacks increased in size and ferocity, with each large formation of bombers accompanied by a hundred or more fighters.

With the targets now exclusively the RAF fighter bases, the British really began to feel the pressure. Despite their most vigorous efforts, they could not break up the huge aerial fleets, and many bases were heavily damaged or put out of operation. Locations such as Biggin Hill, West Mailing, Worthy Down, and Andover became the keys to the battle. More than four hundred British fighters had been destroyed, and the number of machines able to take to the air in defense grew smaller and smaller every day. From Dowding on down, the RAF commanders sensed the threat of imminent defeat. These relentless attacks continued through September 5, and by that date the defenders were scrambling desperately just to get a few fighters into the air—and still the waves of German bombers came on.

The events that would save the day for England were put into place, as are so many things in war, by an accidental occurrence, the effects of which were amplified by a commander's crucial error. In the case of the Battle of Britain, the accident occurred during the second phase of the battle, and was the result of a German bomber getting separated from its formation, carrying a full bomb load, and flying over England after night had fallen. The Germans had been specifically ordered to avoid bombing London, for fear of triggering British reprisals against German cities. The crew of this lost bomber was *certain* they were not over London when they dumped their bomb load and turned around to head for home.

They were wrong. The bombs fell on a small part of that blacked-out city, and Churchill quickly seized upon this as an excuse to strike directly at Germany. During the latter part of August, Bomber Command had conducted several air raids over Berlin and other German cities. The damage inflicted was minimal, but the strategic consequences were great—both Goering and Hitler were furious and humiliated by the violation of Nazi air space. At the very time when the RAF was decimated by the destruction of its bases, virtually down for the count, the Germans changed tactics.

The Third Reich would have its revenge! Therefore, the Luftwaffe was ordered to concentrate its efforts against London, to punish the insolent English for the effrontery of their attacks against German cities. The timing of this decision could not have been more beneficial to the RAF. Beginning September 7, and continuing for the rest of that month, the Luftwaffe conducted day and night air raids against the British capital. The defending air force, at last able to recover from the relentless pressure against its air bases, gathered strength throughout the month and inflicted great losses upon the Luftwaffe bombers and fighters. Bomber Command, in the meantime, began to strike the concentrations of German barges, and by the end of September had destroyed 10 percent or more of the potential invasion craft.

With victory still judged to be a possibility, Hitler ordered Sealion postponed—first to September 15, then to September 21, 24, and 27—to give Goering's air force time to prevail. But the trend of the fighting was now clear: it had become a battle of attrition, under conditions that the Germans could not hope to win. By October, the daylight attacks against London were suspended as too costly, though the nighttime raids would continue through the winter and, off and on, for the duration of the war. But the latter was mere terror bombing, and though tens of thousands of Londoners would lose their lives, the "Blitz" would never come close to breaking the indomitable British morale.

As to Sealion, on October 12 Hitler ordered it postponed until 1941. By the time that year progressed into spring, and weather that would have made the invasion feasible, the Nazi dictator's attentions had turned to a new enemy: the USSR. The war would continue for years, of course, but never again would England have to fear the threat of German landings and occupation.

Even so, during those desperate days of August and September of 1940, the Luftwaffe came very close to accomplishing its goals—and if the Germans had gained air superiority over England and the channel, it is very likely that the invasion could have occurred, and could have been successful. If a more capable commander than Goering had been in control, history might be very different. Fortunately for the cause of freedom, his mistakes defeated his air force when it stood at the very brink of triumph.

Those mistakes have now become a part of history:

Goering tried to use a tactical air force to accomplish a strategic mission.

He failed to appreciate the "home field advantage"—aircrew recovery, and much less fuel consumed flying to battle—that a defending air force has against an attacker. Nor did he grasp how radar would influence modern aerial warfare.

Finally, he allowed his enemy to goad him into abandoning his plan, at the very moment when that plan was about to succeed. This was a mistake from which he would never recover.

PEARL HARBOR

Hawaiian Islands, December 1941

DOUGLAS NILES

The story is so well known that the very name has become a metaphor for any stunningly successful surprise attack. World War Two had been raging for more than two years, but it came to the United States of America out of the sunny skies of that "Day of Infamy," a beautiful Sunday morning in Hawaii. Attacking without warning on December 7, 1941—*before* any declaration of war—naval air forces of the Empire of Japan struck a devastating blow against a powerful U.S. Navy fleet and the attendant Army Air Forces on the island of Oahu. The attackers sank the whole battleship force of the Pacific Fleet and shot up great numbers of American aircraft as the planes were lined up on the ground. (Only two U.S. fighter planes even got into the air during the attack.) Losing only a few dozen of the nearly four hundred planes that participated in the air raid, the Japanese fighters, bombers, and torpedo planes flew back to their ships, leaving a harbor and several army bases in flames, and a nation stunned.

Of course, the Japanese airplanes that struck on that sleepy Sunday morning did more than rudely awaken the navy base and its surrounding army installations—they aroused an entire nation, the "sleeping giant" that Admiral Yamamoto so eloquently described, and turned it into the most terrific war machine that the world had ever seen. In many ways, the Pearl Harbor attack proved to be a very bad thing for the Japanese in the long run. They had not only awakened, but infuriated, a very powerful foe, and the seeds of that fury would be harvested in the ashes of Hiroshima and Tokyo, and in the once-unthinkable concept of the Japanese empire's military surrender. Those consequences, however, lay far in the future. In the immediate aftermath of the attack—it seems an exaggeration to call it a battle—it was obvious to both sides that the Japanese had won a colossal tactical victory.

The plan for the attack was Admiral Yamamoto's brainchild, first presented to the navy staff and cabinet in February of 1941. The plan was perfected by skilled aerial tacticians led by Admiral Genda. The concept was bold, innovative, and daring: to use a fleet of fast aircraft carriers to race across the Pacific Ocean before war was declared, striking not with the heavy guns of battleships but with the highly trained air groups of the six carriers. Diplomatic efforts were to be timed so that the breaking of relations with America occurred minutes before the attack commenced. In the event, this was about the only aspect of the attack that didn't go according to plan—the official announcement was delivered shortly *after* Secretary of State Cordell Hull learned of the attack—but this wasn't much of a liability since, all along, the Nipponese military had known that their diplomats would have to be sacrificed in the name of secrecy and surprise.

Many of the attacking pilots were confident veterans of the

war Japan had been waging in Manchuria and China throughout most of the 1930s. Contrary to the expectations and assumptions of Western "experts," those pilots flew airplanes as well as any in the world. In the case of the frontline Japanese fighter, the Zero, there was no Allied machine in the Pacific or Asian theater that could come close to matching it. (The British Spitfire was a close competitor to the Zero, but the Spits were retained for use against the Germans in the European theater.) The plan for the attack had been revised, rehearsed, simulated, and perfected over the course of the previous year. Some of the bomber and torpedo attack groups conducted as many as fifty practice missions in preparation for the real attack.

Of course, there were tremendous obstacles to overcome. Surprise was determined to be paramount, so much so that if the fleet were discovered en route to Hawaii, the whole operation was to be canceled. Bombing an empty harbor would be a waste, but how could the Japanese be certain that they would catch their quarry in port, instead of at sea? How should the planes be armed? Torpedoes were the optimal weapons for inflicting lethal damage against large and well-armored ships, but what if the American ships were protected by torpedo nets? And Pearl Harbor was known to be relatively shallow, not much more than thirty or forty feet deep. Was it even possible to conduct a torpedo attack in these waters without having the "fish" run right into the bottom?

Undaunted, the Imperial Japanese Navy (IJN) went to work on these problems. Staff officers and diplomats conducted extensive intelligence work through the consulate in Honolulu, among other things learning that the fleet was nearly always in port on the weekends. Further observations confirmed that the Americans were not using torpedo nets to protect the dreadnaughts berthed along "Battleship Row." Meanwhile, Japanese naval aviators practicing in the similarly shallow Kagoshima Bay developed a plywood attachment that prevented a torpedo from making a deep dive after it entered the water. Additional innovations included fitting fins to huge, sixteen-inch armor-piercing shells—projectiles that would normally be fired from a battleship's guns. These could be dropped by horizontal bombers, and would plunge through many decks of a target's superstructure to explode deep within the bowels of the ship.

Throughout 1941, war between Japan and the United States loomed as increasingly inevitable. The Nipponese empire was thirsty for natural resources, all of which lay beyond her borders and current sphere of influence. The Americans had made it clear that any attempt to seize those resources from the Asian colonies of Britain, France, and the Netherlands would be met by military force. In summer, responding to the Japanese move into French Indochina (modern Vietnam), President Roosevelt ordered an embargo of steel and other exports to Japan. This act of sternness virtually guaranteed that war would erupt.

But how, where, and when would it start? Malaya, the Philippines, and the Netherlands East Indies were all possibilities. But the concept of a surprise aerial attack, while daring, should not have been completely unpredictable to the Americans. In fact, there were warnings issued from many different quarters, increasing in urgency as the illusory peace of 1941 ticked away.

There were a lot of reasons to consider the possibility of a surprise attack to start the war. Such had been the Japanese tactic, used to good effect, in all of the modern wars she had waged—most notably when Admiral Togo's fleet decimated the Russian czar's navy with a surprise attack at Port Arthur in 1904. Nippon went on to triumph in the Russo-Japanese War, the first time a non-European nation had defeated a European power in the modern era. (As a young officer, Admiral Yamamoto lost two fingers in that war.) Nor was an air attack against ships in port unprecedented. A little more than a year earlier, the British had sent some two dozen obsolete biplanes into Taranto harbor in Italy, where they had crippled three Italian battleships and two cruisers with torpedoes. As far back as the 1920s, advocates of airpower, such as General Billy Mitchell, had been touting the effectiveness of aerial bombardment against battleships. Mitchell, and others, had even postulated the vulnerability of the great navy base at Pearl Harbor to such an attack. Ambassador Joseph Grew, the American envoy to Tokyo and one of the foremost experts on the potential enemy, had warned specifically in January of 1941 that the United States should beware of a surprise attack against Pearl Harbor.

Nor was the advent of war an utter surprise to the American high command. For some time, the Japanese diplomatic code, Purple, had been an open book to American intelligence services. Although this did not translate into a perfect understanding of the enemy intentions, it was a huge intelligence advantage. More than a week before the attack, President Franklin D. Roosevelt had read a translated intercept detailing Japanese intentions, including orders to destroy code machines in consulates and embassies around the world, and had promptly declared to his staff: "This means war."

Admiral Ernest King, commander of the navy, and General George Marshall, who held a similar post in the army, both perceived the danger from Washington, D.C., and passed on their concerns to their respective commanders in Hawaii. The messages were specific and alarming—one from King included the phrase "This is a war warning." Although these messages were not phrased as direct orders, and probably could have been even more specific than they were, the chiefs of their branches of service fully believed their forces in Hawaii to be far more alert than they actually were.

Unfortunately, none of these warning signs or cautions seemed to resonate with the two men who were in charge of the American military forces on Oahu.

Admiral Husband Kimmel had been the Commander in Chief of the U.S. Pacific Fleet (CINCPAC) since February of 1941. General Walter Short was in command of all army ground and air forces on Oahu. The two men had enjoyed long careers in their respective services. In Hawaii, they frequently golfed together, but when it came to any kind of exchange of important and even crucial information relevant to their responsibilities, they were woefully tight-lipped with each other.

Short was not terribly interested in his job, and took no steps to prepare his command for war. He failed to order aerial reconnaissance of the waters around Hawaii, even though he was strongly encouraged to do so by Washington. His later explanation for this terrible negligence was that he didn't have enough aircraft to search in all directions, so he didn't feel it worthwhile to search even the likely quadrants to the west and north. He had radar sets available to him, but didn't put any trust in the new technology—though for more than a year the British had been proving the importance of radar in defending against air attack, with stunning success. Short had more than a hundred P-40 fighters under his command. While they were outclassed by the Zeroes, they were still the most modern fighters in the American arsenal. He never ordered routine aerial patrols over the island. His primary order was, in fact, counterproductive, as he ordered his aircraft lined up close together to prevent sabotage by enemy agents presumed to be lurking among Hawaii's civilian population. When the attack came, Short's fighters in their neat, closely packed rows were easy pickings for the Japanese. Also in anticipation of sabotage, the army's antiaircraft ammunition was locked away so securely that it took nearly four hours for his troops to be ready to shoot back. By then, of course, the attackers were long gone.

Kimmel, on the other hand, seemed to hoard his crucial information like a miser guarding his gold. When one of his own subordinates, Admiral Newton, took a task force to sea in the days before the attack, Kimmel did not inform him that he had received a "war warning" from Washington less than a week earlier. Kimmel learned on December 3 that the Japanese embassies and consulates had been instructed to destroy their codes and code machines, but he didn't share this information with General Short, nor did he seem to process this crucial intelligence to arrive at any practical conclusion about Japanese intentions and timing. He assumed his port was being protected by the army, but he did not make any effort to confirm that the army was conducting aerial searches around the island, or that its radar was being employed on anything more than an experimental basis. (The navy used radar on some of its ships and had more experience with the fledgling technology than did the army, but traditional practice dictated that it was the army's duty, not the navy's, to protect the port and the ships that were anchored there.)

In Washington, from the president on down through the military chains of command, there was little follow-up to the initial warnings. Marshall had ordered Short, for example, to fly continual air reconnaissance of the seas around the islands, but never confirmed that his orders were being carried out. (Of course, it can be argued that he shouldn't *have* to confirm this!) Both chiefs encouraged and expected interservice liaison between their theater commanders, but didn't press enough to see that such communication actually occurred.

A huge part of the American command failure at Pearl Harbor was rooted in this interservice rivalry and suspicion. These factors resulted in a catastrophic failure in communication between the U.S. Army and the U.S. Navy. Commanders in both services deemed it necessary to maintain a gulf between their branches that could only be detrimental to the nation's security. For example, the reporting of the Magic intercepts (the crucial messages gleaned from the Purple code) to the White House was the responsibility of the army on the even-numbered days of the month, and the navy on the odd-numbered days! They were not allowed to share the information, for "security reasons." Furthermore, President Roosevelt—a former secretary of the navy—loved his ships and his sailors, and perhaps gave them more credence, and paid too little attention to the sphere of the army than was strictly useful.

Interservice rivalries are not uncommon within national military establishments, and, in fact, it can be argued that the rivalry between the Imperial Japanese Army and Navy was even more deleterious to Japan's war effort than they were in the American services. Yet rarely has the suspicion, evasion, and outright deception between branches of military serving the same government ever been brought into as tight a focus as at Pearl Harbor.

Even on the day of the attack there were opportunities to react to the enemy plans and intentions with at least some effectiveness. One of the most galling examples is in the area of radar. The army was just getting to know this new technology, and had erected a small, mobile radar station 230 feet above sea level at Opana, on northwest Oahu. Because of staff limitations for this low-priority device, it was only operated between 0400 and 0700 hours. (It should be remembered that General Short had displayed virtually no interest in radar, and his disinterest inevitably trickled down through the ranks.) On December 7, it happened that the crew of the Opana station was waiting for a tardy transport truck, due to take them to breakfast. With nothing else to do, these two enlisted men kept the radar set running after seven A.M. They detected a massive flight of aircraft coming from the northwest, and quickly and urgently reported this news to their commander. That young lieutenant, only four days on the job, dismissed the report as representing a flight of twelve American bombers flying in from the northeast. (His exact words have been quoted as "Don't worry about it.")

An hour or so earlier, the destroyer USS *Ward*, on patrol outside of Pearl Harbor, had intercepted and fired upon a small submarine that had been trying to sneak into the port. The midget sub was depth charged and sunk, and the *Ward*'s captain immediately relayed this news to Pearl Harbor headquarters. The report of this alarming encounter didn't make its way up to Admiral Kimmel for several hours, at which time the air attack was well under way.

When it came, the attack was delivered with ruthless efficiency, in two waves of more than 150 aircraft each. All eight of the American battleships were hit and incapacitated. (It turned out that only two of them were permanently lost.) Aboard the navy ships, at least, the ammunition for the antiaircraft batteries was readily accessible. Despite the surprise, some guns were shooting back within five minutes. The attacking aircraft of the second wave suffered twice as many losses as the first, ample evidence that even a small amount of warning greatly increased the effectiveness of the defense.

Of course, it could have been worse. It is widely known that had the American aircraft carriers been in port and destroyed, their loss would have dramatically delayed the U.S. recovery. Furthermore, the extensive dry docks, and the massive "tank farm"—the installation consisting of the major fuel reserves of the Pacific Fleet—was left untouched by the enemy aircraft. In fact, many Japanese flyers, including the flight leader, Commander Mitsuo Fuchida, begged Admiral Nagumo—the task force commander—to authorize additional air strikes. Nagumo decided that enough damage had been done, and didn't want to risk counterattack by American forces. In reality, there was little the navy could have done, so the Japanese commander's caution was a rare bit of bright news in the bleak tally of this disastrous day.

The navy ships were helpless to maneuver because they were caught in port, but, in the end, this liability may have proved a boon. Ships that were sunk in a harbor could possibly be refloated, whereas if they had gone down in the ocean they would have been lost forever. Any way one looks at it, however, the army garrisons were almost tragically hamstrung by their lack of readiness. Not only was their ammunition locked away and their airplanes sitting ducks, but there were no trenches or air raid shelters to protect the garrisons from bombs and strafing machine guns. A hapless flight of twelve unarmed B-17s, flying in from the mainland, arrived in the midst of the attack, and suffered greatly both from the Japanese and from trigger-happy American gunners, who, by that time, were only too willing to shoot at anything and everything in the sky. Bases at Hickam Field, Wheeler, and Kaneohe were all shot up, with barracks and dining halls blown up, sometimes while they were full of men.

There is an old axiom of war that holds that one should not plan for what the enemy *will* do, but for what the enemy is *capable* of doing. Both Admiral Kimmel and General Short failed to adhere to this truism. They were men of long experience in crucial positions of command, yet—despite the evidence amassed over twenty-seven months of World War—they were unable to grasp the changing nature of military conflict or think in terms of realistic enemy capabilities. They lived with a mind-set shaped by previous wars, and subscribed to an antiquated notion of interservice rivalry that not only cost them their careers, but the lives of more than two thousand of the men and women under their command.

MIDWAY

Admiral Yamamoto's Failures at Midway

Pacific Ocean, June 1942

DOUGLAS NILES

For six months, they had been utterly unstoppable. Arrayed against the greatest powers of the Western world—with industrialized Britain and the United States at the top of the list—the armed forces of the Empire of Japan ran rampant across the Pacific Ocean and Southeast Asia. The Imperial Japanese Army seized the vast, resource-rich colonies of the embattled European powers, while the Imperial Japanese Navy (IJN) surged across the South Seas, snatching outposts of American, British, and Dutch power, landing and occupying the lightly garrisoned holdings north of Australia. India, Hawaii, and the continent Down Under felt the shadow of potential invasion.

The Japanese offensives had been met by courageous, but ultimately futile, resistance. In places as diverse as Malaya, Bataan, Rangoon, and Wake Island, Allied soldiers were outmaneuvered and ultimately overwhelmed. At Singapore and on Bataan, huge armies surrendered, dooming tens of thousands of men to a hellish captivity that, for the survivors, would last the duration of the war. Sure, the Japanese had suffered a small setback in May of 1942, at the Battle of the Coral Sea, when a naval landing force intending to take the last Allied base on New Guinea was forced to turn back following an inconclusive carrier battle. But even that had been a victory, in a sense, since the IJN had only lost a small escort carrier, while the U.S. Navy had sacrificed the *Lexington*, one of only four precious fleet carriers in the Pacific. Furthermore, the USS *Yorktown* had been badly damaged—the Japanese were certain that she would be out of action for many months.

The key to most of these successes had been the First Carrier Strike Force, the *Kido Butai*, commanded by Admiral Chuichi Nagumo. Centered around six fast, modern aircraft carriers, each with a complement of some sixty aircraft, the *Kido Butai* had launched the attack on Pearl Harbor, struck ports on the Australian mainland, defeated a British task force in the Indian Ocean, and returned triumphantly to the homeland. Not only had the strike force not lost a ship, it had not so much as been hit by an enemy shell or bomb! Well might this fleet, and Admiral Nagumo, be considered master of the seas.

In truth, the only real setback to Japanese plans, operations, and self-confidence had been almost purely symbolic on America's part. In April, General Jimmy Doolittle had led a flight of sixteen B-25 bombers on an air raid over the Japanese homeland. Launching these traditionally land-based aircraft from the aircraft carrier *Hornet*, Doolittle and the planes of his little flight carried a total of only sixty-four 500-pound bombs. Yet their presence over Japan caused consternation and dismay, and brought shame to the Japanese military, as they dropped those bombs on targets in Tokyo and several other cities. While no real damage was done by the raid, the very fact of a sea-launched air attack over the emperor's homeland was enough to humiliate the navy, and provoke a determination to strike a counterblow.

The mastermind of this counterblow was the same admiral who had conceived and ordered the attack on Pearl Harbor in December of 1941, and who had overseen the complicated and successful operations across the whole of the vast Pacific during the subsequent months: Admiral Isoroku Yamamoto. Admiral Yamamoto knew that the American carrier force was the only real threat to IJN mastery of the Pacific, and he set about to create a plan that would compel those carriers to battle, and to annihilation, at the hands of the veteran pilots and air groups of *Kido Butai*.

Yamamoto knew that in order to force the Americans to risk their precious carriers, he would have to threaten an objective that his enemy could not afford to sacrifice. To this end, he chose Midway Atoll, a base consisting of two small islands, Sand and Eastern, and a lagoon, all surrounded by a coral reef. Some thousand miles west and north of Hawaii, Midway was the only American installation within reasonable striking distance of the Japanese. The loss of the atoll would result in a grave threat to Hawaii itself, a threat that the U.S. Navy could not allow.

At his disposal, Yamamoto had plenty of force with which to accomplish this mission. He could bring special naval landing forces—elite assault troops—on transports from the Mariana Islands, and gain air superiority over the objective with the fighters and bombers of *Kido Butai*. He had a fleet of fast battleships, including the world's largest—the *Yamato*—that would allow him to pummel the island's defenses into coral dust before the landing. Skilled at air, land, and sea combat, the IJN could form a juggernaut wherever it desired to go.

Instead of gathering all of these forces into an unstoppable battle fleet, a hammer of naval power that could inevitably crush any and all American opposition, however, Yamamoto proceeded to draw up a plan that would separate his naval assets into smaller fleets scattered across a huge swath of the North Pacific Ocean. For the first time, *Kido Butai* would be sent into battle at less than full strength. Two carriers, *Shokaku* and *Zuikako,* would return to Japan for refitting, repair of battle damage, and replenishment of air groups that had suffered losses at Coral Sea.

Furthermore, Yamamoto had allowed a dangerous complacency about American capabilities to influence his planning. With the unbroken string of victories behind him, he seems to have gone about the preparations for Midway as if he was attempting to create a work of art, like an elaborate dance, instead of a sound military operation. In fact, his plan would require elaborate choreography, and involved some seven task forces spread across the whole of the North Pacific Ocean. Yamamoto authorized a purely diversionary attack against the Aleutian Islands of Alaska to seize Kiska and Attu, fog-shrouded lumps of tundra between the Pacific and the stormy Bering Sea. Although these islands were American possessions, they had little or no strategic value toward the furtherance of the war effort by either side.

As to surface ships, with the American battleship fleet having yet to recover from Pearl Harbor, the Japanese held a clear advantage. *Kido Butai,* despite its emphasis on aircraft carriers, included an escort of two fast battleships—by themselves, more dreadnaught power than the United States could put to sea. Several heavy cruisers were also included in the fleet, and each of these ships packed more punch than any Allied cruiser afloat. Yamamoto had many more battleships at his disposal, but he decided to hold his great dreadnaught fleet, with *Yamato* as its flagship, back from the main area of action. Although he wanted the gunnery of these powerful ships to plaster any American vessels that came within range, his deployment of the fleet virtually insured that they would never even catch a whiff of the battle that would be fought hundreds of miles to the east. While many of the battlewagons were too slow to keep up with the carriers, several—including *Yamato* herself—could have sailed with the First Carrier Strike Force without slowing down the flattops.

But a dance requires coordination among every dancer on the stage. Underlying Yamamoto's far-flung deployments and intricately timed maneuvers were the key flaw in his plan: for the operation to work as designed, the enemy was required to behave exactly as the admiral expected him to behave. If the American fleet had followed the steps in the assigned dance of battle, the IJN would surely have smashed it at Midway. If the Americans did anything other than what Yamamoto expected, his widespread dispersal of force contained the kernels of unprecedented disaster.

Later during, and after, the war, the Japanese began to understand the mind-set that had led them to disaster beginning in the summer of 1942. They called it the Victory Disease, and it represented a sense of sublime overconfidence, based on the unbroken string of victories, but also on a careless underestimation of their foes. In the end, it was a disease that would prove fatal.

The United States, meanwhile, had been learning about war. The aircraft carriers *Enterprise*, *Hornet*, and *Yorktown* had raided Japanese outposts, while their screening vessels had gained experience in fleet operations, and in protecting the vital flattops. At the same time, intelligence drawn from the Japanese naval code had been progressing amazingly well. Under the leadership of Commander Joseph Rochefort, USN, American code breakers had been working diligently to crack the complex cryptography employed by the Japanese navy. By the summer of 1942, they had succeeded in gleaning enough information to decipher the gist of many important messages. A little creativity was often enough to put the information gatherers over the top.

When it became clear that the next Japanese objective was code-named AF, Rochefort's staff had Midway broadcast a message "in the clear" (that is, uncoded) reporting that the island's seawater condenser had broken down. When, a short time later, the Japanese listening station in the Marianas radioed a coded report that AF was short of fresh water, Rochefort had his confirmation: AF was Midway, and Midway was the target of the upcoming, and major, Japanese offensive.

Admiral Chester Nimitz, Commander in Chief of the Pacific Fleet (CINCPAC), knew that he would inevitably be overmatched in numbers of ships, especially battleships. But he knew this would be a carrier battle, and he did everything in his power to muster every carrier in the fleet to the vicinity of Midway Island. Foremost among these were the *Enterprise* and *Hornet*, recently out of the Coral Sea engagement. Nimitz ordered them to steam north at flank speed. The *Yorktown* was a tougher problem—she had been badly damaged during the battle. Initial estimates suggested at least six weeks of necessary repairs.

In the event, under CINCPAC's forceful urging, the ship was rendered seaworthy—and capable of air operations—after a two-day stop at Pearl Harbor. Under the command of Admiral Frank Jack Fletcher, the *Yorktown* sailed to a rendezvous at "Point Luck," joining the other two American carriers (commanded by Admiral Ray Spruance). All these ships gathered northeast of Midway before the Japanese submarines assigned to watch Pearl

Harbor had even arrived on station to form a picket line. At the same time, Nimitz had packed tiny Midway with as many troops and land-based planes as he could. Coastal batteries were installed, barbed wire strung, and mines set around the entire perimeter.

Thus, as *Kido Butai* sailed within air range of the island, the partners in Yamamoto's dance were already out of sync with the choreography. The events of the early morning of June 4 should have done nothing to enhance his confidence—and perhaps the admiral might have made some changes. But here was another key flaw in the great admiral's plan: he and his headquarters were aboard *Yamato,* hundreds of miles from the carriers, and both fleets needed to observe strict radio silence for secrecy. So Yamamoto had *no way to control events* once they started to develop! The conduct of the battle was now in the hands of the stolid and unimaginative Nagumo.

By dawn, *Kido Butai* had been sighted by American observers in a lumbering PBY scout plane. Thanks to intermittent cloud cover, the aircraft was able to avoid the Japanese fighters, and provide fairly steady and accurate location reports on the Japanese carriers. The first land-based bombers from Midway launched at about the same time as *Kido Butai*'s first attacks against the island took to the air. In fact, the two bomber forces passed each other on the way to their respective targets.

The good fortune that had marked almost all Japanese operations throughout the war held firm for the first hours of that fateful day. American bombers based on Midway included army B-17s and B-26s, and old SB2U Vindicator dive bombers (derisively called Wind Indicators by their pilots), as well as some of the more modern SBD Dauntless dive bombers and TBF torpedo planes, flown by marine pilots. They made as many as seven separate attacks on the IJN carrier fleet. Their pilots displayed incredible courage, and many of them did not return, yet they failed to score a single hit against the enemy fleet.

In the meantime, the planes of Nagumo's first wave savaged both Eastern and Sand Islands, the two small specks of land holding the Midway installations. They were met by marine fighters, the pilots every bit as courageous as their comrades in the bombers. But the Japanese Zeroes brushed aside the obsolete Brewster Buffaloes and inflicted heavy losses. Fierce antiaircraft fire took a toll on the bombers, however, and after the Japanese had dropped their bombs and turned back to their carriers, flight leader Tomonaga radioed Nagumo to report the need for a second attack on the island's installations. The planes for this second wave were already armed and on deck of the four Japanese fleet carriers, but they carried torpedoes and armor-piercing bombs, weaponry intended to be used against the American carriers whenever they appeared.

It was here that Lady Luck began to turn her favor upon the U.S. Navy. After dithering rather longer than was helpful, Nagumo decided to have his second-strike planes reloaded with bombs for a ground attack. His crews went to work in a frenzy, interrupted now and then as the carriers maneuvered to avoid the valiant but futile attacks of the Midway-based planes. Meanwhile, Admirals Spruance and Fletcher, lurking undiscovered to the northeast of *Kido Butai*, took the step that would reduce Yamamoto's elaborate dance to the battle equivalent of a pratfall. Though the range was long and the risk was great, they ordered the American air groups from *Yorktown*, *Enterprise*, and *Hornet* to take off, fly to the Japanese fleet, and attack. Because of the distance involved, a coordinated attack was impossible—the planes that launched first would have wasted too much fuel as they circled their carriers waiting for subsequent groups to join up—so they would go in separately.

The American carriers included air groups of three types of planes: dive bombers, torpedo bombers, and fighters. Some fighters were held back as combat air patrol (CAP) to protect the fleet, while the rest were dispatched toward the First Carrier Strike Force. The torpedo and dive bombers were armed and sent, flying in separate groups. Some got lost; the dive bombers from the *Hornet* would eventually land on Midway Island without ever seeing the enemy. Some got through, only to make a doomed attack, an aerial "Charge of the Light Brigade." These were the torpedo bombers, who got there first and attacked at sea level. They suffered horrendous losses—all fifteen of the *Hornet*'s torpedo planes were shot down, with the other two squadrons decimated as well—and, like the land-based bombers, failed to score a hit. But their sacrifice unwittingly accomplished a crucial objective: they drew all the deadly Zeroes down almost to sea level.

By 10:20 in the morning, Nagumo's force had avoided some ten attacks without suffering a hit. In the meantime, his own scouts had spotted the American carriers, and his crews were busy re-rearming the planes, making ready for an urgent attack on that highest of high-priority targets. Although his defending fighters were at low altitude, they had fuel and ammunition remaining, and were climbing again toward their usual defensive position above the fleet. It is almost certain that he did not even imagine how much his fleet, and the whole balance of power in the Pacific Ocean, was about to change.

The American dive bombers from the *Enterprise* and *Yorktown* arrived over the enemy carriers at the same time, approaching from different directions. The two squadrons split up and dove to the attack. In five minutes, they dropped bombs through the crowded flight decks of three of the four Japanese aircraft carriers. The ships, packed with fuel hoses, bomb carts, and fully loaded planes, ignited like tinderboxes. It soon became obvious that *Akagi*, *Soryu*, and *Kaga*—all fully engulfed in flame—were lost. Admiral Nimitz's gamble had disrupted Admiral Yamamoto's choreography beyond repair.

To be sure, the IJN was not finished. The one remaining carrier, *Hiryu*, would launch several strikes, enough to cripple the battle-scarred *Yorktown* with bombs and torpedoes. Here again, however, American damage control proved decisive. After the first strike left *Yorktown* burning and listing, she was repaired and under way—though not capable of flight operations—when the planes of the second strike came over. So certain were the Japanese that this was a different ship that they again attacked the impotent aircraft carrier, rather than seeking out the undamaged *Enterprise* and *Hornet* just over the horizon. Those ships, meanwhile, dispatched the strikes that found, hit, and sank the *Hiryu*.

By the time the sun set on that fateful June 4, all four Japanese carriers had been sunk or mortally damaged. Yamamoto hurried eastward with his great battleships, but he was much too far away to have an impact on this battle. The invasion was called off, the transport fleet retiring to the Marianas, while the remnants of *Kido Butai*—a carrier strike force without any carriers—withdrew in shock and shame. Perhaps Yamamoto already understood that, in those five minutes, the momentum of the Pacific war had reversed itself for once and for all.

GUADALCANAL

Japanese Underestimations in the Solomons, August–November 1942

DOUG NILES

So, it's been a nice run, except for that little setback at Midway. And even the bumbling Americans have to get lucky once in a while! But now you have a serious challenge before you: clear the Allies off the island of New Guinea. They only have one outpost there, Port Moresby, on the southern coast. You are determined to kick them off of this, the second largest island in the world. This important objective will clamp the lid on Australia, and solidify the boundary of your Greater East Asia Co-Prosperity Sphere.

You don't have time for distractions, for sideshows. Yet now, on August 7, just such a distraction has come along to bother you. A few months earlier, your forces captured the Solomon Islands, practically without a fight. They are, for the most part, useless rotting jungle, but far to the south, in Tulagi, you have established a seaplane base. Just across the sound from Tulagi, on a larger island, your men have started building an airfield. It is this airfield that seems to be the American objective.

In a place called Guadalcanal.

The attack on Guadalcanal embodied a lot of firsts for the United States military in the Pacific theater of World War Two. It was the first time a significant ground force—an entire division—went on the offensive in the war. It was the first amphibious assault in a theater in which virtually every subsequent campaign would begin with an amphibious assault. And it was the first time that territory held by the Japanese was taken away from them.

The operation, code-named Cactus, came together in a hurry, after aerial reconnaissance photos showed the existence of the nascent airfield. Near the very southern terminus of the Solomons, Guadalcanal as a Japanese base would create a major threat to the sea lines of communication between Australia and the west coast of the United States. Bombers based there could force convoys to detour far to the south or face the risk of aerial attack. The field could not be allowed to become operational, but there was much debate as to how to interfere with the enemy plans.

In American command circles, the Solomon Islands lay astride the barrier between General Douglas MacArthur's South West Pacific Area (SWEAPAC) and Admiral Chester Nimitz's Central Pacific Area (CINCPAC). Since the navy had the available forces when the mission was assigned—including the First Marine Division, which would do the initial fighting on the ground—Nimitz was given overall command. His chief in the South Pacific Area was Vice Admiral Robert Ghormley.

The operation was thrown together in a hurry, with a brief rehearsal of the landing that was described as an unmitigated disaster, and then the marines were shipped into the waters off Guadalcanal, a place that would soon be known as Ironbottom Sound. Operation Cactus came to be known as Operation Shoestring to the marines, who fought so desperately to hold on to the airfield, and the island. At the start of the battle, they had significant help, especially air cover from Admiral Frank Fletcher's carriers, including the *Enterprise*, *Wasp*, and *Saratoga*.

The initial landings went remarkably well and, except for some initial resistance at Tulagi, all of the objectives were taken in the first two days, with virtually no interference from the Japanese. On Guadalcanal, these enemy troops consisted mainly of conscripted labor forces, put there to build the airfield, and they had very little stomach for fighting. By August 8, Vandegrift's marines had established a defensive perimeter around the airfield. Navy engineers quickly began work aimed at completing the field, which would become operational by August 20.

Things did not go nearly so well at sea and in the air, however. As soon as he learned of the invasion, Admiral Inouye on Rabaul sent a series of air raids against the American ships. Fletcher, handling his carriers rather clumsily, judged that he had lost too many fighters for safety and withdrew his flattops on the night of August 8. A day earlier, Admiral Mikawa had set sail from Rabaul with a powerful cruiser force. In the dark, shortly after midnight on the morning of August 9, his cruisers savagely mauled two groups of American and Australian cruisers covering the transports that were still loaded with tons of Vandegrift's supplies. Aided by faulty Allied deployment, wherein the defensive force was split into two groups and failed to communicate with each other throughout the battle, Mikawa won a major tactical victory in the Battle of Savo Island. The Japanese proved superior in night gunnery and ship-handling, and their "Long Lance" torpedoes were far more deadly than the shorter-ranged and unreliable American weapons.

As a consequence of this disastrous engagement, Admiral

Ghormley authorized the withdrawal of the U.S. Navy from the waters around Guadalcanal. The marines watched the transports, laden with much of the food, ammunition, and other supplies they would need to survive, sail away. Feelings of abandonment ran rampant. Yet, from Vandegrift on down, determination was an even stronger force.

Mikawa, on the other hand, failed to follow up on his stunning victory in several crucial ways. First, in the hours after winning the stunning victory at Savo Island, he neglected to continue onward, when a few more miles would have carried his lethal surface force into the midst of the helpless, anchored transports. He did not know that the American carriers had withdrawn, and he feared air attack during the day. So, content with destroying the American warships with barely a scratch to his own fleet, he turned and headed back to Rabaul.

The Japanese commanders knew that the Americans would have to be driven back from the airfield, but they seriously underestimated the strength in ground troops required for this task. Their attention still focused on New Guinea, they sent dribs and drabs of reinforcements, landing small detachments at night to the east and west of the marines' perimeter. This failure to capitalize quickly on control of the sea would cost them the battle.

The newly completed airfield was named Henderson Field, after a marine corps pilot killed during the battle of Midway. On August 20, the first squadrons of marine aircraft, primarily F4F Wildcat fighters and SBD Dauntless dive bombers, arrived. These machines, flown by pilots who lived in jungle conditions much like those faced by the marines on the front lines, would form the nucleus of the "Cactus Air Force," and during the coming months they would make the difference in the fight for the island. Reinforced by more marines and a handful of army pilots flying obsolete P-400s, they ruled the skies during the day, even while the IJN controlled the sea every night.

The first land attack against the marines was in regimental strength. Led by Colonel Ichiki, whose detachment had landed east of the perimeter, it struck the well-entrenched marines along the coast, at the mouth of the Tenaru River. In a savage night of frontal attacks, the Ichiki detachment was utterly shattered. The remnants withdrew to the east, with the colonel taking his own life to atone for the failure of his offensive.

But this failure didn't convince the Japanese leadership that they faced a more formidable opponent than they had originally guessed. Instead, they simply continued to reinforce the island with the small increments of reinforcements that they could send down the "Slot," the channel between the two parallel chains of Solomon Islands. The Japanese admirals still did not make a full-scale effort to retake the island. Instead, the troops were brought down in small numbers aboard destroyers, or on destroyers that had been converted into high-speed transports. They were put ashore at night, and slowly mustered under General Kawaguchi, who was determined to make a multipronged attack.

The rest of August provided further bad news for the U.S. Navy. In the battle of the Eastern Solomons (August 22–25), the two carrier forces clashed, with the IJN losing the light carrier *Ryujo* and the Americans suffering serious damage to the *Enterprise*, one of the four fleet carriers remaining in the Pacific Fleet. That clash resulted in more or less a draw, but on August 31, the *Saratoga* was torpedoed by a Japanese submarine and knocked out of action for three months. Even worse, on September 15, the *Wasp* was torpedoed and sunk by another sub attack.

Over it all, the planes of the Cactus Air Force had begun to make the waters around the island very dangerous for the Japanese during the hours of daylight, as the dive bombers sank vulnerable transports and even the occasional warship, and the fighters exacted increasing unacceptable losses among the land-based fighters and bombers that made the six-hundred-mile flight down to Guadalcanal from the major Japanese base at Rabaul.

On land, General Kawaguchi painstakingly marched his men over jungle ridges and through swampy rivers, bringing his force in position to attack Henderson Field from the inland side, to the south. The marines of Edson's Raiders and the Parachute Battalion were dug in along a grass-topped elevation only a few miles from the field. With greater emphasis placed on defending the coastal approaches, the ridgetop line was thin, with several notable gaps. It was here that Kawaguchi chose to attack.

The Japanese troops on the line of battle were weary and short of supplies. They couldn't bring any heavy equipment, such as artillery, with them on the jungle trails. Still, they charged up the hill in frenzied waves, rushing into the marine foxholes with bayonets fixed. They were met by a barrage of artillery, machine gun, and small arms fire. Over the course of several days the battle raged, with occasional groups of attackers breaking through the marine lines, only to be cut off and wiped out before they could threaten the field. After more than a dozen attacks against the hilltop, which would forever be known as Bloody Ridge in the histories of the U.S. Marines, the strength of Kawaguchi's infantry was spent. The survivors retreated through the jungle, fighting starvation and disease.

After this failure, the Japanese finally began to get serious. The headquarters of the Seventeenth Army arrived and, under the command of General Haruyoshi Hyakutake, assembled two divisions—some twenty thousand men—with the intention of making a major, concentrated attack. Once again, however, the rugged terrain in the interior of the island, and the crude communication inherent in the wilderness environment, caused the great attack to go in without coordination. In a series of piecemeal attacks on October 23–25, thousands of Japanese soldiers died, and the American position was never seriously endangered.

The battle for the seas remained a bitter struggle. On October 13–15, the IJN brought down battleships, cruisers, and destroyers to pound the marine positions and the airfield with their big guns. Many planes were destroyed on the ground. It was during this month, however, that the USN began to regain the initiative, with improvements in tactics and command. Admiral William Halsey replaced Ghormely on October 18. Over October 26–27, the two sides engaged in another carrier fight, the battle of the Santa Cruz Islands. Though the Americans lost the redoubtable *Hornet*, the Japanese lost more than a hundred planes, and their irreplaceable pilots. The tide had shifted for good, and in later battles—the Naval Battle of Guadalcanal and the Battle of Tassafaronga—American gunnery and night-fighting skills really began to come into their own.

By November, the Second Marine Division began to arrive, reinforcing the First. Army units, beginning with the 164th Infantry and finally including the entire Americal Division, were also landed. On December 9, Army General Alexander Patch finally relieved Vandegrift and the First Marines. By the end of the year there were more than fifty thousand American forces on the island, to face some twenty thousand Japanese, and the writing was on the wall. The Americans attacked relentlessly, pushing the enemy to the far western end of the island. Recognizing the battle as lost, the Japanese evacuated some thirteen thousand troops during the first week of February.

While both sides made many mistakes in the Battle of Guadalcanal, the mistakes of the Japanese high command, including Admirals Inouye, Mikawa, and Tanaka, and Generals Kawaguchi and Hyakutake, were serious enough to cost them the battle.

They included:

- failure to take advantage of the U.S. Navy withdrawal during the first month of the battle
- a continual inability to recognize the importance of the battle, until it was too late
- piecemeal tactics of reinforcement and attack that dissipated whatever local superiority could be assembled before it could be brought to bear.

STALINGRAD

General von Paulus's Disaster at the Battle of Stalingrad

Stalingrad and the Volga Basin, USSR, September 1942–February 1943

DOUGLAS NILES

Imagine that you are General Friedrich von Paulus. You've reached a position, command of a great army, thanks not so much to your incredible skills, but because you get along very well with the most powerful man around. And if Adolf Hitler likes you, the world—at least the Nazi world—is your oyster. In your case, this favor has been enough to lift you out of the long career of staff work that seemed destined to frame your contributions to World War Two. And you are good at staff work, and especially operational planning. Indeed, the detailed arrangements for Operation Barbarossa, the great invasion of the USSR during the summer of 1941, were your masterpiece.

Now, in 1942, you have been elevated beyond the role of planner, given command of the Sixth Army. This is a mighty engine of war, one of the key spearheads in the great summer offensives of 1942. It has driven across vast swaths of the Russian steppes, crossed great rivers—most recently the Don—and now stands poised to reap the greatest prize of the campaign. Only sixty miles away stands the great city on the Volga, a center of transportation and industry of huge strategic value—and even greater symbolic value, for it is named after the very man who controls the entire Soviet state.

It is the city of Stalingrad.

During the first year of the Nazi-Soviet War, the Wehrmacht made its dual thrust for Moscow and Leningrad, only to be thwarted in the very suburbs of these key cities. In 1942, Hitler's strategic objective changed, and he determined that the great effort against the Russians should be made in the south, with the ultimate objectives being the oil-rich territories of the Caucasus and, possibly, a breakthrough into Persian and Arabian territories in the south. By the end of July 1942, the Germans had savagely ripped apart the Red Army wherever it tried to stand against them. The mighty fortress of Sevastopol and the entire Crimean peninsula fell, the Donets River was crossed, and the panzer spearheads filled in the great bend of the Don River and quickly pushed their way across that formidable barrier.

From the Don, the German tanks continued on, with Kliest commanding Army Group A as it plunged southward. Advanced echelons would actually reach the foothills of the Caucasus Mountains and the shore of the Caspian Sea. Army Group B, with von Paulus's Sixth Army in the lead, broke across the Don, with the objective of Stalingrad. This great manufacturing city—it had been called Tsaritsyn before the Soviet dictator changed its name—was key to control of the Volga River.

But Hitler, as he did so often, just *had* to tinker with the plan. The other major component of Army Group B, beside the Sixth Army, was the Fourth Panzer Army. This Hitler diverted southward, to help Kliest, and thus left von Paulus to accomplish his objective without the necessary strength.

Still, the Sixth Army pressed onward, and by August 23 reached the Volga north of Stalingrad. More divisions came up, and, instead of attempting to encircle his objective and cut it off from support, the commanding general fed those new arrivals into the meat grinder that the city was to become. He pressed his attacks from the north, west, and south, along the whole perimeter of Stalingrad, an elongated, narrow city that extended for more than ten miles up and down the west bank of the Volga.

At the same time, two Soviet armies, under the overall command of General Vasily Chuikov, turned the city into a fortress. The Russians contested every building, every street and alley of the vast metropolis. They turned factories, grain elevators, and train stations into bastions, and though they were driven steadily back toward the banks of the Volga, they made the Germans pay for every bloody inch of ground gained. The great tractor factory at the northern end of the city had been converted to tank production for the war. Now, as shells fell on and around it, the production line continued to operate, cranking out T-34 tanks that literally rolled off the assembly line, out the factory doors, and into the battle. The Soviet defenders were aided by massive artillery formations on the east bank of the river, guns that could pound the enemy with impunity, safe from ground attack behind the impermeable barrier of the Volga.

Stalin was utterly determined that the city, his namesake, should not fall. He ordered all available reinforcements to that sector of the front. Because the Germans had failed to encircle the city, had in fact made no effort to cross the Volga north or south of Stalingrad, these newly arriving troops could be ferried across the river in great numbers. Chuikov used them to prop up crumbling positions across his front, and as September cooled into October, the lethal struggle continued unabated.

Another of Stalin's moves would prove crucial: he placed his most brilliant commander, Marshal Georgi Zhukov—the man who had saved both Leningrad and Moscow the previous year—in command at Stalingrad. He ordered Zhukov to plan a counter-attack, and instructed him, under penalty of death, to keep those plans an utter secret. Even Chuikov, conducting the desperate defense of the city, was not to know of the impending operation designed to come to his rescue.

Von Paulus maintained his attack with single-minded, bull-dog determination. In a few places, his forces actually broke through to the river, and everywhere the Soviets were pushed into ever smaller pockets on the west bank. But they always maintained some ground, including the all-important Ferry Landing, where most of the Soviet reinforcements arrived. Though Chuikov pleaded for more men, these reinforcements were limited by Zhukov to just the bare minimum needed to maintain the defense. Many of these new men were pulled from the Siberian theater, and they were as tough and hardy fighters as the Nazis would face anywhere in the war. They added to the defensive strength and held tenaciously as November began and the Russian winter loomed.

As to the rest of Zhukov's available troops, he had big plans. Hundreds of thousands of German troops were crowded into the contested city, but the Sixth Army had two long, tenuous flanks that were thinly held by Rumanian troops. Although their nation had been strong-armed into the Axis and compelled to join the fateful invasion of Rumania's ancient enemy, Russia, these troops were less well equipped, and far less motivated, than their German comrades in arms. Furthermore, they were holding very long stretches of front because the Sixth Army had moved so far ahead of the rest of the German-controlled territory.

Zhukov's attack was timed to coincide with two crucial factors, one strategic and the other tactical. The former was the Western Allied landings of Operation Torch, as American and British forces took Casablanca, Oran, and Algiers from Vichy France, attracting Hitler's attention to a new and clearly menacing threat. The tactical advantage was the first hard freeze, as cold weather hardened the muddy steppes and opened up the whole, vast landscape to speedy tank operations.

The attack opened on November 19, with two powerful "fronts" (the Soviet equivalent of army groups) striking the Third Rumanian Army holding the line of the Don River to the west and north of Stalingrad. The South-West Front, under General Nikolai Vatutin, smashed southward, armored spearheads racing many miles on the first day of the attack. The Don Front, under Marshal Konstantin Rokossovsky, attacked closer to Stalingrad, driving for von Paulus's headquarters. Between them, they shattered the Rumanians, quickly surrounding five divisions and sending many more reeling backward in defeat.

On November 20, the second jaw of Zhukov's double envelopment thrust west and northward from the region south of the embattled city. The Stalingrad Front, commanded by General Andrei Yeremenko, punched through the Fourth Rumanian Army and drove deep into the Axis rear. By November 23, the two massive pincers had met in the vicinity of Kalach, on the Don, trapping about a third of a million enemy troops within a deep encirclement.

With this sudden and decisive counterattack, the Battle of Stalingrad changed from a Nazi offensive into a struggle for survival. The Russian winter closed in with its usual fury, and the

Sixth Army pocket fought to hold the Soviets at bay, while the men strived to stay warm, and scrabbled to find enough food to keep themselves alive. Hitler himself took command of the situation, declaring Stalingrad to be a "fortress," as Goering, chief of the German air forces, pledged that the Luftwaffe would supply the surrounded army until the Nazis could once again resume the offensive.

Like most of Goering's promises, this one would prove to be far beyond his capabilities. Within the encircled army, desperate hunger began to spread and, by December, soldiers were dying from lack of food. In the meantime, Zhukov kept up relentless pressure, eventually bringing seven armies to bear against the surrounded Germans. The Axis troops resisted with their usual skill and élan, but it was clear that unless something dramatic happened, the Sixth Army was doomed.

The German answer to Marshal Zhukov, the commander who was sent to rescue embattled sectors, was Field Marshal Erich von Manstein. As commander of Army Group Don, he gathered his most powerful armored forces under the command of General Hermann Hoth, and ordered Operation Winter Storm, designed to relieve the besieged troops in Stalingrad. The "Hoth Group" attacked on December 12, driving toward Stalingrad from just west of due south, driving into the Soviet Fifth Shock Army. The panzers were outnumbered by the Russian armor, but they made steady headway, pushing against determined opposition until they were about thirty-five miles away from the trapped Sixth Army.

Manstein contacted von Paulus by radio and urged him to try to break out. If the two German forces could have connected, it is possible that an opening could have been maintained that would have allowed the bulk of the Sixth Army to make it out of the Stalingrad deathtrap. But von Paulus would not move without authorization from Hitler, and when the fürhrer was consulted, he insisted that his besieged troops stay in place—that they not give up any of the ground they had captured, even though by this time that ground represented nothing more than a place for tens of thousands of Germans to die.

The Soviets counterattacked Hoth on Christmas Eve, with the Fifth Tank Army, the Second Guards Army, and the Fifty-first Army attacking side by side. The Hoth Group was overwhelmed and, fighting furiously, was forced all the way back to, and across, the Don. The Sixth Army's fate was sealed. Starvation and frostbite were rampant among the surrounded Germans, and crushing fatigue wore down the men until they could barely stand, much less function as the efficient soldiers they once had been.

But still they didn't give up. Soviet armies pressured the Stalingrad pocket from all sides, and somehow the starving, freezing troops found the strength to resist. By January, Zhukov brought even more strength to bear, and now it was the Germans who clung to every block, every street of bloody, ruined ground, while the original defenders pressed home their irresistible attack. On January 8, 1943, Rokossovsky gave von Paulus the opportunity to surrender, but the German general, again ordered by Hitler to continue resisting, refused. The Russians drove on, until the Nazi forces were trapped in two pockets in the rubble of Stalingrad.

Hitler had one last card to play, and it was typical of his madness that it embodied a taunt and a merely symbolic reward. On January 30, he promoted von Paulus to field marshal, the highest ranking in the German military hierarchy. He also reminded him, pointedly, that no field marshal in the entire history of Germany had ever surrendered.

It was no use. The very next day, January 31, von Paulus and his men in the southern pocket of Stalingrad capitulated. Two days later, the last group of Germans, in the northern end of the city, surrendered. The Battle of Stalingrad was over. The Soviets captured nearly 100,000 Germans, with an equal amount dying during the battle. This loss was bad enough, but because of the terrific symbolism each side had imbued in this battle, the real defeat was even greater. It was the end of Germany's offensive against Russia. From here on, the Soviets would be on the attack, and the Wehrmacht would be defending, and retreating, until the final brutal battle—in some ways eerily similar to Stalingrad—was enacted in the rubble of Berlin itself.

Much of the disaster at Stalingrad can be laid at the feet of Adolf Hitler himself. Even so, a better field commander could have handled the battle with more subtlety, and emerged, if not with a victory, at least with much of his army intact. But not von Paulus.

Instead:

- He tried to batter his way into the city along the whole of its broad front, instead of trying to encircle and isolate the crucial Soviet strong point.
- He vastly underestimated the Russian determination to hold Stalingrad at all costs.
- Finally, von Paulus failed to try to break out when Manstein's relief force was only a few dozen miles away. In his unfailing obedience to his master's orders, the general/field marshal, as did so many other Germans during this war, sealed his own doom.

KASSERINE PASS

General Fredendall's Fiasco at Kasserine Pass

North Africa, February 1943

DOUGLAS NILES

The Axis and Allies had been fighting over the continent of Africa since 1940, in battles centered along the coastal deserts of Libya and Egypt. After a long run of successes, doing a lot with a little, German Field Marshal Erwin Rommel's *Panzerarmee Afrika* had at last been checked by autumn of 1942. At the Battle of El Alamein, British Field Marshal Bernard Montgomery's Eighth Army would finally push the Desert Fox into his longest retreat, permanently removing the Axis threat to the Suez Canal, and, one by one, capturing the key Libyan ports of Tobruk, Benghazi, and Tripoli.

At the same time, the Western Allies launched their first combined operation, a three-pronged landing in the Vichy French territories of western North Africa. Key ports—it was always about the ports, on that Saharan coast—were seized in French Morocco and Algeria. But the real objectives of the operation, the Tunisian ports of Bizerte and Tunis, were judged too dangerous for direct attack. Instead, they would be taken by a swift advance from Algiers.

The overall commander of Operation Torch was General Dwight D. Eisenhower. He was faced with a multitude of complexities, not the least of which was the complicated political situation between Free French, Vichy French, British, and American interests in northwest Africa. Ike ended up spending most of his time trying to iron out this mess—with some notable success, to be sure—while he left the actual campaign to his army and corps commanders. The advance on Tunisia was slow. Due to terrible December rains and a startlingly rapid Axis buildup, the drive on Bizerte and Tunis halted in a muddy stalemate. Under the command of the British lieutenant general Anderson, the British First Army and American II Corps took up defensive positions for the winter.

By early 1943, Rommel had completed his long retreat and occupied the Mareth Line, an old but extensive network of formations erected by the French at the Tunisian-Libyan border before the war. Montgomery was slowly coming up, but despite the deliberate pace, Rommel knew his adversary would eventually have enough strength on the border to make a powerful attack. In that event, Lieutenant General Anderson's forces in western Tunisia formed a lethal menace to the *Panzerarmee*'s very survival.

Naturally, Rommel decided to attack. His target would be the American II Corps, the southern end of Anderson's long position. It was relatively unblooded, and, with a dramatic victory, he hoped to infuse the U.S. Army with a significant sense of inferiority on the battlefield. In this effort, he was not much impeded by his rival field commander.

Major General Lloyd Fredendall was loud, forceful, and blustery, the general commander of II Corps and a man with strong ideas about what he wanted, and where and when he wanted it. When it came to the location of his headquarters, for example, he decided that it should be some eighty miles behind the front. His scouts found a cavern located far up a remote canyon, and Fredendall put several hundred of his engineers to work excavating additional underground bunker space. (Later, Eisenhower would comment that he never observed another major headquarters so determined to get itself underground.)

Fredendall also seemed to want direct tactical control of his units. Certainly, this was the case with II Corps' only tank-heavy formation. The First Armored Division of the U.S. Army was just that: the original armored formation of division size, formed between the wars as the harbinger of the slow American progress toward a modern war machine. The division first saw action in the Torch landings, and swiftly overcame the spirited but short-lived resistance of the few Vichy French troops in North Africa who were inclined to resist. As the armored component of II Corps, it formed a key element of the American presence in the war as the Allies faced German forces under Rommel and von Arnhim in Tunisia. The division commander, Major General Orlando Ward, was calm and soft-spoken and respected by his men—but not by his corps commander.

Bypassing the chain of command, Fredendall issued orders directly to Ward's subordinate commanders, outlining their deployments. He placed Combat Command A (CCA), one-third of the division's strength, around the town of Sidi Bou Zid, far in advance of the positions of the rest of the division and the corps. To compound the error, the various components of CCA were widely dispersed. The infantry elements held two important hills, Djebel Lessouda and Djebel Ksaira. They overlooked the tanks and artillery in the flatlands below, but were too far away from each other to offer mutual support.

Eisenhower toured the II Corps positions for the first time on February 13, 1943. He was alarmed by the casual sense of ease—units that had been in position for several days had yet to lay minefields or complete defensive excavations—and he was upset by Fredendall's detachment from the realities of his position. The engineers working on the HQ excavations, he felt, should have been used to strengthen frontline positions. But he was too late to do anything about either problem.

Two of Rommel's veteran *Afrika Korps* formations, the Tenth and Twenty-first Panzer Divisions, attacked CCA on February 14. They swiftly defeated the surprised armor units, and surrounded the infantry on their two isolated hilltops. The Luftwaffe, including the virtually obsolete Stuka dive bomber, ruled the skies as the Americans fell back in disarray. The thousands of soldiers on the two hills spent a dark, terrifying night, with Axis forces in control of the town and plains below them.

The next day, Fredendall ordered a counterattack by another of the First Armored's components: Combat Command B. This tank-heavy formation rolled forward, and the Germans let them come—straight into a trap. At the last second, a barrage of tank and antitank fire, with supporting air attacks, smashed CCB to the point that only four of its nearly sixty tanks escaped. Within the next twenty-four hours, the remaining American troops abandoned their two hilltop positions and tried to escape on foot. More than half were captured or killed.

Rommel rolled on, toward the pass that would give the battle its name. He had breached II Corps, and the entire Allied position lay open before him. But his counterpart, von Arnhim, insisted on taking the Tenth Panzer for his own (ultimately fruitless) use. And under the confused command situation established by Hitler, the Desert Fox had no choice but to release the division. Nevertheless, he fought his way through Kasserine Pass against stiffening resistance and burst northward, toward Tebessa, the key Allied air and supply bases in Tunisia.

The situation was serious, but the momentum of the attack had already been spent. British forces from the Sixth Armored Division came south to make a valiant stand at Thala. They were supported by four dozen howitzers of the American Ninth Infantry Division, guns that had been hauled hundreds of miles over muddy mountain tracks in order to be brought to bear.

Personally observing the curtain of artillery fire across his intended route of advance, having lost half of his armored strength to von Arnhim, the Desert Fox called off the attack. Fredendall's forces were in shambles, demoralized and shaken by their first taste of blitzkrieg. Rommel pulled back through Kasserine Pass, leaving less than a dozen of his tanks destroyed on the battlefield, while the II Corps could only lick its wounds.

And await a new commander. Eisenhower fired Fredendall, though even then the infuriated supreme commander could not bring himself to demote his subordinate and send him stateside in disgrace. But he made up for this lapse with the man he installed in Fredendall's place, a man who had much history yet to write.

His name was George S. Patton.

OKINAWA

April 1945

BRIAN THOMSEN

Considered to be the final land battle of the Pacific theater in World War Two, the overall engagement at Okinawa was really equal parts sea and land conflict, with the Allied forces steamrolling the Japanese attempts at combined sea and air actions, which included numerous kamikaze attacks meant to cripple the naval fleet.

The Allied plan, dubbed Operation Iceberg, involved the greatest armada of land and sea power in the history of the war in the Pacific or Europe (even larger than the Normandy invasion the previous year), involving over fifteen hundred ships carrying over a half million soldiers, all descending on the island of Okinawa, which was not much more than sixty miles in length. Moreover, an additional 183,000 troops and over twelve planes were available to be called on, if necessary. The Allied strategy of focusing an overwhelming force on a concentrated target was designed to hasten an end to the war by sending a message of inevitability by securing a quick, clear, and decisive victory.

It was believed that if Okinawa, the linchpin of the Ryukyu Islands, couild be secured, the Japanese mainland would be rendered defenseless to an Allied invasion.

Initially, things went according to the Allied plans.

On the day of the first landings, the ships laid down a barrage so heavy that, had each shot killed one Japanese soldier, the battle would have been over before it started. The beaches were then bombed and strafed by aircraft. Indeed, only twenty-eight men were lost in the initial landing.

The troops, an initial fifty thousand on the first day alone, hastened off the shore and into the brush, meeting little or no resistance, even capturing two airfields almost immediately.

Such progress and lack of bloodshed continued for a week.

Then the fleet offshore became bedeviled by widespread kamikaze attacks, where the Japanese attitude was "a plane for a ship is a necessary trade-off." These attacks continued for close to ten weeks.

Meanwhile, the men on the beach continued their trek until they reached the southern third of the island, where they met their first resistance, resulting in a combat situation that went on for close to a hundred days, and, as a result, what started out as a cakewalk with lopsided American superiority of armed force turned into an ugly and seemingly unending meat grinder of man-to-man combat.

Indeed, the largest American invasion resulted in the single deadliest campaign in the history of the U.S. Navy.

So what went wrong?

Theoretically, the Allied forces had engineered a plan that

assured victory from day one. Even Colonel Hiromichi Yahara, who devised the defense plans for the island, was quoted after the war saying, "The fact is that we never had a chance for victory on Okinawa."

Ergo, both sides had empirically reached the same overall conclusion.

What that conclusion meant, however, was another story entirely.

To the Allied forces, it meant an honorable surrender would soon be forthcoming.

To the Japanese it meant the complete opposite.

Victor Davis Hanson, in his brilliant *Ripples of Battle*, summed it up this way: "Their plans were also very simple—kill so many Americans, blow up or shoot down so many aircraft, and sink so many ships that the United States . . . would never wish to undergo such an ordeal again."

Therefore, a brutal and savage fight to the end on Okinawa might dissuade the invaders from trying a similar approach to Japan itself, and perhaps make them more agreeable to a negotiated peace rather than an unconditional surrender.

Thus, once one acknowledges that winning is impossible, the stakes change. Losing with honor becomes the objective, a way of thinking that the Allies should have anticipated, given their previous exposure to the kamikaze attacks throughout the war.

On the pragmatic side, the Allies also underestimated the terrain they would be facing.

Okinawa was larger than most of the previous islands they had leapfrogged up on their Pacific rim mission to the shores of Japan, prone to unpredictable weather, and pre-outfitted with man-made and natural formations that would provide cover for the indigenous force who, once in place, just waited for the "invaders" to arrive.

Furthermore, though in terms of heavy weaponry the Allies greatly outgunned the Japanese, the actual ratio of Allied to Japanese troops on the ground, and therefore subject to one-on-one combat (not even regarding the damage done by hidden entrenched snipers and booby traps), was a mere one and a half to one, which is by no means an overwhelming force.

Indeed, the cockiness on the part of the Allied commanders allowed their foot soldiers to walk into the traps set by the wily Japanese leaders. By withdrawing all 100,000 troops to the southern third of the island, the Allies were lulled into carelessness by the huge expanses of deserted terrain they passed through, only to find themselves surrounded by the savage force of deadenders, far from shore and the chance of immediate reinforcements. Moreover, "enemy territory" was well mapped out in advance, with a network of hiding holes and fortifications, hidden supply dumps, and lines of communication, so the immediate and imminent advantage had to go to the Japanese despite the one-and-a-half-to-one ratio against them.

The defenders had had over a year to craft their fortifications and traps, and the local climate made it virtually impossible to gain accurate and clear aerial reconnaissance.

The Allied forces had a plan, too, and they were unwilling to abandon it just because it proved to be ineffective. Their objective could probably have been achieved faster by a complete withdrawal once the infantry met the unexpected resistance, followed by a more leveling bombardment from both air and sea that would have not only thinned the surviving resistance, but also deprived them of their cover and constructions. Carpet bombing, shelling from sea, and a few good bulldozers might have saved countless American lives.

What should have been an easy victory resulted in a quarter of a million deaths in just ninety days—ninety days of the bloodiest and most savage fighting the war had seen.

And when it was all over, the Japanese had indeed sent their message: for our honor we are willing to fight to the end and give up our lives, provided we make sure you give up yours as well.

On an interesting and ironic side note, this, too, had unintended consequences.

Just as the Allies had not foreseen the outcome of their assured victory, the Japanese did not and could not have foreseen the results of the lesson they gave through their savage resistance.

Indeed, an invasion of Japan would be costly in Allied blood and was to be avoided at all costs.

The alternative, however, was not a negotiated surrender, but the savage lessons of Hiroshima and Nagasaki.

THE SIX-DAY WAR

June 5–11, 1967

EDWARD E. KRAMER

" . . . [a] desolate country whose soil is rich enough, but is given over wholly to weeds—a silent mournful expanse. . . . A desolation is here that not even imagination can grace with the pomp of life and action. . . . We never saw a human being on the whole route. . . . There was hardly a tree or a shrub anywhere. Even the olive and the cactus, those fast friends of the worthless soil, had almost deserted the country."

—Mark Twain, 1867
The Innocents Abroad

Israel was small and barren, roughly the size of New Jersey, but on May 15, 1948, it became the official homeland to the Jewish people. With the expiration of the British Mandate on May 14, 1948, the flag that rose was one designed by the First Zionist Congress shortly after Mark Twain's historic visit in 1867. It bore a pure, white background with two stripes, resembling a prayer shawl and symbolic of the transmission of Jewish tradition. The Star of David at the center was the symbol worn by 6 million

Jews who perished in the Holocaust, which ended just three years prior. The new State of Israel was recognized that day by the United States, and three days later by Russia.

The Holocaust's "Final Solution" took form in December 1941 at a meeting in Berlin between the grand mufti of Jerusalem, Haj Amin al-Husseini, and the Nazi führer of Germany, Adolf Hitler. Hitler promised the Arab leader that after securing a dominant military position in Europe, he would send the Nazi war machine into the Arab world under the guise of liberating the Arabs from British occupation. About two months later, the infamous Wannsee Conference took place, in which the Nazis produced their plan to exterminate the Jews of Europe.

While captured Nazi leaders were tried at Nuremberg, al-Husseini escaped and became the major force to bring Hitler's program of genocide to the Arab world. Returning to the Middle East, the mufti ordered death to any Arab who opposed him, which served to groom his nephew Mohammed Abdel Rahman al-Husseini to instigate violence against the Jews and spread Nazi hatred throughout the Arab world. Mohammed Abdel Rahman al-Husseini later changed his name to Yasser Arafat.

While the United Nations blessed the new state, seven Arab nations surrounding it declared war within the first twenty-four hours and bombed Tel Aviv. Since the slow, diplomatic process did not fit their cause, they all vowed to march into Israel and push the Jews into the sea. Armies from Egypt, Jordan, Syria, Lebanon, and Iraq invaded the new nation, which owned no heavy artillery, tanks, or airplanes.

Throughout the battle, Arab leaders, like the exiled mufti (and his nephew Arafat) and the Arab Higher Committee for Palestine, encouraged Arabs to leave Israel, so they would not be part of the imminent devastation to follow. With the promise that they would be rewarded with the homes and property of the dispensed Jewish people, the Israeli Arabs temporarily emigrated into neighboring countries. When the war ended thirteen months later, Israel signed separate cease-fire agreements with Egypt, Jordan, and Syria, drawing new borders with 50 percent more land than the original UN partition allotted. Many of the Arab nations that accepted their emigrated cousins suddenly expelled them, building cities of dissident refugee camps to house them until the next great war.

The Arab world, with a population of 45 million to Israel's 600,000, would not forget their loss. While they had come together to destroy the Jewish people, they possessed no coordinated military effort. They actually cared very little for each other, as well. But, with a unified common enemy—the State of Israel—the governments of the Arab League States drafted resolutions and agreements to structure their efforts and planned a militarily surprise that would devastate the new county. Throughout the conflict, the United Nations time and again failed to intervene.

On October 10, 1960, the Israeli foreign minister Golda Meir challenged Arab leaders to meet with Prime Minister David Ben-Gurion to negotiate a peace settlement between Israel and its neighbors. Egypt's President Gamal Abdel Nasser responded that his country would never recognize the Jewish state and that the Arab nations "shall not enter Palestine with its soil covered in sand. We shall enter it with its soil saturated in blood." Arab leaders from Syria, Jordan, and Iraq followed the lead in preparation for a historic war—one that would finally eradicate the Jewish state.

Rogue attacks grew more and more frequent, often from Syrian fire from the Golan Heights, across the UN-sanctioned demilitarized zone established to protect Israel from invasion. On April 7, 1967, Israel retaliated, launching an F-1 air assault against Syria, shooting down six of its new MiG-21 fighters, then flying unhampered over Damascus. The Soviet Union, an arms supplier to Syria, Egypt, and most of the Arab world, offered to help facilitate military plans to unify the Arab assault on Israel.

A consulting Soviet delegation met with Egyptian leaders on May 13, revealing that Israel had concentrated eleven to thirteen brigades in preparation for an imminent assault along the Syrian border. When the Soviet claims came to light, Israel denied any military buildup or aggressive intent. Middle East peacekeeping forces, the United Nations Truce Supervision Organization, stationed on the Syrian border to safeguard Israel from Arab terrorist attacks, also denied the Soviet claims. Days later, Syrian troops lined the Golan Heights, ready to respond to Israel's imminent attack. Battle-ready, Nasser announced, "The Jews threaten to make war. I reply: Welcome! We are ready for war."

Jordan's King Hussein signed a defense pact with Nasser on May 30, joining the Egyptian-Syrian military alliance and placing troops on both sides of the Jordan River under Egyptian command. The Iraqi president Abdur Rahman Aref announced, "This is our opportunity to wipe out the ignominy which has been with us since 1948. Our goal is clear—to wipe Israel off the map." His army then joined the alliance with Egypt, Jordan, and Syria.

No longer waiting for the Israeli invasion, later revealed to be Soviet disinformation meant to destabilize the region in hopes of additional military sales, the new Arab coalition was ready to attack the Jewish state. Algerian, Saudi Arabian, Iraqi, and Kuwaiti armies set station on the Egyptian, Syrian, and Jordanian fronts. A combined air force of 810 planes, 2,880 tanks, and nearly half a million troops prepared for the battle of all battles.

While Jewish ethics requires mercy toward all, it demands vengeance on and salvation from an enemy. In Deuteronomy, the song of Ha'azinu reads, "I will render vengeance to My enemies, and will repay those who hate Me." But, in Psalms, the song goes even one step further: "[T]o execute vengeance upon the nations, to execute upon them the judgment written: it is an honor to all his pious ones." On June 4, the cabinet held an emergency meeting, giving the prime minister and the minister of defense the authority to do whatever was necessary to defend the State of Israel. The course was clear: Israel had no choice but a preemptive strike.

The following dawn, the Israeli Defense Force launched an offensive code-named Moked, in English, "focus." In the first two hours, over three hundred Egyptian bombers, combat planes, and helicopters were destroyed. Before the day's end, the Israeli air force destroyed Jordan's military airfields in Amman and Mafraq, as well as most of the Jordanian combat fighters, then eliminated the Syrian and Iraqi air forces for good measure.

On the ground, Israeli tank units gained one population center after another. But it was the recapture of the last remnant of King Solomon's Temple, the Western Wall, on June 7, that the people of Israel experienced firsthand. By the end of the day, IDF forces also captured the biblical Judea and Samaria, and ancient towns of Shechem, Shiloh, Bethel, Bethlehem, and Hebron. Israeli troops penetrated the Egyptian army along three main axes to reach the Suez Canal and the Gulf of Suez in just four days. By June 8, IDF forces controlled the entire Sinai Peninsula.

Perched in the Golan Heights, the Syrian army remained well fortified against both land and air attacks. From their armored bunkers across miles of trenches, Syrian gunners had harassed the Jewish farmers and fishermen for nineteen years. The Israeli air force bombarded their infantry battalions for two days, then launched a paratrooper assault from behind enemy lines backed by tanks from the ground. By June 10, even the Syrian deployment collapsed, and remaining troops were in retreat.

By the end of the sixth day, the war was done. It was a three-stage offensive orchestrated with near perfect precision. While it cast Israel as a new military power, it cost the small nation the lives of seven hundred Israeli soldiers, with another twenty-five hundred wounded. Yasser Arafat escaped Israel into Jordan dressed as a woman, carrying a baby. Conservatively, Arab casualties exceeded fifteen thousand; however, no official figures have ever been released. Unlike almost any other war in military history, the victor was cast as an occupier, a label Israel has retained for the past thirty-eight years.

In 1981, Israel returned the Sinai to Egypt after President Anwar Sadat acknowledged the legitimate existence of the Jewish state. The Golan Heights, a major strategic position, remains under Israeli control. Gaza and the West Bank (Judea and Samaria) are now home to over 2 million Arab refugees who have been refused homeland in neighboring Arab countries. While they live in near-poverty conditions, the communities do receive some $300 million annually from their Arab brethren for arms and explosives to launch small-scale military strikes upon Israel, and to reward families whose children die while deploying explosives into Israeli communities.

"The Egyptian, the Babylonian, and the Persian rose, filled the planet with sound and splendor, then faded to dream-stuff and passed away; the Greek and the Roman followed, and made a vast noise, and they are gone; other peoples have sprung up and held their torch high for a time, but it burned out, and they sit in twilight now, or have van-

ished. The Jew saw them all, beat them all, and is now what he always was, exhibiting no decadence, no infirmities of age, no weakening of his parts, no slowing of his energies, no dulling of his alert and aggressive mind. All things are mortal, but the Jew; all other forces pass, but he remains. What is the secret of his immortality?"

—Mark Twain, 1897
Concerning the Jews

When the Philistines invaded Israel nearly two thousand years earlier, one group entered from the south of Beersheba, where they fought with the tribes of Abraham, Isaac, and Ishmael. Another group, coming from Crete after being repulsed from an attempted invasion of Egypt by Rameses III, seized the southern coastal area, where they founded five settlements (Gaza, Ascalon, Ashdod, Ekron, and Gat). In the Persian and Greek periods, settlers from the Mediterranean islands overran the Philistine districts. All successful invasions came from the coastal regions, pushing inward, while the Arab nations—ignoring their feigned Philistine heritage—continue to do just the opposite. It may also be worthwhile to note that Israel, deeded to the Jewish people in Genesis, the first book of the Bible, is itself a prophetic name—translated to English as "he who will fight the mighty."

DIEN BIEN PHU

Vietnam, 1954

BILL FAWCETT

In many ways, the history of the last fifty years of not only the United States but much of the world resulted from a battle that should not have been fought. When the French reoccupied French Indochina after World War Two, this included Vietnam. Where there was an expectation by the French government and returning residents that this meant they would simply go back to business as it had been before the war, this was no longer possible. Having watched the Japanese, another Asian people, easily defeat the French forces in their country, the Vietnamese were no longer willing to passively accept the domination and exploitation of their country by these same Frenchmen.

The French, having air power, modern weapons, experienced veterans, and the French Foreign Legion, felt they would have no problems suppressing any poorly armed revolt that lacked their military advantages. Nine years later, almost everyone, including the Paris government, agreed that they had been wrong. Before the battle of Dien Bien Phu was ever fought, the fate of French Indochina had really been settled. But two factors kept the French from conceding control and withdrawing. There were three factors actually, if you include Gallic pride.

The first factor was that the Vietminh were supported by the communist governments of China and Russia. This meant that, in the era of McCarthyism and domino theory, every other major Western power encouraged the French to continue their attempts to suppress the Vietnamese—who were, after all, communists. Among those who were most supportive or demanding of this was the United States.

The second factor in keeping the French fighting in Vietnam was one man. This was the commander of the French forces in Vietnam, Henri Navarre. General Navarre still viewed the Vietminh as barely armed peasants. He decided their only advantage was the ability to hit and run. Navarre also knew that the Paris government had already begun truce talks. He had to win fast or have no chance to win at all. So he decided on a way that he could force the Vietnamese military commander, Vo Nguyen Giap, to fight him in a more traditional type of battle, a conflict where the French advantage of air power, artillery, and armor would allow him to finally destroy the Vietminh in one decisive combat. You might note here that we are seeing, once more, a commander chasing the illusion of that one perfect, all-deciding battle, and, by so doing, dooming yet another army to disaster.

The only way to draw the Vietminh into a traditional-style battle was to create a challenge they could not resist, even with peace talks imminent. To do this, Navarre, in late November, occupied and began to massively reinforce and fortify a base near the Laotian border in a valley that had formerly held only the small and militarily unimportant village of Dien Bien Phu.

The valley itself was completely surrounded by steep, jungle-covered mountains and connected to the outside world only by winding trails. General Navarre was sure this location in the middle of such difficult terrain meant that his forces would face, at most, rifle-armed peasants, exhausted and demoralized by the sheer effort needed to just reach the battlefield.

Being located about two hundred miles due west of Hanoi, the only access for the French to the valley was by the airstrip the French built in the center of their base. Thousands of men landed, labored to prepare the base, and then settled down to slaughter the human wave attacks that Navarre was sure would follow. Weeks went by and, aside from the occasional sniper, nothing happened. Literally months passed and, while thousands of Vietminh occupied the mountains around the camp, no major attacks occurred. Instead, Giap used porters and bicycles to bring in tons of supplies and even modern artillery that had been broken down into manageable pieces.

On March 13, 1954, with the settlement talks with Paris threatening to make the battle a nonevent, Giap decided to attack. He, too, wanted a military resolution to occur before terms were agreed upon by his government. It was now the rainy season and clouds rendered the French air force useless. They were unable to even fly in the level of supplies that were needed once the fighting began. These seasonal rains meant that the valley floor soon became what was basically one large puddle of mud. Tanks sank up to their chassis and became no more than immobile pillboxes. Where the French expected the lightly armed Vietnamese to be slaughtered by their artillery and armor, that armor rusted in the dank climate, and when Giap finally attacked, the Vietnamese guns far outnumbered the French artillery. Hundreds of guns, many the latest Russian models, had been broken down and carried on bikes, backs, and donkeys across hundreds of miles of jungle and reassembled on the mountainsides. Men would carry a single artillery round for days to deliver it to where a battery could fire hundreds every hour. After the Vietminh artillery had smashed many of the French defenses, the mass attacks Navarre had desired finally began. Far from being slaughtered, the Vietnamese successfully overran position after position. Then the attacks would stop, and the Vietnamese artillery would once more pound every part of the French camp in the valley that was spread out below them. Giap's guns, supplied with shells by a second army made of thousands of peasants carrying them in on their backs, literally fired day and night.

Navarre had badly underestimated both the determination and the ability of the Vietnamese. But he had his battle and was determined to fight it, despite the fact that the French had lost all of their advantages. So the French fought a desperate defense. Even after the airstrip was first destroyed, then overrun, hundreds of French Foreign Legion volunteers continued to parachute into the valley. Most died in the air or when they landed among the Vietminh. A few actually made it into the contracting French perimeter, but despite their heroism and valor, the legionnaires accomplished little beyond increasing the number of prisoners eventually taken by the Vietminh.

At the end of April, over a month after Giap's offensive began, the area of Dien Bien Phu that remained under French control was limited to a small corner of the former camp that measured only a few hundred yards on each side. The rain had continued to fall constantly, as was usual for that area that time of year, which still ruled out any use of air power. No landing even remained for the French to use had they desired to evacuate those remaining. The French were trapped. Still, the artillery slammed into the defenders day and night, stopping only when hundreds of Vietnamese attacked in desperate charges, which always began with the first men throwing themselves onto the barbed wire, dragging it down with their bodies to allow others to pass over them. More supplies were dropped from the cloudy sky, at the cost of dozens of French aircraft downed, with most of it falling outside the small perimeter. A final push by Giap on May 1, 1954, was the last. The camp's command center was captured, and all of the battered French soldiers and legionnaires surrendered. The conference settled on terms, and within months the French occupation forces left Vietnam. Under the agreement, the area was split into two new countries: North Vietnam, under Giap and the Communists, and South Vietnam, controlled by those considered friends of the Western powers.

The French loss at Dien Bien Phu was as important in demonstrating that even a modern European army could be defeated as it was for creating two new nations. That loss and "communist victory" led directly to the U.S. involvement in the failed defense of South Vietnam. It also most certainly hurried the dismantling of the last vestiges of the pre–World War Two colonial system all over the world.

The Greeks created the word "hubris," but it accurately describes General Navarre's belief that he could take on the Vietnamese in a location and tactical situation that in every way favored their enemy. The French even gave away the initiative and still expected to win the "decisive" battle. Instead, they guaranteed their own defeat and gave the Vietnamese a great advantage in their political negotiations with Paris. It really comes down to the fact that Navarre and his officers simply underestimated their opponents. In order to draw Giap into a traditional-style, set-piece battle, the French commander put his forces in a position that took away all of their advantages. When you lose your own strengths and play to the enemy's, as this book shows, almost inevitably you lose, often disastrously. The Roman legionnaires were defeated by this mistake at Teutoburg Forest and Carrhae, and the French legionnaires at Dien Bien Phu suffered the same fate, for the same reason, almost two thousand years later.

EPILOGUE

This book ends at what arguably can be considered the first of the modern wars. It ends with the first loss of a Western nation in Vietnam. The mere use of that word "modern" rather answers the obvious question: Have things changed? That there are no further wars and battles in this book does not in any way imply that there are no modern bad generals. We still have, as today's media tends to tell us often and loudly, our full share of military incompetents. But even with the fertile material of modern blunderers, modern battles are not included for two reasons. One is that it is still too soon to understand the full consequences of some of these recent acts of command stupidity. The second is that a writer cannot, this close to any event, remove opinion and politics from any analysis of these mistakes or even from identifying them. Or perhaps it is just too hard to write about those mistakes when some of the men and women who died because of today's command disasters were people we personally knew.

INDEX

BOOKS BY BILL FAWCETT

HOW TO LOSE A BATTTLE

Foolish Plans and Great Military Blunders

ISBN 0-06-076024-9 (paperback)

This engrossing and fact-filled compendium chronicles the worst military defeats (both famous and obscure) throughout history. Whether a result of lack of planning, miscalculation, a leader's ego, or spy infiltration, Bill Fawcett offers an illuminating look at what caused each of these battlefield blunders.

IT SEEMED LIKE A GOOD IDEA . . .

A Compendium Of Great Historical Fiascoes

ISBN 0-380-80771-8 (paperback)

Throughout the annals of history, the best of intentions—and sometimes the worst—have set in motion events with a vastly different outcome than originally intended. William Forstchen and Bill Fawcett explore the watersheds of history that began as the best of ideas and ended as the worst of fiascoes.

YOU DID WHAT?

Mad Plans and Great Historical Disasters

ISBN 0-06-053250-5 (paperback)

History has never been more fun than it is in this fact-filled compendium of historical catastrophes and embarrassingly bad ideas.

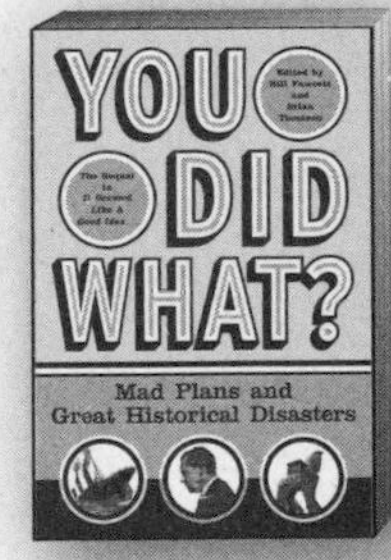

HUNTERS & SHOOTERS

An Oral History of the U.S. Navy SEALs in Vietnam

ISBN 0-380-72166-X (mass market)

In this remarkable volume, fifteen former SEALs share their vivid, first-person remembrances of action in Vietnam —brutal, honest and thrilling stories of covert missions and ferocious firefights, of red-hot chopper insertions and extractions, revealing astonishing truths that will only add strength to the SEAL legend.